I0521096

ROOT-TO-RISE

HOW TO LOVE LIFE

A Soulful Guide to Living with
Balance, Purpose, and Fulfillment

CHANDRA LYNN, M.B.A.

GLOWLIVING.COM

Copyright © 2025 by Chandra Lynn, M.B.A.

Published by Chandra Lynn, M.B.A., Glow Living (Publishing Division of Glow Marketing LLC) All rights reserved.

This is a work of nonfiction. Some names, identifying details, and personal characteristics of individuals have been changed to protect their privacy.

No part of this publication may be reproduced, stored in a retrieval system, or transmitted in any form or by any means—electronic, mechanical, photocopying, recording, or otherwise—without the prior written permission of the author or publisher, except in the case of brief quotations used in critical articles, reviews, or educational settings as permitted by U.S. copyright law.

Disclaimer: This book is intended for informational and personal development purposes only and is not a substitute for professional medical, psychological, or psychiatric advice, diagnosis, or treatment. The author is a certified life coach, not a licensed therapist. Readers are encouraged to seek support from licensed healthcare providers or mental health professionals for issues requiring clinical care.

ISBN (Paperback): 979-8-9986859-0-3

ISBN (eBook): 979-8-9986859-1-0

Cover design: Patrick Boyer, UrbanCowboy.net

Grateful acknowledgement is made to Robbins Madanes Training for content related to human needs psychology and the Emotional Triad, as taught in their coach certification training materials.

Root-to-Rise™, Glow Living™, and Glow Marketing™ are registered trademarks of Chandra Lynn, M.B.A.

For inquiries, contact: Glow Living / Glow Marketing LLC
info@glowliving.com chandralynn.com glowliving.com glowmarketing.com

Printed in the United States of America First edition

♥For Kai

CONTENTS

PHASE II: RESILIENCE

PHASE III: RISE

INTRODUCTION

"The tree is me. I am rooted in truth and reaching for purpose. With deep, strong roots, I rise through every storm into the light of who I'm here to be."

CHAPTER 1

A NEW BEGINNING

Introducing Root-to-Rise

W hat were you going to be when you grew up? Did that vision come true, or did life take unexpected turns? Maybe you achieved certain milestones but still feel unfulfilled. Perhaps you're at a crossroads, wondering if you're truly living the life you want, or just going through the motions.

If you've ever felt this way, you're not alone. Many of us wake up one day realizing that success and fulfillment aren't always the same. We chase dreams, hit goals, and yet, deep down, something still feels...off. We wonder: *Is this all there is?*

But instead of slowing down to reflect, we distract ourselves. We work harder. We stay busy. We scroll. Because facing these questions means admitting that something needs to change.

I know this feeling intimately. And I want you to know this book is for you.

My journey didn't start with a clear roadmap. It began during a time of instability and emotional conflict, and over time, it led to resilience and reinvention. For years, I built my life around one core belief: *I will never depend on anyone for anything.* I was fiercely independent, ambitious, and determined to create my success. But that belief—one that had protected me early on—became a barrier I didn't even realize was holding me back.

Because I didn't grow up with a clear roadmap, I spent years trying to figure life out the hard way, through trial and error, and with emotional grit. Eventually, I realized I needed something to guide me, not just through success, but toward real fulfillment. That phase spanned my teens into early adulthood, and each choice became a step toward both freedom and complexity. *Root-to-Rise* became that roadmap. And now, it's here to support you too.

This book is not a memoir, or just another collection of motivational ideas. It's a guide to help you reclaim the parts of yourself you may have ignored or buried. The *Root-to-Rise* method you'll discover in these pages offers a simple yet profound way to realign your life from the inside out. You'll learn how to ground yourself in what matters most—your roots—so you can rise into your fullest potential with clarity, confidence, and emotional freedom.

You will receive tools to assess your current situation, pinpoint obstacles, and create meaningful change in any area of your life, including health, relationships, career, family, and friends. The transformation begins with awareness. And your journey starts here.

Before I guide you through the *Root-to-Rise* process, I want to share where it came from—my story of struggle, resilience, and transformation. As you read, I invite you to reflect on your own story too. You don't have to have lived the same experiences to recognize the feelings, including the pressure, the turning points, the desire for something more. I hope that in knowing more about my path, you'll feel more supported on yours. What follows is the heart behind the framework and, soon, the tools to help you rise.

A Family Legacy of Transformation

I grew up in a family where helping others heal wasn't just an idea; it was a way of life. My grandfather was a psychologist, and my grandmother was a licensed marriage and family therapist. They spent late nights volunteering on a suicide crisis hotline. Deep conversations about what really drives human behavior surrounded me from an early age.

My grandmother had a gift for seeing past the surface. She could sit with someone for just a few minutes and ask one question that unlocked their heart. She taught me the power of being truly seen and heard. Even then, I knew I wanted to help people the way she did.

While my grandparents dedicated their lives to healing others, my own early life was full of uncertainty. My parents separated when I was three. There were custody and financial woes that wove themselves into the fabric of our everyday lives. As a child, I absorbed those dynamics in ways that shaped how I viewed love, safety, and control. I came to believe that financial dependency was the root of conflict. So I made a vow to myself, quietly and fiercely: *I will never depend on anyone for money. Ever.*

That belief became my silent engine. It fueled my ambition, helped me build a successful career, and gave me a sense of safety in the face of uncertainty. It also planted deep patterns I wouldn't recognize until much later. The seed of self-reliance grew into something bigger. I struggled to trust others, to lean on anyone, or to fully commit to partnership.

Eventually, that inner drive led me to make several truly tough decisions for my needs, despite the emotional consequences.

From Reinvention to *Root-to-Rise*

I've reinvented myself more than once. The first time was when I left Oklahoma at age 14, where I had been living with my mom, and moved back to California.

We had some tough seasons. My mom worked long hours in a demanding, male-dominated industry, doing her best to provide for us. Sometimes we had to stretch what we had, and her perseverance left a deep impression on me.

I remember one day coming home hungry and searching the fridge for something to eat. All I spotted with potential were eggs, flour, salt, and water. I mixed the ingredients, poured them into a hot muffin tin, and waited. When I opened the oven, they had puffed up, golden and hollow—popover magic!

It felt like a small miracle. Like I had made something out of nothing and that moment stuck with me. If I could figure that out on my own, maybe I could figure out my life too.

That's when another belief took root: *I have to be resourceful. I have to make it on my own. No one's coming to save me.*

That belief shaped everything. It gave me strength and also built walls. Becoming fiercely independent, I filtered every major life decision through that lens, a lens shaped by a child's perspective, trying to make sense of adult realities. Still, it fueled my ambition, pushed me to take risks, and gave me a sense of control in a world that often felt unpredictable. Over time, I've learned that what we often call control is really a deeper longing for safety and security.

As a genuine "California-girl" struggling to feel at home in what felt like a foreign land, I made a bold choice to leave Oklahoma and move back to California to live with my dad. Claiming independence came at the price of a strained relationship with my mom, which has had a lasting impact on me.

At 17, I did it again. I told my dad I wanted my own place with an older boyfriend. He gave me two options:

1. Stay home and have financial security through college.
2. Move out and be on my own.

My drive for independence, and the desire to step fully into my life, led me to choose the harder path. I moved out. I kept moving forward, driven by independence.

By my mid-twenties, I had earned an MBA in marketing. By 40, I had built a thriving career in the music industry, launched a consulting business, lived with a long-term romantic partner, and had a son. On paper, I had made it.

And yet, I had reached another turning point. I had grown beyond the version of me who built that life, and it was time to realign with what I truly needed next.

I had focused on two areas of my life—parenting and career—at the expense of others. My roots had weakened in areas like my romantic relationship, my self-esteem, and my friendships. I didn't fully realize how these different parts of life acted like roots, each one essential to my overall strength, balance, and ability to grow.

I had been surviving on grit, but I wasn't thriving. That's when depression and dissatisfaction set in, and I knew it was time for another change.

I realized the discontent I felt wasn't failure; it was feedback. With the quiet inner signal my roots had shifted, I knew it was time to rise into a new version of myself, no matter how difficult or messy the transition. Growth doesn't always look graceful. And sometimes the hardest part is forgiving ourselves for how we fumble through it.

The Spark Behind *Root-to-Rise*

That realization hit me hard: my life was out of balance. It wasn't one thing; it was *everything*. The breakdown of a twenty-one-year romantic relationship. The pressure to be a perfect parent. Running a business while feeling alone in the decisions. Grieving the loss of my life partner and death of both grandparents, stepmom, and a few close friends. And underneath it all, the exhaustion of trying to hold everything together. This awareness sent me on a quest, not just for more success, but for *deeper fulfillment*.

During this difficult season—when it felt like everything was unraveling—the depression weighed heavy in my chest, like a stone pressing down, making it hard to breathe. I kept showing up to yoga, week after week, moving through the poses, just trying to hold myself together.

Then, one day, something shifted. My dear friend and yoga teacher, Kristen Dessange, introduced me to a fundamental principle and cue within yoga practice that I had never considered before: *root to rise*. She explained that before we can extend upward, we must first ground down.

In yoga, "root to rise" is both a physical instruction and a deeper metaphor. It's the act of pressing firmly into the earth, creating strength, stability, and alignment in the lower body, so that the upper body can lift and expand with grace. It's about finding a balance between grounding and growing, between effort and ease. What began as a cue for proper posture suddenly struck me as a profound life lesson: *to truly rise in any area of life, I first had to get rooted—in my body, my values, my truth.* That single phrase held the wisdom I didn't even know I was searching for.

I was in Tree Pose (sanskrit: Vrksasana), balancing on one leg, tears welling up in my eyes. My body wobbled. My breath caught. But something deep inside me held steady. And then, a thought surfaced, clear and undeniable: *I don't have to fight so hard. Growth doesn't have to be a battle. I can root down first and rise from there.*

That moment brought clarity. The years of pushing, forcing, and striving suddenly made sense. My ambition pushed me to rise without consciously rooting. I was building without a strong inner foundation.

As I reflected on this experience, I saw "root to rise" as a metaphor for life. The different areas of our lives—our health, relationships, family, career, and friendships—are like the roots of a tree. When we nourish and balance them, they create a strong core, both in our body and in our life. From that solid foundation, we can rise: reaching, achieving, experiencing, and ultimately giving back.

And what do we offer when we rise? The fruits of our labor. These are not only the rewards we reap, but the unique gifts and contributions we share with the world. They symbolize our purpose in our fullest, most authentic expression. The fruit on this book's cover reminds us of what's possible when we tend to our roots and rise with intention.

From that point forward, I shifted how I approached everything. I stopped thinking I had it all figured out and started exploring the roots I had neglected. Through deep personal work, in-depth coach certification training through Robbins-Madanes Training (RMT), and spiritual growth, I created what would become the trademarked *Root-to-Rise* method that you will learn in this book. It became the foundation not just for my healing, but for the work I now share with clients who are also seeking balance, clarity, and direction.

Along the way, I've come to appreciate that every relationship—whether nurturing, challenging, or transitional—played a part in my growth. Even when things were difficult or unresolved, each connection helped me learn something vital about myself. This book is born not only from my healing, but from the influence of those who shaped me, stretched me, and ultimately helped me rise.

Turning Pain into Purpose

By the time I had that awakening in Tree Pose, I had brought my insights to others. I launched Glow Living as a space for emotional seekers, people like me who were yearning to live more authentically and love life. I then poured myself into developing the *Root-to-Rise* method as an online course, leading workshops, and giving away content freely, hoping to reach those who needed it most.

Then the pandemic hit. Suddenly, it felt like the entire world was tired of Zoom, and I assumed people needed a break from screens. So I pivoted. I began writing this book.

What started as a passion project quickly became an enormous undertaking. I had no outside budget or publisher, just my vision, drive, and deep desire to be of service. But without a sustainable income stream, I burned out. I lost money, and with it, the means to grow the impact I had dreamed of. I lost my spark. Somewhere along the way, I disconnected from my why.

So I pressed pause. I focused on providing marketing services—the thing that paid the bills—and I quietly shelved the book.

After stepping away from the book project and returning to marketing, I thought I was on a path of quiet recovery. But then, everything shifted.

My best friend of over 40 years died by suicide.

Grief cracked me open in a way nothing else had. I asked myself all the impossible questions: *Could I have done more? Should I have seen it coming? Why wasn't my coaching enough?* Eventually, through the waves of sorrow, something beautiful emerged. I transmuted the pain into purpose. I previously lost touch with the spark that once fueled me—my reason for creating Glow Living in the first place. And in the depth of grief, I reconnected to a purpose even greater than following in my grandparents' footsteps.

I came to this truth: *If my words, my voice, my story—if even one piece of what I've created—can offer someone hope, then it's all worth it.*

This book, this method, and this mission are part of my healing, and also my *legacy*. If something were to happen to me, I want my son to have this guidebook—a map to help him navigate life with strength, clarity, and love. That's what this book really is: an offering born from heartbreak and hope. A roadmap for anyone ready to rise again, even after heartbreak, burnout, or loss.

And most of all, this is my way of saying: *you don't have to do it all alone.* The belief that I should never depend on anyone once shaped my life, and in many ways, it protected me. But now I know the deeper truth: *we all need each other.*

I've learned to receive support, to lean into the wisdom others carry, regardless of age, background, or role. Sometimes, a 14-year-old holds the exact insight a 55-year-old needs to hear. When we stay open, we become both students and teachers in every season of life.

This book is my offering for anyone who needs a hand, a mirror, or a map. And in writing it, I've allowed myself to depend on something bigger than independence: *connection.*

And now, after years of testing, refining, and living this process, I'm offering it to you in its most complete form yet.

This Book as a Lifeline

When we stop growing, we disconnect from our purpose. We feel stuck. Lost. Numb. This book is an invitation to awaken. It's a framework for navigating transitions, rebuilding confidence, and aligning your life with what matters most to you.

It's also a lifeline. It's something you can return to anytime you feel overwhelmed, uncertain, or in need of encouragement. When the world feels heavy or confusing, these pages offer more than inspiration. They offer tested tools, grounding practices, and a voice that believes in your potential. You'll find exercises that can help you shift your mindset, realign with your values, and take action, even if it's just one small, courageous step. Sometimes, that's all it takes. One moment of clarity. One split-second decision. One question that sparks a breakthrough.

I'll share stories, mine and those of others, to show you what's possible. And I'll give you the tools to do the work yourself.

Before you turn the page, take this one small but powerful step:

➢ Grab your journal. Write down one area in your life where you feel stuck or disappointed, where things didn't turn out how you hoped. Tuck it away.

The *Root-to-Rise* method will soon unfold as the *Root-to-Rise* Framework which includes a main infographic, coaching prompts, and a map. As you move through it, you may uncover insights that help you break free or find peace. At the end of this process, I invite you to look back at this journal entry and evaluate how you've grown.

Guidance for the Journey

You'll notice that I shift between storytelling, practical coaching, and educating throughout this book. That's intentional. Some chapters are deeply personal, while others are more instructional. I believe that transformation happens when we integrate knowledge with heart, and when we understand the *why* behind our patterns and also feel seen in our lived experience. I invite you to receive this book like a conversation between us: real, honest, and grounded in tools that work.

CHAPTER 2

A PATH TO LOVE LIFE

The Root-to-Rise Method

I f you've made it this far, you already know something in your life needs to shift. Maybe you've been feeling stuck, overwhelmed, or out of balance. Maybe you've pushed forward so long that you haven't taken time to question if your life genuinely aligns with what fulfills you.

The good news? You don't have to figure it all out at once. That's exactly what the *Root-to-Rise* method helps you do.

Refer to the *Root-to-Rise* Infographic at the end of this chapter for a visual representation of the method's framework. It shows how your roots and rise elements interact and how a strong foundation allows for sustainable, meaningful growth. Don't worry about taking it all in now. I will build this infographic at the end of each section so that you will understand it as we go.

This method isn't about chasing an unrealistic ideal. It's about creating a life that supports you from the inside out so rising into your full potential feels natural, fulfilling, and deeply aligned.

True transformation doesn't happen by reaching for something "out there." It happens from the ground up by strengthening what's already within you.

How the *Root-to-Rise* Method Works

I put the method into a framework to offer a clear, compassionate path forward—one rooted in universal truths, hard-won wisdom, and the core needs that connect us all. It's designed to make personal growth feel empowering rather than overwhelming. And to be accessible to anyone, regardless of gender, background, geography, or belief system.

It mirrors the way a tree grows, from the roots up. Before it reaches toward the sky, a tree invests in growing strong, deep roots that provide stability, nourishment, and resilience. Without them, even the tallest tree is vulnerable to the slightest storm. The same is true for us.

In nature, there's a principle called "as above, so below" which means the health of what's visible above ground is a direct reflection of what lies beneath. In our lives, this translates to our careers, relationships, health, and fulfillment, which can only thrive to the degree our internal foundation is solid.

Many of us try to rise without first doing the root work. We aim high without strengthening what's below. We chase success, love, or meaning without realizing that rising too fast or too soon, without inner stability, can lead to burnout, collapse, or a lingering sense that something's missing.

The root work isn't always glamorous. It asks for honesty, patience, and commitment. But it's essential. By nurturing your Life Root System—the five foundational areas of Health, Family, Relationships, Career, and Friends—you create the strength and balance needed to rise with clarity and power.

The framework also introduces six universal human needs that shape how we think, act, and feel: Security, Variety, Self, Intimacy, Growth, and Transcendence. These needs are present in every life root, and when they go unmet or are met in unhealthy ways, we start to feel disconnected, stuck, or unfulfilled.

By evaluating how well these needs are being met in each root area, you'll see exactly where things are out of alignment, and how to bring them back into balance. This is where real transformation begins.

What Happens After You Evaluate Your Roots

Once you understand how your core needs are being met—or not—you'll move into the next phase: clearing the obstacles that have been holding you back. This includes things like limiting beliefs, perfectionism, procrastination, low standards, and persistent worry or fear. You'll learn how these patterns form, why they persist, and how to break free of them at last.

Next, you'll build emotional resilience. You'll learn how to shift your emotional state using an RMT tool called the Emotional Triad, protect your energy, and work with the concept of Energy Arrows so you can stay grounded even in challenging environments.

When life throws its inevitable storms such as loss, change, stress, you'll know how to withstand the elements without falling apart completely, and how to put yourself back together if you do. You'll reclaim your energy, shift your mindset, and move through life's hardest moments with more grace and strength.

And finally, you'll rise, not just in the surface-level sense of achieving goals, but in the deeper sense of living in alignment with your highest self. You'll set clear intentions, take aligned action, and begin living a life rooted in your values, powered by your purpose, and full of meaning.

This isn't about perfection or performance. It's about progress, presence, and personal freedom.

Your Compass & Your Map

The *Root-to-Rise* Infographic will serve as your visual compass as we move through this work together. Later in the book, you'll create your own *Root-to-Rise* Map, a personalized guide to transformation based on your reflections, needs, and intentions.

This map will become your tool for navigating future decisions, recalibrating when life shifts, and staying grounded when things get messy. It's not just a plan, it's your North Star that serves as a reflection of who you are and what truly matters to you. As you move through the root chapters, you'll find a short North Star Reminder at the end of each one. These reflections help you clarify what you truly want, why it matters, and how you're willing to grow.

Every step from here is about deepening your roots, clearing your path, and rising into something greater.

Want Extra Support Along the Way?

To help you go even deeper, there's a *Root-to-Rise Companion Workbook* available. It includes guided journaling prompts, reflection exercises, and practical tools designed to help you apply everything in this book to your real life, step by step. If you learn by doing (or love to write things down), this workbook will become your trusted partner on the path. You can find it wherever this book is sold or at glowliving.com.

Are You Ready to Play Full Out?

Before we go any further, pause and ask yourself: How *willing* am I to fully commit to this process? Not just to read this book but to apply what's in it.

To reflect. To journal. To do the exercises. To be honest with yourself. To take action.

Ask yourself:

➢ How willing am I to challenge myself to go all in on this journey?

➢ How willing am I to show up with courage and honesty?

➢ How willing am I to take real action instead of staying stuck in old patterns?

Because the depth of your willingness will determine the depth of your transformation.

Your Journey Begins Now

This isn't about adding more pressure to your life. It's about removing the weight of what no longer belongs. By the end of this book, you'll have:

- ☑ A deeper understanding of the hidden forces shaping your life
- ☑ A clear path toward the future you want
- ☑ Your own *Root-to-Rise* Map to guide your next chapter

So take a deep breath. You're exactly where you need to be.

You can use the workbook alongside this book or revisit it any time you need a reset. Think of it as your personal transformation journal and safe space to get honest, go deep, and track your rise.

ROOT-TO-RISE INFOGRAPHIC

RISE

HIGHER PURPOSE
What do you want to be known for?

RISING UP
- Life's Key Question
- Bucket List
- Goals & Aspirations
- Accomplishments
- Connections/Relationships
- Milestone Events

BALANCING LIFE
- Yoga & Meditation
- Gratitude
- Self-care
- Prioritizing Roots

CONNECTING TO AUTHENTICITY
- Tap into Your Heart
- Aligning Others
- Your Lens

WITHSTANDING THE ELEMENTS

- Winds of Change
- Storms/Upheaval
- Grief & Loss

NAVIGATING EMOTIONS
Triad:
- Body/Mind/Spirit
- Physiology/Focus/Meaning

CLEARING OBSTACLES

- Nourishing Needy Roots
- Honoring Driving Needs
- Pain Points
- Getting Unstuck
- Fears & Limiting Beliefs
- Double Binds
- Leveraging you Tap Root

FOCUS MIND   **MEANING SPIRIT**

PHYSIOLOGY BODY

RESILIENCE

HUMAN NEEDS

Transcendence
- Moving past the self to serve others
- Connecting to higher purpose
- Contribution
- Sharing
- Service
- Providing

Growth
- Growing
- Pulsating energy
- Progress
- Learning
- Feeling momentum
- Advancing
- Breaking free

Intimacy
- Nurturing
- Valuing relationships
- Belonging
- Feeling passion
- Having desire
- Striving for unity
- Togetherness

Self
- Self-esteem
- Self-worth
- Significance
- Importance
- Pride
- Importance
- Perfection

Variety
- Change
- Transitions
- Storms
- Challenges
- Trauma/Crisis
- Chaos
- Variety
- New/Different
- Spice of Life
- Surprise
- Fear

Security
- Certainty
- Safety
- Rootedness
- Grounded
- Comfort
- Stability
- Predictability
- Protection
- Commitment

LIFE ROOT SYSTEM

HEALTH/FITNESS	FAMILY	RELATIONSHIPS	CAREER	FRIENDS
Nutrition	Parents	Self	Time & Money	Introvert v. Extrovert Needs
Food/Beverage	Caregivers	Romantic Partner	Contribution	Who are they?
Supplements	Siblings	Commitment	Heart-based/ Passion vs Corporate	Values alignment
Fitness/Exercise	Partner	Chemistry	Hobbies/Craft	Reflection of you
Massage/Body Work	In-laws	Compatibility	Who you are:	What do you offer?
Wellness vs. Illness	Children	Communication	• Strengths/ Weaknesses	What do they offer?
	Chosen		• Leader vs.Worker	Elevate
			• Visionary vs. Operational	Support
			• Analytical/ Data-minded	Experience

TAP ROOT
What feeds your soul deeply?

ROOTS

www.glowliving.com
#glowliving
#roottorise
#lovelife

© All Rights Reserved. Glow Living/Glow Marketing LLC 2025

GLOWLIVING
love life.

**PHASE I:
ROOTS**

Part One

ROOTS

Keep nourishing your journey and stay connected for soulful
updates, fresh tools, and free resources.
Sign up at GlowLiving.com.

CHAPTER 3

LIFE ROOT SYSTEM

The Foundation of Your Rise

I n the *Root-to-Rise* Framework, we focus on five essential areas of
life, referred to as the Life Root System. Just like a tree needs
strong roots to thrive, so do we. Each root represents a
foundational area that supports our well-being. The strength of these
roots depends on how well we're meeting our fundamental human
needs across all aspects of life. This chapter is about assessing your
roots, identifying areas that need growth, and strengthening the
foundation that will allow you to rise into your full potential.

Why We Need Strong Roots

A tree with deep, healthy roots can weather storms. Without them, it
may grow tall, but it remains vulnerable, easily uprooted by strong winds
and unable to reach its full height. The same is true for us. When our
roots are weak or unbalanced, we may achieve success in some areas,
but struggle with lasting fulfillment.

Strengthening our roots provides:

- **Stability:** A solid foundation gives us resilience in the face of
  challenges.
- **Identity:** Our roots connect us to our sense of self, shaping
  our beliefs and values.

- **Purpose:** A deep understanding of what sustains us helps us find meaning and direction.

- **Connection:** Strong roots help us form meaningful relationships and nurture the ones we have.

When our foundation is strong and balanced, we're better equipped to handle adversity, make empowered choices, and experience deeper joy and fulfillment.

This section will help you evaluate your roots, identify their strengths and weaknesses, and create a plan to fortify them. By doing so, you'll set yourself up for a steady, sustainable rise and grow with clarity, resilience, and purpose.

Life Root System

Each of the five roots you'll explore is essential to building a grounded, fulfilling life. They include Health, Family, Relationships (Self and Romantic Partner), Career, and Friends.

While we'll explore the six core emotional needs in depth later, you'll see them referenced in each root chapter because they're always present, quietly shaping our choices. These needs—Security, Variety, Self, Intimacy, Growth, and Transcendence—influence how stable or strained our root areas feel. As you read, notice which needs are driving your patterns, and which might be unmet or out of balance. This awareness will deepen your reflection and prepare you for the Needs section ahead.

1. Health: The Root of Vitality

Without health, everything else in life becomes secondary. If we're struggling with illness, exhaustion, or chronic stress, we simply don't have the energy to fully engage in other areas of life. Strengthening this root may involve:

- Prioritizing physical health through movement, nutrition, and rest.

- Addressing mental health with self-care, mindfulness, or therapy.
- Healing self-esteem and body image issues to cultivate self-love.

The key is embracing health as a lifestyle, not a quick fix.

2. Family: The Root of Connection

Family is often our earliest and strongest root. For some, it's a source of love and support. For others, it may represent loss, dysfunction, or unhealed wounds. In *Root-to-Rise*, family isn't just about blood ties; it's about the people who shape us deeply, whether they are biological relatives, chosen family, mentors, or caregivers. This section will help you:

- Evaluate the strength of your family relationships.
- Identify areas that need healing or nurturing.
- Create meaningful connections and set boundaries where needed.

For parents, this root also includes parenting to foster love, security, and emotional growth for the next generation.

3. Relationships (Self and Romantic Partner): The Root of Love

Whether you're in a relationship, seeking one, or focused on self-love, this root plays a critical role in your emotional well-being. It's about how you give and receive love, how you relate to yourself, and what you believe you're worthy of. In this section, you will:

- Reflect on how you show up in romantic relationships, or why you may avoid them.
- Identify patterns of attachment, people-pleasing, or self-sabotage that may block deeper intimacy.
- Explore your relationship with yourself including your inner dialogue, self-respect, and emotional needs.

- Clarify the qualities you need in a partner or in your solo life to feel fulfilled.
- Learn how to create emotional safety, set healthy boundaries, and deepen your capacity to love and be loved.

Whether shared with another or rooted within, this form of love is essential to your rise.

4. Career: The Root of Purpose & Prosperity

Our careers offer more than just a paycheck. They provide structure, identity, purpose, and a way to contribute our gifts to the world. In this section, you will:

- Reflect on whether your current career aligns with your passions and strengths.
- Identify any blocks preventing success or satisfaction.
- Redefine what career fulfillment and prosperity look like for you.

Even if you're in a season of transition, caretaking, or reinvention, this root helps you clarify how to express your purpose and meet your needs through meaningful contribution.

5. Friends: The Root of Support & Joy

Friendships are essential to a thriving life. They provide joy, connection, emotional support, and perspective in a way no other relationships can. In this section, you will:

- Evaluate the quality and reciprocity of your friendships.
- Identify which connections uplift and energize you.
- Recognize patterns in how you initiate, maintain, or avoid connection.

Friendships grow. The key is learning how to invest in the ones that feed your soul and lovingly release those that no longer align with your growth.

Breaking Free of Low-Quality Patterns

We all have needs, and we all meet them. But not every strategy is healthy, empowering, or sustainable. Sometimes, we settle for low-quality ways of getting our needs met, such as staying in toxic relationships, working unfulfilling jobs, or neglecting our well-being out of habit or fear.

Ask yourself:

> ➤ Where have I settled for "just okay" instead of thriving?
>
> ➤ What limiting beliefs are keeping me from strengthening my roots?
>
> ➤ How willing am I to challenge those beliefs and create new, healthier patterns?

In *Root-to-Rise*, we don't just name those pattern, we change them.

Strengthening Your Roots

As you work through each chapter, you'll assess the current state of each root and determine what shifts, big or small, you can make to grow stronger and more aligned. When your roots are healthy and integrated, you become more resilient, joyful, and fully empowered to rise.

At the end of each root chapter, you'll find a North Star Reminder. This isn't just a summary, it's a compass. In the *Root-to-Rise* Framework, your North Star represents the vision you're rising toward: a life aligned with your deepest needs, values, and purpose. These reminders help you pause, reflect, and reconnect to what matters most in each area of life. Like a traveler checking the stars for direction, you'll use these touchpoints to stay oriented as you grow.

When your roots are strong and your North Star is clear, you won't just move forward, you'll rise with intention.

Your foundation is everything. By strengthening and balancing your roots, you create fertile ground for your next chapter. It's time to root down, rise up, and live with clarity, connection, and purpose.

CHAPTER 4

ROOT 1: HEALTH

The Root of Vitality

Your health is the root from which everything else grows. When your physical and mental well-being are strong, you have the energy, clarity, and resilience to show up fully in every area of life. But when your health is off—even slightly—everything can feel harder. Minor challenges become overwhelming. Simple joys feel out of reach.

That's why I begin with health. As we age, it becomes the foundation for longevity, energy, emotional resilience, and even self-worth. Without it, rising becomes nearly impossible.

A 2021 study led by Harvard's Human Flourishing Program found that physical and mental health were two of the strongest predictors of overall well-being and life satisfaction (VanderWeele et al., 2021). Regular movement, nutritious eating, and quality sleep all contribute significantly to lower rates of anxiety, depression, and chronic illness.

It's important to acknowledge that not everyone starts from the same place. Some people are born with chronic health conditions, acquire serious illnesses, or experience limitations outside their control. In these cases, health doesn't always mean reaching peak performance. It may simply mean managing symptoms, conserving energy, or adapting to new ways of living.

Rooting into health doesn't mean chasing perfection. It means honoring your body's reality, your emotional needs, and your capacity in each season of life. Whether you're seeking healing, stability, or simply more peace in your day-to-day, you deserve to feel supported and empowered in that pursuit.

From Survival to Vitality

Imagine someone who is chronically ill. Their focus is survival—not joy, not growth. And yet, many people living with illness or disability rise in extraordinary ways. They do this not by ignoring their limits, but by accepting them with courage, creativity, and grace. Often, their energy goes to managing symptoms, not building dreams. Compromised wellness affects relationships, creativity, and careers.

Thriving looks different for everyone. Your version of vitality might not involve a marathon. It might be reclaiming joy in a quiet moment or finding strength in asking for help.

Now picture someone who radiates health: strong, vibrant, grounded. Clarity and energy mark their movements through life. They're not constantly managing pain or exhaustion. They're building, loving, giving.

Take a moment.

> ➢ Which version am I living today?

> ➢ On a scale of 1-10, how have I prioritized my health?

The Real Cost of Neglect

Neglecting your health doesn't just impact your body, it affects every part of your life.

- **Chronic disease risk:** Poor nutrition, inactivity, and lack of sleep increase the risk of diabetes, heart disease, and stroke.
- **Mental health strain:** Neglecting self-care fuels anxiety and depression.

- **Exhaustion:** Low energy leads to burnout, resentment, and disengagement.

- **Financial stress:** Medical costs skyrocket without preventative care.

- **Reduced joy:** Poor health diminishes your ability to enjoy and participate in life.

The CDC reports that 6 in 10 U.S. adults live with a chronic illness, and 4 in 10 live with two or more. Many are preventable through healthier lifestyle choices.

I have friends who were told they were pre-diabetic. Their doctors gave them a clear roadmap: change your diet, move more, rest better. Some made lasting changes. Most didn't. They started strong but lost steam, or never fully committed.

Why? Because knowledge isn't enough. Change requires self-compassion, structure, and support.

If you were told that your future could involve injecting insulin every day, wouldn't you act? And yet, so many don't. This isn't about shame, it's about reclaiming your power before life forces your hand.

The High Price of Pushing Through

I once worked with a dear friend and colleague named Chris. He was one of those people everyone loved—loyal, sharp, warm-hearted. He worked in sales and was constantly on the road, chasing deals, hitting goals, never slowing down. Even when he started struggling with chronic pain and gout, he kept pushing. He'd joke about the discomfort, brush off the concern, and self-medicate just to make it through another trip.

He told himself he'd take care of it after the next quarter, after the big client meeting, after things slowed down. But "after" never came. His body was screaming for help, but he didn't listen. And eventually, the pain became something much worse.

Chris passed away far too young and was survived by beautiful daughters.

His loss shook me to my core. It was a devastating reminder that ignoring your health doesn't just affect you, it affects everyone who loves you. We lost a beautiful human being because he didn't feel like he could take a break. He was so focused on sales performance that he didn't give himself permission to pause, ask for help, or put his health first.

I share this not to scare you, but to wake you.

You matter. Your presence matters. And your well-being has a ripple effect. Prioritizing your health isn't selfish; it's an act of love for everyone who depends on you, learns from you, and walks beside you.

My Story: From Self-Loathing to Strength

While Chris ignored his body's cries, I realized I had been waging my own quiet battle against mine. Poor health isn't only about what we eat or how much we move. It's also about the thoughts we feed ourselves. The way we see our bodies can shape, and sometimes sabotage, our health just as powerfully as any physical habit.

For much of my life, I believed I was overweight and practiced a subtle form of self-loathing. I don't think others saw me this way, but it was my inner narrative. No matter what I tried, I couldn't achieve the image I wanted. When discouraged, I spiraled into frustration and self-loathing.

After giving birth to my son, I'd had enough. I was tired of fighting my body. I fully committed to following a proven strength-training program. No shortcuts. No second-guessing.

It changed everything.

For the first time, I wasn't guessing. I wasn't working against myself. I built strength, confidence, and clarity. I no longer saw my body as the enemy. I felt pride. When I reached a major goal, I threw a celebration with close friends. I handed out thank-you cards with a photo of my progress and the words:

"She Believed She Could, So She Did."

That phrase became a mantra. It wasn't about the number on the scale. It was about who I became through that process: someone empowered and embodied.

Now, I train because I care. I move because I love my body, not because I want to fix it. I train for strength, travel, and longevity.

If you've ever battled body image, negative self-talk, or the cycle of defeat, please know: you can rewrite your story. You have more power than you think.

Your health determines how you show up in every other area of life. Whether you feel energized or depleted, confident or self-critical, connected or lost. Your relationship with your body affects everything.

Small, Sustainable Shifts

You don't need to change your whole life overnight. Big transformation happens in small, consistent steps. Your journey is unique. What supports your health may look different from someone else's, especially if you live with chronic conditions, disabilities, or limitations.

Honor your reality. There's no shame in starting from where you are and defining wellness on your own terms.

Check in with yourself:

- Am I moving regularly in ways that feel good?
- Are my meals nourishing and mood-supportive?
- Am I well-rested or running on fumes?
- Do I have ways to reset like breathwork, nature, or journaling?

If something feels off, pay attention to it and get help if you need it. Choose one small shift this week. Not from shame, but from love. Because your body deserves to feel alive.

Asking for Help Is Strength

You don't have to go it alone. Whether through therapy, a fitness coach, a holistic practitioner, doctor, or supportive family and friends, getting support can help you stay accountable and aligned.

This journey is about consistency. It's about meeting your needs with kindness and creating a lifestyle that sustains your energy, joy, and presence.

When your health root is strong, every part of your life benefits. And you'll rise—not by force, but by flow.

North Star Reminder

Your Health root is the foundation for how you move through the world physically, mentally, and emotionally. When it's strong, you have the energy, clarity, and resilience to rise into your purpose.

As you continue through this book, you'll reflect on what you truly want for your health, why it matters to you, and what you're willing to do to create lasting well-being. You'll capture those intentions in your *Root-to-Rise* Map later in the Rise section.

CHAPTER 5

ROOT 2: FAMILY

The Root of Connection

Our families can be our greatest source of love, support, and belonging—and sometimes, our greatest source of pain. Whether your family roots feel deep and strong or shallow and fragile, this area shapes who we are at our core.

For many, family is a place of safety and a foundation of unconditional love. For others, it represents loss, conflict, or unresolved wounds. No matter where you fall on this spectrum, you can nurture and strengthen your family roots. That might mean healing old hurts, setting boundaries, or redefining what "family" means to you now.

A 2017 study published in *The Journal of Family Psychology* found that individuals with close, supportive family relationships reported higher emotional resilience and lower levels of depression and anxiety, especially during times of stress or crisis.

The Importance of Family

When we invest in our Family root, we build:

- **Stronger relationships:** Nurturing family fosters deep, supportive bonds.
- **Emotional support:** Feeling like someone has your back creates security.

- **Belonging:** Healthy dynamics help us feel seen, valued, and grounded.
- **Traditions and values:** Family helps shape what we pass on.
- **Legacy:** How we love and show up now affects future generations.

And family isn't only about blood. Some are born into families that protect and uplift. Others build their own chosen family with people who truly see them and show up without condition.

Family & Childhood Wounds

Almost everyone carries some level of childhood wounding, even those with well-meaning parents. That's because growing up requires individuation, the process of discovering who we are separate from our caregivers' expectations.

Some wounds are subtle: maybe feeling unseen or emotionally neglected. Others are more acute, stemming from loss, abuse, addiction, or abandonment. Regardless of scale, early family dynamics shape our beliefs about love, connection, and worth.

A 2021 study from the *Child & Adolescent Psychiatry and Mental Health* journal found that unresolved childhood trauma correlates with increased emotional reactivity and self-esteem issues in adulthood.

If your Family root feels broken or painful, the most powerful first step is acknowledging the pain then consciously choosing to heal.

One way to start is by asking:

- ➢ What did my family dynamic teach me about love and connection?
- ➢ What kind of family do I want to build now?
- ➢ What patterns am I willing to release so I can create something better?

You don't have to repeat what you came from. You get to choose where you go next.

Whose Love Did You Crave the Most?

Here's a question that unlocks deep insight:

> ➤ Whose love did I crave most growing up, and what did I feel I had to be to receive it?

For me, it was my grandmother. A therapist with incredible presence, she made me feel seen and inspired. But I also felt I had to be emotionally intuitive, aspirational, and wise to earn her love.

Those traits shaped me in powerful and painful ways. When I embody them, I feel grounded. When I drift, I feel disconnected from myself.

Sometimes we discover strengths we've developed in beautiful ways. Other times, we find limiting beliefs that no longer serve us. Either way, awareness is power.

Redefining Family

For a long time, I thought blood defined family. Over time, life taught me otherwise. I learned that family comprises the people who show up. They are the ones who stand beside you, not just because they're related, but because they choose to.

I've lost people I assumed would always be there. Their absence carved a painful truth into my heart: *the opportunity to express love isn't endless.* We don't always get another birthday, another conversation, another "someday" to say the words that matter.

That's why I don't wait anymore. I say the thing. I send the message. I let people know what they mean to me. Love that stays locked inside the heart is love that goes unfelt.

So pause for a moment and ask yourself:

➤ Who has shown up for me, again and again?

➤ Who feels like family, even if they don't share my DNA?

➤ Have I told them what they mean to me?

Take a moment to reflect, and then take action because the time to express love is always now. Your words and presence can shape the family you choose and the legacy you leave behind.

Parenting: A New Generation of Roots

Whether you are a biological parent, stepparent, adoptive parent, or simply a loving presence in a child's life, *you matter.*

Some people always knew they wanted children. Others, like me, felt unsure.

I didn't know if I wanted kids. I immersed myself in the music industry, working nights and weekends, attending concerts and events. My identity was bound to my career, and I was worried about how motherhood might change that. I also knew that having a child would make me emotionally vulnerable in a way I hadn't experienced before.

My unexpected pregnancy shocked me. At the doctor's office, when the staff congratulated me, I sat in the room and cried. I felt fear, confusion, and a deep apprehension about the unknown. It took almost two weeks for me to sit with those emotions and decide.

And then I did.

I embraced the experience fully, pouring my heart into being the best mom I could be. Leaving my job brought insecurity, but I did it anyway. I shifted into consulting and hired a nanny so I could work from home and stay close to my baby. The thought of missing even a moment with him saddened me. I took him everywhere, including concerts. His first backstage pass was at a John Mayer show. One of the other artists on the bill, Sheryl Crow, stopped in her tracks, smiled, and told me how adorable he was. In that moment, I felt the worlds I loved—motherhood and music—collide in the most beautiful way.

He grew up in the music industry with me, worked alongside me, and went on to study the music industry at UCLA. He's the light of my life. And I never felt like I sacrificed anything. He's added more value to my life than I ever could've imagined.

Parenting is difficult. It stretches you. It asks you to make peace with uncertainty, redefine who you are, and pour yourself into someone else. But it can also be one of the most fulfilling, growth-oriented, love-drenched journeys of your life.

As parents, one of the greatest gifts we can give our children is the ability to stand on their own. Our job isn't to keep them tethered to us, it's preparing them for independence, even though it means one day facing the bittersweet ache of an empty nest. Every small milestone matters: learning to make their own meals, dress themselves, manage their own laundry, and care for their lives builds real-world confidence. Each act of self-sufficiency reinforces their self-esteem and shows them they are capable, resilient, and trustworthy. While letting go is never easy, knowing we've raised them to thrive is one of the greatest rewards of parenting.

Moving Forward: Own Your Family Story

Parenting isn't just about raising children. It's about raising yourself along the way. It's messy and meaningful and stretches your capacity for love, patience, and identity.

Ask yourself:

- ➤ Have I created a safe emotional environment?
- ➤ Have I invited joy, curiosity, and spontaneity into our routine?
- ➤ Are we emotionally close and able to be real with each other?
- ➤ What am I learning as a parent?
- ➤ How am I leaving a legacy of love and healing?

Your Family root doesn't have to be perfect; it just has to be nurtured.

To strengthen this root:

- Reassess the relationships that define "family" for you.
- Acknowledge old wounds, and choose to heal over repetition.
- Build meaningful connections with people who feel like home.
- Speak your love out loud, while you still can.
- Choose to parent with presence, not perfection.

North Star Reminder

Your Family root is not just part of where you came from. It's a key component of your Life Root System. Strengthening it will guide you toward greater emotional balance, connection, and legacy.

As you continue your journey, you'll reflect on what you truly want for your family relationships, why that vision matters to you, and what you're willing to do to strengthen this root. You'll capture those intentions in your *Root-to-Rise* Map later in the Rise section.

CHAPTER 6

ROOT 3: RELATIONSHIPS

The Root of Love—Romantic & Self

A h, romantic relationships...my favorite topic. And let's be real, they're also one of the hardest areas of life to keep in balance. Some people might say making money or chasing big goals (like writing this book!) is harder, but I believe that navigating relationships, both with a partner and with ourselves, is one of the greatest challenges we face.

Why? Because relationships mirror us. They reflect our strengths, but they also expose the parts we still need to heal. They force vulnerability upon us, stretch us to grow, and challenge us to be fully seen.

Codependency & The 51% Rule

Romantic relationships naturally involve some level of interdependence. But when that turns into codependency—when one person consistently sacrifices their well-being to care take or rescue the other—it creates imbalance, resentment, and burnout.

I learned a powerful lesson about this in a past relationship with someone who was struggling in his career. As a marketing consultant, I couldn't help myself, so I dove in to support him. I created branding materials, helped him clarify his message, even drafted outlines for things he could say to promote himself. But none of it landed. He didn't use them. He wasn't moving forward, not because he lacked support, but because he lacked internal motivation.

One evening over dinner, I remember looking at him and saying, not with frustration, but with clarity, *"I can't want this more than you do."* That moment helped me understand the importance of setting healthy boundaries, not just to protect my energy, but to clarify what I'm truly responsible for. Over-functioning in relationships is often self-abandonment disguised as care.

That became a turning point for me. I realized I had been carrying more than my share, not just of the work, but of the desire. I came up with the 51% rule: that in every relationship, each person has to be at least 51% responsible for their own growth, healing, and success. Hopefully more!

It doesn't mean we don't support each other. It means we don't carry someone who is unwilling to walk for themselves.

If you're giving more energy to someone's life than they are, pause and ask yourself:

➤ Am I helping or rescuing?

➤ What would happen if I stopped over-functioning?

➤ Could I redirect that energy toward supporting my growth?

Healthy love is generous, and not self-abandoning.

Vulnerability & Emotional Safety

For years, I thought I was great at being vulnerable. I shared openly. I wore my heart on my sleeve. Or so I thought.

But during one of the most difficult seasons of my life, I shut down. I didn't reach out. I didn't admit how much I was struggling. Somewhere deep down, I believed that, as a coach and a leader, I had to stay strong and put together.

I've since learned that true strength includes softness. Vulnerability isn't a liability, it's a bridge to connection.

According to researcher Brené Brown, vulnerability is the birthplace of love, belonging, and creativity. Without it, connection stalls. With it, we create emotional intimacy and trust.

If vulnerability is hard for you, start small. Say what you feel. Ask for what you need. Let someone see you—not just your polished parts, but your real ones. The right partner will respond with love, not judgment.

And if they don't? Maybe they're not your person.

Turning Conflict Into Connection

Conflict is inevitable. But it doesn't have to be destructive.

What matters is how we fight, and whether we use challenges as doorways to deeper understanding. One powerful tool I've found helpful is Nonviolent Communication (NVC), developed by Marshall Rosenberg PhD. It encourages us to observe without judgment, name the feeling we're experiencing, identify the unmet need behind it, and make a clear request with compassion.

Instead of blaming or defending, this method helps you communicate from your core, not your ego. It creates space for both people to be heard, seen, and supported.

The next time tension arises, pause and ask:

> ➤ Am I reacting from fear or responding from love?

> ➤ Am I trying to win or trying to understand?

Conflict isn't the enemy. Disconnection is.

When a Relationship No Longer Serves You

One of my favorite quotes is by Henry David Thoreau: *"There is no remedy for love but to love more."*

I believe that's true. And sometimes, loving more means loving yourself more—enough to walk away from a relationship that no longer honors your needs, growth, or truth. If a relationship consistently leaves you feeling small, unsafe, or unseen, it may be time to ask:

➤ Are my needs being met in healthy ways?

➤ Am I staying from love or from fear?

➤ What would it look like to let go with compassion?

"Conscious uncoupling," a term coined by Katherine Woodward Thomas and made popular by Gwyneth Paltrow and Chris Martin, offers a path to ending relationships with grace. It's about honoring what was, releasing with care, and choosing to heal over blame.

Letting go is hard. But staying in a connection that drains you is harder.

Being single isn't a waiting room before "real life" starts. It's an invitation to deepen your relationship with yourself, reconnect with your joy, and build a life you genuinely love.

Use this season to heal past patterns, explore what truly fulfills you, discover how to meet your own needs with joy, and learn to love yourself...not as a placeholder, but as a priority.

This is also a time to reflect on your attachment patterns, including how you connect, how you protect yourself, and where you may be unconsciously repeating old relational dynamics. The book *Attached* by Dr. Amir Levine and Rachel Heller is a powerful resource for exploring this. Grounded in advanced relationship science, it helps readers identify whether they tend to be anxious, avoidant, or secure in relationships, and why that matters. Understanding your attachment style can reveal hidden patterns and empower you to create more secure, fulfilling connections going forward.

Tools like Internal Family Systems (IFS) therapy and Imago Therapy can also be incredibly helpful here. IFS helps you uncover and work with different "parts" of yourself including your protectors, fears, and inner child. Imago explores the unconscious patterns behind why we're drawn to certain people, and how to create healthier relationships from now on.

Reflect with curiosity:

➢ What patterns repeat in my relationships and why?

➢ What parts of myself am I ignoring, criticizing, or hiding?

➢ What do I truly need, not just in a partner, but in life?

The more whole you feel on your own, the more powerful and magnetic your relationships will become.

The Most Important Relationship of All

Before we can truly thrive in romantic relationships, we must first examine the one we have with ourselves. Are we kind to ourselves in moments of struggle? Do we honor our needs, speak our truth, and accept who we are, flaws and all?

Self-relationship is the root beneath all others. When it's weak, we search for love from a place of emptiness, hoping someone else will validate our worth or soothe our wounds. But when it's strong, we bring wholeness, clarity, and emotional availability to every connection.

This is the part of your love life you have full control over. And it's where the most powerful healing begins.

Ask yourself:

➢ How do I speak to myself when I fall short?

➢ Do I meet my own needs or expect someone else to?

> Am I choosing relationships that honor me or reflect how I secretly feel about myself?

No relationship will ever rise higher than the one you have with you.

Whether you're in love, in healing, or in between, the Relationships root asks you to return to yourself again and again. It invites you to lead with vulnerability, balance giving and receiving, communicate with truth, and show up fully. It reminds you that you don't have to settle, over-function, or stay stuck.

To strengthen this root, focus on fostering intimacy through honesty and emotional availability. Practice balancing support with self-responsibility by honoring The 51% Rule. Embrace conflict as a gateway to deeper connection. Let go when staying would mean betraying yourself. And most importantly, create a life you genuinely love, even before someone else enters it.

Your relationship with yourself is the root from which all of your relationships grow.

Reflection Prompts

Take a few moments to explore the relationship you have with yourself and others.

> What patterns or roles do I often play in love?

> What emotional needs feel unmet, and how do I typically try to meet them?

> What qualities do I need in a partner—or in my solo life—to feel truly fulfilled?

> Where might I be ready to set a boundary or shift a pattern to deepen my capacity for love?

North Star Reminder

Your Relationships root holds your deepest desires for connection, growth, and shared purpose. Nurturing this root, within yourself and with others, aligns you with the love and partnership that reflects your truth.

And just as importantly, are you aware of your emotional needs? When we don't recognize or tend to them, we may seek validation, soothing, or love in ways that reinforce our wounds instead of healing them.

As you continue this journey, you'll define what you want in your relationships, why it matters to you, and what you're willing to do to cultivate the love and intimacy you deserve. You'll capture these intentions in your *Root-to-Rise* Map later in the Rise section.

CHAPTER 7

ROOT 4: CAREER

The Root of Purpose & Prosperity

Our careers are more than a paycheck. They provide structure, fulfillment, and a chance to share our unique gifts with the world. Yet, many people struggle with career dissatisfaction, often because they are following a path shaped by societal expectations, family influence, or a narrow definition of success.

To cultivate a strong, healthy Career root, we must determine a professional direction that aligns with our personality, interests, and values, not just what others think we "should" do for money or credibility. Research from Values Institute in a 2023 study called "The Effects of Personal and Workplace Values on Job Satisfaction" indicates that when personal values align with workplace values, individuals experience heightened job satisfaction and are less likely to seek new employment opportunities.

Many people confuse a job with a career, but they are different. A job is a short-term way to earn money or gain experience, often necessary for survival but lacking deep fulfillment. A career is a long-term journey involving skill-building, growth, and purpose. It requires investment in education, training, networking, and staying relevant in a changing landscape.

Your career mirrors your needs, values, and self-worth. Whether you're an entrepreneur, corporate leader, freelancer, or stay-at-home parent, your work contributes to your identity, purpose, and daily structure. No matter which path you choose, the ability to feel progress fuels motivation and momentum. A strong Career root means you're not just working, you're evolving.

If your work leaves you drained, unmotivated, or stuck, it may be because your needs are being neglected or met in unhealthy ways.

Ask yourself:

➤ Am I choosing safety over growth?

➤ Am I chasing external validation instead of internal fulfillment?

➤ Do I feel challenged, connected, and inspired?

Case Study: Terrance's Journey from Rock Stardom to True Fulfillment

Terrance had achieved fame, fortune, and a career as a legendary rock star. He performed in front of sold-out crowds, feeding off the electrifying energy of adoring fans. Yet, when the stage lights dimmed and the roar of the crowd faded, he found himself alone on his luxury tour bus, feeling an emptiness that his success couldn't fill.

Despite reaching the pinnacle of his profession, Terrance felt unfulfilled. He had spent years believing that once he made it big, he would finally feel satisfied. But the reality was different. His success had brought financial stability and recognition, but it lacked deeper meaning, romantic connection, and a sense of balance.

Terrance's internal conflict stemmed from competing desires. As a child, he envisioned being a musician, traveling the world, and making a name for himself. However, he had also longed for a family, and a stable home life filled with love and connection. His career had been his primary focus for years, but as he aged, he realized that touring kept him from the deeper relationships he longed for. He felt trapped: the very success he had worked so hard for was now in conflict with the life he truly wanted.

This misalignment between his career and his growing human needs—love and connection, personal fulfillment, and stability—left him feeling lost. His subconscious roadmap had led him to a life that no longer served him, and he knew something had to change.

Terrance reached out for support, realizing that the version of success he had chased no longer matched his true desires. He began a process of self-reflection, asking himself key questions:

✓ What truly fulfills me beyond fame and recognition?

✓ What do I need in my life to feel a deeper sense of connection and purpose?

✓ How can I redefine success in a way that aligns with my needs?

Through this process, he realized he had outgrown the version of himself who once longed to spend years on the road. Now he craved meaningful relationships, creative expression on his own terms, and a lifestyle that aligned with his values.

Terrance made a bold decision. He shifted his primary focus from touring to composing and producing music in a home studio. While he still had to tour occasionally to keep his fans engaged and make money, this transition allowed him to continue his passion for music while also building the stable and fulfilling personal life he desired.

By rewriting his roadmap, Terrance created a career that supported his deeper human needs. He set clear boundaries around his work, choosing projects that allowed him to be present with his family and nurture personal relationships. He also embraced new opportunities, mentoring young artists and using his industry experience to support others.

Terrance's journey is a powerful example of how success isn't just about external achievements. It's about aligning your career and life choices with your core human needs. When he shifted his focus from chasing fame to creating a life rich with meaning, he found the satisfaction he had been missing all along.

His transformation teaches us:

- Success is personal. Define it on your own terms, not by societal expectations.
- Our needs evolve. What once fulfilled us may no longer serve us, and that's okay.
- Changing course is not failure; it's growth. Aligning your life with your deepest values is the ultimate achievement.

If you resonate with Terrance's story, consider examining your own career path. Are you living according to your true vision or are you following a path that no longer fits? Rewriting your roadmap may be the key to a more fulfilling, purpose-driven life. This may require slight tweaks to your priorities or a major pivot. The key is finding clarity around what you want and being courageous enough to take the first step.

A career is more than just a way to make a living; it's an essential root of life that meets several core human needs. Whether you're an entrepreneur forging your own path, a corporate professional climbing the ladder, or a parent balancing both work and family, your career plays a significant role in your sense of identity, contribution, and fulfillment. To create a career that truly supports you, it's essential to define success on your own terms, align your work with your values, and embrace both the challenges and rewards that come with it.

Entrepreneurs & Artistic Spirits: Navigating the Unknown

For those who choose the road of entrepreneurship or artistry, the career path can be uncertain and often unpredictable. Unlike traditional careers, these fields don't always provide stable income or clear advancement structures. Yet, what they offer is the freedom to pursue work that is deeply fulfilling, creatively rewarding, and uniquely suited to one's personal vision.

Terrance's story illustrates this well. As a musician, he had achieved fame, yet he felt disconnected and unfulfilled. His original vision of success—touring the world and playing sold-out shows— ultimately left him yearning for a sense of stability and deeper purpose. By reassessing his career choices, he transitioned to a path that aligned with his need for connection while still honoring his passion for music.

If a non-traditional career path appeals to you, accept that it will be nonlinear. The key to sustaining a creative or entrepreneurial career is developing strong business skills, building financial stability, and cultivating a support system that helps you weather the inevitable ups and downs.

Building financial stability as an entrepreneur or artist begins with treating your work like a business, not just a passion. That means learning to manage cash flow, diversify your income streams, and price your work or services with confidence. It also involves budgeting for slower seasons, investing in tools or education that support your growth, and setting clear financial goals aligned with your values. For some, it means marketing and monetizing your gifts in ways that feel authentic, such as through personalized offerings, licensing, product sales, or creating passive income with digital assets.

Financial empowerment isn't about chasing fame or riches, it's about creating a sustainable foundation so your art or vision doesn't suffer under financial stress. When you pair creativity with strategy, freedom becomes possible in your work and in how you live.

Reflection Prompt:
Making Your Creative Career Sustainable

If you're walking the path of entrepreneurship or artistry, take a few moments to reflect:

➤ What does *financial stability* mean to me in this season of life?

➤ Which of my skills or talents could I monetize more intentionally?

> What one small action could I take this week to move toward sustainable income without sacrificing my values or creativity?

Remember, building a purpose-driven career doesn't mean compromising your authenticity. It means supporting it with intention, structure, and self-respect.

Climbing the Ladder: The Power of Relationships

Whether you're in a corporate setting, a small business, or building something of your own, success isn't just about how skilled you are, it's about who you know and how well you build relationships. People hire, promote, invest in, and collaborate with those they trust and enjoy working with. Our human need for connection, belonging, and recognition deeply fuels career growth. Advancing your career doesn't happen in isolation; it happens through conversations, shared experiences, and mutual value.

To grow professionally, emotional intelligence matters just as much as technical ability. Building strong relationships means showing up with integrity, genuine interest, and consistent follow-through. When you express curiosity about others' journeys, ask meaningful questions, and offer your support without strings attached, people remember how you made them feel. Simple gestures like a thank-you message, a thoughtful introduction, or remembering someone's win create lasting trust.

It also helps to seek mentors who can guide you and to become a mentor yourself when the opportunity arises. Both roles expand your influence and deepen your understanding of the industry and the people in it. Over time, you build your personal brand based on your actions and your relationships. Being generous, trustworthy, and easy to work with opens doors.

Relationship-building isn't just a "nice to have," it's a career strategy. When done authentically, it becomes one of your most valuable long-term assets. Prioritize people, and your career will rise on a foundation of connection, community, and mutual growth.

Parenting & Career: Balancing Two Roles

If you're a parent or caregiver, your career decisions do more than impact your income. They shape how your children view work, fulfillment, and possibility. When you make aligned career choices, you model self-respect, resilience, and the courage to pursue a life that feels meaningful. And the impact doesn't stop there.

Your choices teach your children what's worth striving for. They learn how to set boundaries by watching how you protect your time. They learn how to handle stress by observing how you respond to challenges. They absorb your beliefs about money, ambition, balance, and self-worth, often more from what you *do* than what you say. When you choose purpose over pressure, integrity over approval, or creativity over conformity, you give them permission to imagine new ways of living. You show them that success is personal, and that their future doesn't have to come at the cost of their well-being.

Overcoming Fear & Self-Doubt in Your Career

Many people hold themselves back professionally because of self-doubt. They worry they aren't skilled enough, experienced enough, or connected enough. Nobody starts as an expert.

The need for growth and significance plays a huge role in career fulfillment. People often feel stuck because they are waiting to feel ready. But progress happens when you take action, not when you wait for perfection.

Elizabeth Gilbert's *Big Magic* is an excellent resource for overcoming creative fears. She reminds us that even if someone has done an idea before; You bring a unique voice and perspective to your work. The key to overcoming self-doubt is to step forward despite the fear, recognizing that your skills and confidence will grow as you move forward.

Live-Work Balance:
Defining Success on Your Terms

A fulfilling career is important, but it's not everything. At the end of life, few people regret not working more. Many regret not spending enough time with loved ones, prioritizing their passions, or taking care of themselves.

That's why I prefer to call it live-work balance instead of work-life balance. Life comes first. A successful career should support your overall well-being, not consume it. A healthy balance contributes to:

- **Mental & physical health:** Reduces stress and prevents burnout.
- **Stronger relationships:** Fosters deeper connections with family and friends.
- **Productivity & satisfaction:** Keeps you engaged and motivated.
- **Personal growth:** Leaves room for hobbies, self-care, and learning.

The key is to define success not just in financial terms, but in terms of how much time and energy you have to enjoy your life fully.

Progress = Joy:
The Power of Growth in Your Career

One of the most essential human needs is growth. No matter your career path, feeling a sense of progress—whether it's learning new skills, advancing in your industry, or developing personally—creates joy and fulfillment.

- A sense of accomplishment builds confidence and job satisfaction.

- Personal development happens when you challenge yourself to grow.
- Career advancement provides more opportunities, recognition, and income.
- A clear sense of purpose keeps you engaged and motivated.
- A competitive edge makes you valuable in your field and open to new possibilities.

Your career is a significant part of your identity and daily life. The key is to shape it in a way that meets your core needs, fuels your passions, and allows you to experience both success and personal fulfillment. Whether you're an entrepreneur, corporate go-getter, balancing work with family, or redefining success, your career can be a source of joy, growth, and purpose.

Define Success on Your Own Terms

Ask yourself:

➢ On a scale of 1 to 10, how well is my career meeting my needs?

➢ Am I in a job for survival, or am I building a career that fulfills me?

➢ If fear or self-doubt weren't a factor, what would I pursue?

Success isn't one-size-fits-all. Align your career with your values, strengths, and purpose, not just financial gain. Focus on growth and progress, knowing that even small steps create momentum. If you crave variety, explore a career path or multiple paths that fulfill different aspects of your identity. When live-work balance is a challenge, set boundaries that honor both personal and professional fulfillment. Your career should support the life you want to live, not consume it. Choose a path that supports your life and allows you to rise with purpose, joy, and sustainability.

North Star Reminder

Your Career root reflects your values, purpose, and evolving sense of identity. When aligned, it becomes a powerful channel for contribution, growth, and fulfillment.

As you move forward in this book, you'll define what you truly want from your career, why it matters to you, and what you're willing to do to create a work life that supports your rise. You'll add these insights in your *Root-to-Rise* Map during the Rise section.

CHAPTER 8

ROOT 5: FRIENDS

The Root of Support & Joy

Romantic relationships and jobs may come and go, but genuine friends can be lifelong witnesses and supporters of your journey. Friendships are one of the most fulfilling aspects of life because they provide love, connection, growth, and belonging—all essential human needs. When we prioritize our friendships by staying connected, communicating openly, and nurturing the give-and-take balance, these relationships can become our greatest sources of fun, support, and personal expansion.

Friendships matter because they hold us through the storms and celebrate us in our joy. A well-nurtured Friends root supports us when the other roots are challenged. When we struggle in our romantic relationships, family dynamics, career, or health, our trusted friends can "hold our basket" which offers us a safe space to vent, gain perspective, and receive guidance from people who genuinely want the best for us.

In times of transition or hardship, strong friendships can mean the difference between feeling isolated and feeling deeply supported. Life is full of ups and downs, and having a circle of true friends ensures we don't have to navigate those moments alone.

Understanding the Value of Strong Friendships

When life gets busy, friendships are often the first thing we push to the back burner. While good friends will probably understand, nobody likes to feel neglected. Prioritizing our friendships isn't just about making time for others, it's about investing in the relationships that uplift us.

Some of the most powerful benefits of close friendships include:

- **Emotional & Social Support:** Friends provide a safe space to process emotions, reduce stress, and receive guidance during life's challenges.

- **Better Mental Health:** Strong friendships reduce rates of depression, anxiety, and loneliness.

- **Joy & Well-Being:** Spending time with friends brings laughter, fun, and connection, which fuels happiness and resilience.

- **Personal Growth & Expansion:** Friends challenge us with different perspectives, push us to grow, and encourage us to step into our potential.

- **Longevity & Physical Health:** Studies show people with strong friendships live longer, healthier lives.

The Art of Being a Great Friend

Friendship is a unique kind of intimacy, different from romance or family ties. It's chosen, not inherited.

Friendship is a two-way street. We choose our friends, and they choose us, which means they can also choose to walk away. It's essential not to take friendships for granted. If we want strong friendships, we have to be strong friends.

Unlike romantic relationships, we don't always talk about expectations in our friendships—but we should. Asking a friend, *"What do you need from me right now?"* can deepen trust instantly.

This simple question allows them to tell you whether they need someone to just listen (without fixing), provide honest feedback to help them see clearly, or give emotional reassurance and a reminder they're not alone.

We often assume what our friends need, but asking removes the guesswork and creates deeper trust and intimacy. Just knowing that someone cares enough to ask is sometimes enough to meet their need for love and connection.

Navigating Challenging Friendships & Setting Boundaries

Some friendships that start strong can eventually become draining, toxic, or unbalanced. This happens when one person takes more than they give, repeatedly crosses boundaries, or doesn't respect your growth.

It's important to identify unhealthy patterns and set clear boundaries. Friendships, like all relationships, require mutual respect and effort. If you avoid a friend or feeling exhausted after spending time with them, ask yourself:

➢ Is this friendship still serving my highest good?

➢ Have I clearly communicated my needs and boundaries?

➢ Am I holding on out of habit, guilt, or fear?

If the friendship still holds potential, it may be worth a courageous conversation. Not all friendships need to be cut off, but not everyone should occupy the top tiers of your trust and time. This isn't about punishment, it's about clarity. Your energy is sacred, and your inner circle should comprise people who truly support your growth.

Chandra's Friendship Journey

Having worked in music marketing my entire career, I've built friendships with people all over the world. While this has been amazing, it also meant that I didn't have many local friendships because I was always traveling or busy with work.

After having my child and transitioning to working from home, I felt the need for local friendships and a genuine sense of community. I longed for a space like in the TV show *Cheers* but not a bar, a place where I felt deeply connected.

I started opening myself up to new friendships by attending yoga classes, reconnecting with people from my past, and attempting to meet like-minded individuals. The result? A life-changing group of women who became my sacred community. Through yoga and fitness at a gym, I met incredible women who supported me through major life changes including breakups, dating, career shifts, parenting struggles, and personal growth. Together, we not only practiced yoga but also formed deep bonds of self-discovery through travel, women's circles, and shared experiences.

What I love most is that we don't live in the land of the unspoken. We tell each other what we mean to one another, and we actively plan time together because we truly desire that connection.

Strengthening Your Friends Root

You don't need dozens of close friends. A few good ones—who see you, support you, and grow with you—can change your life. Friendships are one of the most enriching parts of being human, but like any meaningful relationship, they require attention and intention.

Clear expectations and ongoing communication build every strong friendship. Not everyone needs the same level of connection. Some friends love daily check-ins, while others feel nourished by one meaningful conversation every few months. Instead of assuming, take the time to ask how often they like to connect and what kind of support feels good to them right now. This kind of clarity reduces disappointment and strengthens trust.

The deeper your friendships, the stronger your foundation. And from that foundation, you can rise—connected, supported, and with a feeling of belonging.

Ask yourself:

➤ On a scale of 1–10, how supported do I feel in my friendships?

➤ What actions can I take to deepen connection with people I care about?

➤ Have I been showing up as the friend I want to attract?

➤ Do any friendships need boundaries, upgrades, or a loving goodbye?

By investing in your friendships with presence, care, and vulnerability, you're nurturing a root system strong enough to support you through every season of life.

North Star Reminder

Your Friends root is a vital source of joy, connection, and resilience. It helps you weather storms and celebrate wins with people who truly see and support you.

As you continue on this journey, you'll reflect on what you want from your friendships, why that connection matters, and what you're willing to do to deepen and protect the bonds that help you rise. You'll bring these reflections in your *Root-to-Rise* Map later in the Rise section.

CHAPTER 9

TAPROOTS

What Grounds You

I n order to break through the obstacles holding us back from rising, we need to summon energy from the source that feeds our roots most deeply...our Taproot. When you connect to what is most meaningful in your life, you unlock an endless source of strength to grow and achieve what you desire.

A taproot is a type of root system found in plants, characterized by one thick root that grows deep into the soil. It anchors the plant and draws nourishment from far beneath the surface. Like a carrot or an oak tree, your Taproot reaches down to your core, giving you stability and resilience.

In the *Root-to-Rise* Framework, your Taproot is your spiritual anchor. It fuels the five root areas of life and sustains your ability to meet your deepest human needs. Without it, your rise may feel directionless or easily shaken. But when nourished, this foundation helps every other part of your life flourish.

Discover What Grounds You

A "life taproot" refers to the core values, passions, or beliefs that give your life meaning and purpose. It's the deep-seated, essential part of your identity that guides your decisions and direction.

Taproots are deeply personal and may evolve over time. Your culture, upbringing, personal experiences, or unique view of the world might shape yours. Some common examples include:

- **Family & Relationships:** A sense of belonging, love, or responsibility.
- **Career or Service:** Finding purpose in meaningful work or creative expression.
- **Personal Growth & Development:** Pursuing learning, healing, creating, or self-mastery.
- **Spirituality or Faith:** Drawing strength from a higher power or sacred purpose.
- **Contribution to Others:** Uplifting others through service, activism, or generosity.

For me, my Taproot is the love I have for my son. When I think of him, I want to grow into the best version of myself. I know my choices—how I show up, communicate, and handle relationships—are shaping his view of life. That awareness fuels my commitment to live with clarity and intention.

Some people are driven by helping others, feeding people, nurturing beauty, creating art, or spending time in nature. Taproots come in many forms, and yours is uniquely yours.

When life feels overwhelming, your Taproot grounds you. It keeps you centered when you're tempted to stray and fuels your growth when you're ready to rise. It reminds you of who you are and why you started, especially when fear, fatigue, or uncertainty creep in.

Exercise: Identify Your Taproot

Your Taproot is your deepest source of strength. It keeps you going when life feels hard. It's the well of motivation, purpose, or love that you can draw from when you need to dig deep.

Step 1: Reflect & Journal

Use any or all of the prompts below to help uncover your Taproot.

- ➤ **Reflect on Your Values:** What principles do I want to live by (e.g., honesty, compassion, responsibility)?
- ➤ **Identify Your Passions:** What brings me joy or purpose?
- ➤ **Consider Your Strengths:** What do I do naturally and well?
- ➤ **Reflect on Your Experiences:** What shaped my beliefs?
- ➤ **Look to Role Models:** Who inspires me and why?
- ➤ **Imagine Your Legacy:** What impact do I want to leave behind?

Still unsure, try these prompts:

- ➤ What keeps me moving forward when I want to quit?
- ➤ What truly feeds my soul and authentic self?
- ➤ What is the deeper reason behind the things I do?
- ➤ Where do I draw positive energy from when I need it most?

Step 2: Capture It in a Phrase

Summarize your Taproot in a succinct statement:

A value: *"Love always guides me."* A person: *"For my children."* A belief: *"I am here to serve."* A feeling: *"Freedom and growth fuel me."*

Step 3: Write It Down

My Main Taproot:

Other Important Taproots (optional):

Pro Tip: Anchor Your Taproot for Daily Focus

Your Taproot is your most important, non-negotiable priority. It's the root that, when nurtured, strengthens all other areas of your life. To reinforce it:

- Set a daily intention tied to your Taproot
- Create a mantra (*"I prioritize my health so I can show up fully"*)
- Use a visual cue such as bracelet, wallpaper, or mirror note

When life feels chaotic or unclear, return to your Taproot. It's your why and foundation for everything else.

North Star Reminder

Your Taproot is the deepest truth that grounds you. It's your guiding principle, core belief, or soul-level why. When everything else feels uncertain, this is the part of you that stays steady. As you continue rising into your fullest expression, come back to this Taproot often. You'll add it to your *Root-to-Rise* Map in the Rise section of this book as a reminder to let it anchor your choices, fuel your growth, and remind you of who you are at your core. A strong Taproot keeps you aligned, resilient, and rooted in meaning—no matter what life brings.

CHAPTER 10

ROOTS RECAP

I n this section, you explored the Life Root System with each representing a vital area of your well-being. Just like a tree needs strong, stable roots to grow tall and weather storms, your life needs nourishment at the foundational level to support balance, resilience, and long-term fulfillment.

Each root reflects a distinct part of your life:

- **Health** gives you the energy and strength to engage fully.
- **Family** grounds your identity through connection and care.
- **Relationships** deepen intimacy and self-awareness—whether with a partner or within yourself.
- **Career** offers purpose, growth, and a platform for contribution.
- **Friends** bring joy, support, and a sense of shared experience.

Together, they create the ecosystem that supports your rise.

At the center of it all is your **Taproot**, your spiritual anchor and deepest source of meaning. While the five roots represent your external life, your Taproot runs beneath them, drawing from your core values, purpose, and passions. It's what fuels your motivation when life gets hard and reminds you why your growth matters. When your Taproot is strong, everything else becomes more sustainable.

One of the most powerful takeaways from this section is the importance of checking in with your root system regularly. Are your foundations solid? Are your choices aligned with your truth? Many people drift into imbalance, not because they aren't trying, but because they're unconsciously meeting emotional needs in low-quality ways. That's where burnout, resentment, and misalignment begin.

This framework invites a different approach; one of conscious design. By regularly tending to your roots—and reconnecting to your Taproot—you build a life that supports your full expression, not just your survival.

But even with strong roots, something deeper drives how these areas feel, and that's where we're headed next.

> ➤ What were my most important takeaways from this Roots section?

Now that you've explored your roots, it's time to understand why they feel balanced or out of sync. The next section introduces the six core human needs—the hidden drivers shaping your decisions, relationships, and fulfillment. Once you understand how these needs are playing out in your life, you'll be able to meet them with more intention, compassion, and clarity.

ROOT-TO-RISE INFOGRAPHIC
PHASE ONE: ROOTS

LIFE ROOT SYSTEM

HEALTH/FITNESS
- Nutrition
- Food/Beverage
- Supplements
- Fitness/Exercise
- Massage/Body Work
- Wellness vs. Illness

FAMILY
- Parents
- Caregivers
- Siblings
- Partner
- In-laws
- Children
- Chosen

RELATIONSHIPS
- Self
- Romantic Partner
- Commitment
- Chemistry
- Compatibility
- Communication

CAREER
- Time & Money
- Contribution
- Heart-based/Passion vs Corporate
- Hobbies/Craft
- Who you are:
  - Strengths/Weaknesses
  - Leader vs. Worker
  - Visionary vs. Operational
  - Analytical/Data-minded

FRIENDS
- Introvert v. Extrovert Needs
- Who are they?
- Values alignment
- Reflection of you
- What do you offer?
- What do they offer?
- Elevate
- Support
- Experience

TAP ROOT
What feeds your soul deeply?

ROOTS

www.glowliving.com
#glowliving
#roottorise
#lovelife

© All Rights Reserved. Glow Living/Glow Marketing LLC 2025

GLOWLIVING
love life.

Part Two

NEEDS

HUMAN NEEDS

 Transcendence

 Growth

 Intimacy

 Self

 Variety

 Security

CHAPTER 11

UNDERSTANDING HUMAN NEEDS

Have you ever stayed in a job you didn't like and couldn't figure out why? Or kept going back to a relationship that wasn't good for you? Or felt inexplicably stuck, even when everything in your life seemed "fine"?

Most people never stop to question why they do what they do. But understanding your behavior—really seeing the hidden drivers underneath—is how everything shifts. We all do things that make little sense on the surface. But underneath every choice is something deeper: core emotional needs silently steering the wheel.

These hidden forces are our emotional needs. They shape the way we show up in relationships, the goals we chase, the beliefs we hold, and the patterns we repeat until we learn to bring them into the light.

These needs are why we say yes when we want to say no, strive for achievements that don't fulfill us, or resist change even when we crave it. They're not flaws, they're part of what makes us human, and they're running the show whether or not we realize it.

I believe we can transform our lives in a single second. One decision—one moment of clarity—can change everything. That might sound dramatic, but people do it all the time. Whether it's leaving a toxic job, committing to a new habit, or finally letting go of the past, change begins with a conscious choice.

Understanding why we do what we do—why we stay in situations that don't serve us, seek validation that doesn't fulfill us, or resist change even when we crave it—is the first step toward real transformation. This part of the book is about uncovering the hidden forces that guide you, so you can make aligned, soul-honoring decisions as you chart your course forward.

What Are Human Needs?

Fundamental emotional needs, inherent in every person on the planet, demand fulfillment, whether healthy or unhealthy. These needs are not surface-level desires. They're not preferences. They're the fuel behind everything we do.

The idea of human needs psychology was first introduced by psychologist Abraham Maslow, who proposed a hierarchy of needs, beginning with physical survival and progressing toward self-actualization. Later, I learned in my coach certification training that Tony Robbins and Cloe Madanes built on this work to define six core emotional needs that drive all human behavior.

I've adapted their work into the *Root-to-Rise* Needs Framework, aligning each need with the Life Root System so you can see how they play out in your day-to-day decisions and patterns.

These are the six human needs we'll explore:

1. **Security:** The need for stability, safety, and comfort.
2. **Variety:** The need for excitement, change, and new experiences.
3. **Self:** The need to feel important, valued, and unique.
4. **Intimacy:** The need for deep connection with yourself and others.
5. **Growth:** The need for progress, learning, and personal evolution.

6. **Transcendence:** The need to contribute beyond yourself and align with a greater purpose.

We all have these needs, but we prioritize them differently. And we meet them in different ways—some healthy, some not.

So the question is:

Are you meeting your needs in ways that nourish you or in ways that keep you stuck?

Why Understanding Human Needs Changes Everything

You may not have thought about these needs before, but they've shaped every major decision you've made. Let's look at a few real-world examples:

- You stay in a job you don't love, not because it excites you, but because it makes you feel secure.
- You return to an unhealthy relationship, not because it's good for you, but because it meets your need for connection or significance.
- You jump from one new project to the next because your nervous system is wired to seek variety.

When we're unaware of our needs, we meet them in reactive, automatic, and often destructive ways. But when we notice them, we get to choose how to fulfill them, consciously and intentionally.

This awareness puts you back in the driver's seat.

How Human Needs Impact Your Roots

How well your needs are met in each of your five roots affects them. For example:

- If your need for Security is unmet in your career, you might feel constant stress around finances or job stability.

- If your need for Intimacy isn't met in healthy ways, you might cling to unfulfilling relationships or isolate yourself entirely.

- If your need for Growth is ignored, you may feel bored, restless, or uninspired, even if life looks good on the outside.

In each area of life, your goal is to meet your needs at a high, healthy level, ideally at an 8, 9, or 10 out of 10. A 4, 5, or 6 only partially meets your needs, leaving you feeling "fine" but not fulfilled. And when a need drops even lower, it can lead to burnout, anxiety, depression, or crisis.

It's not about perfection, it's about *alignment*. The more you meet your needs in healthy ways, the more resilient, grounded, and energized you become.

The Two Forces That Drive All Change

Often, people don't change because they're in the "just okay" zone. Things aren't terrible, but they're not joyful either.

As Tony Robbins teaches, there are only two things that cause people to change:

1. The pursuit of **pleasure.**
2. The avoidance of **pain.**

Think about the big changes you've made in life. Were they driven by pain you could no longer tolerate or by a compelling vision you were excited to chase?

Now imagine making changes *before* things fall apart. That's what emotional mastery is all about. It's choosing to evolve from clarity, not crisis.

Ask yourself:

➢ Where in my life are my needs being met at a low level?

➢ Where am I just "fine" when I could be thriving?

➢ What am I tolerating that no longer serves me?

This Is the Beginning of Mastery

When asked in an interview: *"Why should we care about these hidden forces?"*

My answer was simple: *"Because they're shaping every decision we make, whether or not we realize it. And once we understand them, we can take control. We can stop reacting and start creating a life that actually works."*

This section is the beginning of that shift.

You're about to learn what's been driving your decisions, and how to change the ones that aren't serving you. You'll explore how each of the six needs shows up in your life, how they interact with your root areas, and how to meet them in ways that empower you instead of drain you.

The next six chapters have a different structure than the more narrative sections of this book. Each chapter is formatted intentionally, offering a consistent framework you can come back to anytime you feel out of balance or stuck. These chapters are more educational by design, with practical tools, reflection questions, and simple strategies to help you better understand how your core needs are shaping your behavior. You're not expected to memorize them. Think of this section as your personal reference guide, a kind of emotional owner's manual you can return to when you're ready to grow in a new direction.

Understanding your human needs, and how they impact your Life Root System, is foundational to the *Root-to-Rise* Framework. Once you learn them, you'll be able to apply them throughout the rest of the book and to your life to create lasting fulfillment.

Let's begin with the first core need: Security.

---

*The concept of human needs psychology is rooted in the work of Abraham Maslow's hierarchy of needs and expanded upon by Tony Robbins and Cloe Madanes. The *Root-to*-Rise Framework adapts and integrates their teachings, showing how these core needs shape our decisions, behaviors, and sense of fulfillment.

CHAPTER 12

NEED 1: SECURITY

The Foundation of Stability

During the pandemic, I spoke with a music photographer whose career had always thrived on live shows and touring artists. Practically overnight, the gigs vanished. No shoots. No backstage passes. No income. *"I built my entire identity around working with musicians,"* he told me. *"And now I feel like I don't know who I am—or how I'll survive."* As a freelancer, he had no employer benefits to fall back on. The lack of structure, safety net, and stability shook him to the core. He even considered leaving the creative field just to feel secure again.

His story isn't rare. When our foundation gets shaken—whether financially, emotionally, or relationally—it affects everything. That's the power of Security. When we don't feel safe, it's nearly impossible to dream, create, or connect. Our nervous system locks down, and life becomes about survival rather than expansion.

Security is the bedrock of our well-being. It's the inner "exhale" that allows us to relax, trust, and feel safe. Without it, we live on edge feeling fearful, anxious, uncertain, and emotionally guarded. This need shows up everywhere: in our relationships, finances, health, homes, communities, and even in our thoughts.

Security looks different for everyone. For one person, it's a million dollars in the bank. For another, it's a stocked fridge. For someone else, it's knowing a loved one will always answer the phone. The details differ, but one truth is universal: when our sense of Security is threatened, everything else becomes harder to access, including joy, connection, creativity, growth.

Just like roots anchor a tree to the Earth, Security anchors you into yourself. It's not weakness to need it; it's wisdom to create it.

The Foundation We Stand On

Security isn't about being boring or risk-averse; it's about creating the internal and external stability that allows everything else to grow. It matters because it supports:

- **Physical Safety:** We need to feel safe in our homes, workplaces, and communities in order to thrive
- **Emotional Well-being:** A stable foundation helps us respond calmly to stress and change
- **Financial Stability:** Knowing that your basic needs are covered reduces fear and gives you space to plan for the future
- **Trust in Relationships:** We feel most free to be vulnerable when we trust that someone won't abandon, betray, or shame us—and if they do, we can trust ourselves to get through it
- **Mental Health:** Chronic insecurity leads to anxiety, overwhelm, and overthinking

The Light and Shadow Sides of Security

Like all human needs, the need for Security has both healthy and limiting expressions.

When Security is a Strength:

- Encourages loyalty, dependability, and commitment
- Provides a strong foundation for long-term planning and growth

- Fosters environments where people feel nurtured and safe

When Security Becomes a Block:
- Leads to avoidance of risk, change, or uncertainty
- Fuels perfectionism, rigidity, or hyper-controlling behaviors
- Encourages staying in unfulfilling relationships, jobs, or habits out of fear
- Causes over-attachment to routine and resistance to new experiences

People with a high need for Security are often the stabilizers in families and teams. They're reliable, grounded, and thoughtful, and if the need dominates, it can lead to stagnation or even emotional paralysis.

The key is to *build* your sense of safety, not cling to it. True resilience comes from knowing you can handle life's ups and downs, not from trying to prevent them all.

Code Words

You can often spot the need for Security in the words used. Here are some **code words** that reveal when this need is driving you or someone else:

Comfort / Comfortable: Seeking ease and peace of mind

Safe / Safety: Prioritizing emotional or physical protection

Stable / Stability: Desiring consistency and control

Grounded / Rooted: Wanting to feel anchored or connected

Predictable: Preferring routines or reliable outcomes

Protected / Defensive: Guarding against vulnerability or harm

Trust / Trustworthy / Loyal: Requiring reliability in relationships

Assurance / Confidence: Needing certainty about the future

Shelter: Wanting physical or emotional refuge

Cautious: Being careful due to fear of instability

Pain-free / Secure: Avoiding anything that threatens the status quo

These words aren't bad; they're signals. When you hear them (especially in your own thoughts), you're learning what your nervous system is asking for.

Needing Security Isn't a Weakness, It's a Core Need

If this is one of your top needs, you might notice these tendencies:
- Craving routine, predictability, or control
- Avoiding conflict or change
- Over-preparing or trying to plan every detail
- Struggling to leave comfort zones, even when growth is needed
- Clinging to familiar situations out of fear, not fulfillment

This is your brain's way of seeking safety. Yet, Security doesn't mean staying still. It means knowing you'll be okay, even when things move.

Practical Questions to Explore Your Need for Security

➢ Where in my life do I feel most secure?

➢ Where do I feel the most uncertain or vulnerable?

➢ How do I typically respond to change or disruption?

➢ Am I holding on to something that no longer serves me just because it's familiar?

➢ What healthy habits, systems, or support would help me feel more grounded?

Simple Ways to Meet Your Need for Security

- Create a grounding morning or evening routine
- Build a financial buffer or review spending to stay on a monthly budget
- Declutter to create a sense of calm and control
- Set consistent work hours or daily rhythms that reduce overwhelm
- Ask for clarity or reassurance in relationships
- Keep a gratitude journal to focus on what's already stable
- Use breathwork, nature, or somatic tools to regulate your nervous system
- Prepare for the future without over-controlling it
- Organize important information (contacts, passwords, paperwork) in one place
- Focus on one area of life at a time instead of scattering your energy

How Security Shows Up in the Roots

Health: Establishing routines for rest, exercise, and nourishment
Family: Feeling emotionally and physically safe with loved ones
Relationships: Trust, reliability, and consistency in connection
Career: Job stability, financial reliability, and role clarity
Friends: Knowing who will show up for you when it counts

Closing Thoughts

Security isn't about playing small. It's about creating the stability that lets you rise strong. When you honor your need for safety, you build a foundation that steadies your heart, clears your mind, and makes space for growth.

It's not about controlling every outcome. It's about knowing that no matter what happens, you have what it takes to navigate it.

Let Security root you, not to keep you stuck, but to help you stand tall.

Now let's explore the need that tugs in the opposite direction, Variety.

CHAPTER 13

NEED 2: VARIETY

Keeping Life Fresh

We all crave surprise, change, and fresh experiences. While Security grounds us, Variety brings us to life. It's the spark that makes us feel excited, curious, and creatively engaged. It's the urge to explore, shake things up, and try something new, not because something's wrong, but because newness makes us feel alive.

Think about a time when every day felt the same…same tasks, same conversations, same four walls. Eventually, even comfort can feel like a cage. You may find yourself scrolling endlessly, daydreaming about travel, rearranging furniture, or craving something—anything— to break the monotony. That's the need for Variety calling out: *wake me up, stir my soul, show me something new.*

A Case of Restlessness: Nick's Story

Nick was a touring guitarist who lived for the road—new cities, packed venues, spontaneous late-night jams. But when his band took an extended break during the pandemic and life quieted down, he struggled. *"It's like I forgot who I am,"* he told me. *"Every day's the same. I feel trapped."*

Without the adrenaline of performing and socializing, Nick's need for Variety was unmet. When he came out of the pandemic, he tried to fill the void by overindulging in partying, binge-watching shows, dating without connection. Inside, he knew it wasn't healthy or meeting deeper needs. What finally helped was discovering healthier ways to stimulate his creativity: producing tracks in different genres, hosting jam sessions with new musicians, and teaching a beginner music class at a local school. Variety meant learning to channel his craving for newness into growth, not destruction.

Sometimes, when the need for Variety goes unmet for too long, we reach for shortcuts—alcohol, drugs, thrill-seeking, shopping, endless scrolling, or emotional drama—to simulate excitement and break the monotony. While these can provide a temporary rush, they rarely satisfy the deeper craving for purpose and creativity. If you've ever used unhealthy coping mechanisms to avoid boredom or feel "something," you're not alone. These behaviors are often unconscious attempts to meet a very real need. The key is learning how to meet that need in high-quality, life-affirming ways.

Using Variety to Spark Your Life

Meeting your need for Variety in healthy ways can dramatically improve your well-being. When this need goes unmet, life can feel flat and uninspired. When it's honored, you feel more awake, playful, and emotionally present.

Here's what Variety supports:

- **Creative Thinking**: New experiences stimulate fresh ideas
- **Resilience:** Navigating change builds adaptability and emotional flexibility
- **Excitement:** Keeps relationships and routines from growing stale
- **Exploration:** Encourages you to try new things and discover hidden passions
- **Motivation:** Disrupts monotony and prevents burnout

People often underestimate how much a lack of Variety can lead to boredom, frustration, or even self-sabotage. It's not indulgent to shake things up. It's essential to feeling alive.

The Light & Shadow Sides of Variety

Like every core need, you can express Variety in ways that support your growth, or undermine it.

When Variety is a Strength:
- Fuels passion, play, and creative flow
- Encourages adaptability and a growth mindset
- Inspires new ideas and fresh perspectives
- Brings energy and novelty into relationships and environments

When Variety Becomes a Block:
- Leads to scattered focus or inconsistency
- Triggers boredom in stable, meaningful situations
- Fuels chaos or restlessness just to "feel something"
- Creates impulsivity, distraction, or escapism
- Makes long-term commitment feel suffocating

Remember, Variety doesn't mean being unfocused or impulsive. It means honoring your need for stimulation in ways that expand your life, not disrupt it.

Code Words

Pay attention to the language you or others use. These words often signal a craving for stimulation, change, or emotional novelty:

New / Different / Unusual / Novel: Seeking contrast or freshness

Exciting / Fun / Spontaneous: Wanting stimulation or play

Adventure / Challenge: Desiring boldness or personal edge

Change / Transition / Shift: Needing movement

Surprise / Thrill / Edge: Seeking risk or activation

Open to Possibility / Exploration: Craving discovery

Bored / Restless / Stir-crazy: Signs of unmet variety

These aren't throwaway words, they're signals from your nervous system that something needs to shift.

When the Need for Variety is Driving Your Life

If Variety is one of your dominant needs, you might notice:

- Starting lots of things but rarely finishing them
- Jumping from project to project (or relationship to relationship)
- Avoiding structure or routine because it feels restrictive
- Creating unnecessary drama or distractions just to break the monotony
- Feeling unmotivated when everything feels the same

None of these patterns make you wrong. They simply reflect a deep need for newness, challenge, and stimulation. The goal is to meet this need in a way that keeps your life vibrant, without unraveling what's working.

Practical Questions to Explore

➢ Where in my life do I feel bored or uninspired?

➢ How do I typically seek stimulation or excitement?

➢ Am I using healthy outlets, or falling into distraction or chaos?

➢ What creative or playful activities light me up right now?

➢ Where could I infuse more fun, flexibility, or experimentation?

Simple Ways to Meet Your Need for Variety

- Try a new hobby, recipe, or workout style
- Rearrange a room or refresh your daily routine
- Plan spontaneous adventures, even small ones
- Take a class just for fun, not productivity
- Journal in a new location or take meetings outside
- Create a "something new" weekly challenge
- Explore a different genre of music, book, or podcast
- Introduce playful rituals like themed nights or surprise plans
- Change your environment with nature walks or creative spaces

How Variety Shows Up in the Roots

Health: Trying new workouts, recipes, or wellness routines

Family: Creating spontaneous adventures or rotating traditions

Relationships: Introducing playful experiences or emotional novelty

Career: Seeking creative projects or evolving roles

Friends: Planning fun, diverse activities and meeting new people

Closing Thought

Variety doesn't have to mean chaos. It simply means staying awake to the richness of life. When you meet this need intentionally—not impulsively—it becomes a wellspring of energy, creativity, and joy.

Honor it. Dance with it. Let it bring color to your world without pulling you off center. Now let's deep dive into Self.

CHAPTER 14

NEED 3: SELF

The Core of Identity

Every person has a fundamental need to feel like they matter. Whether through accomplishments, service, creativity, or presence, we long to feel important, valued, and unique. This is the need for Self: the emotional hunger for identity, significance, and self-worth.

From the time we're young, we scan the world for signs of who we are and what makes us valuable. We listen for praise. We notice who gets attention. We internalize what earns love, and what invites disapproval. Over time, these signals shape our identity. We form beliefs like, *"I'm only lovable if I succeed,"* or *"I have to be the best to be enough."*

Beneath all the striving, a quiet truth remains: you are not your performance. You are not your productivity. You are not your status or your roles. You are your presence, your essence, your being, your truth. Self-worth is not about becoming more. It's about remembering that you were already enough.

A Case of Self-Worth Reclaimed: Ivy's Story

Ivy was a top-performing creative director at a major ad agency. She led award-winning campaigns, mentored junior staff, and always exceeded expectations. But beneath her polished surface was a woman unraveling.

"I don't know who I am without my job," she confessed in a coaching session. "If I don't constantly prove my worth, I feel invisible."

Her entire identity had become entangled with success. She rarely took time off. She feared losing relevance. And compliments never seemed to land. They evaporated before she could believe them.

We worked on separating her value from her output. She began journaling her strengths, setting boundaries with clients, and reconnecting with long-neglected passions. She learned to ask herself, "What do I want?" instead of "What will make me look good?"

Eventually, Ivy left the agency and started a small design studio on her terms. For the first time in years, she felt free. "I'm still creating," she said, "but now it's from a place of caring about others, not fear of being judged."

Ivy didn't stop there. She launched a mentorship circle for mid-career creatives, offering space for women to explore their worth beyond titles and awards. She also began taking on purpose-driven clients, lending her talents to causes she believed in.

Ivy didn't lose her ambition. She reclaimed it, rooted now in impact, self-respect, and joy. In supporting others, she finally saw her own value reflected back. And in helping others rise, she rose too.

Becoming the Source of Your Own Value

When the Self need is met in healthy ways, it creates confidence, clarity, and a sense of purpose. We stop outsourcing our worth and begin living from our truth. We raise our standards, speak up for ourselves, and lead with presence instead of performance.

Here's how the need for Self supports your well-being:

- **Creates Purpose:** Feeling significant gives your life direction and focus

- **Builds Self-Confidence:** You feel grounded and resilient in your decisions

- **Strengthens Relationships:** When you value yourself, you form deeper, more respectful connections
- **Encourages Achievement:** This need drives you to take initiative and show up fully
- **Protects Against Self-Sabotage:** A healthy sense of self-worth reduces the need to seek significance in negative ways

Self-worth is essential not just for personal growth, but for emotional safety. Without it, we become vulnerable to toxic relationships, burnout, and cycles of self-doubt.

The Light & Shadow Sides of the Need for Self

When Self is a Strength:
- Fuels authentic leadership, confidence, and self-expression
- Encourages healthy boundaries and resilience
- Helps you take initiative and stand in your truth
- Supports emotional balance and clarity of identity
- Models wholeness and inspires others to do the same

When Self Becomes a Block:
- Can lead to arrogance, perfectionism, or the need to be right
- May create excessive competition or comparison
- Fuels people-pleasing or over-functioning to earn validation
- Causes self-worth to become tied to performance or external status
- In extreme cases, can lead to feelings of deep inadequacy or hopelessness

One of the fastest ways people try to feel significant is by dominating attention, whether by being the loudest, always needing to be right, or constantly positioning themselves as the one with the biggest problem.

Others may over-identify with roles or status, losing sight of their identity outside of achievement.

Code Words

These words and phrases often reflect a desire for validation, control, or internal significance:

Self-Esteem / Confidence: Trust in your own value

Significance / Status / Influence: Longing to matter or be impactful

Achievement / Recognition / Legacy: Wanting your efforts to be seen and remembered

Validation / Approval / Praise: Seeking reassurance of worth

Power / Control: Desire for influence or leadership

Perfection / Comparison / Competition: Measuring your worth against others

Relevance / Distinction / Special: Needing to feel unique or irreplaceable

Purpose / Identity: Craving clarity about who you are and why you matter

These aren't inherently unhealthy. They're clues about where your need for significance is surfacing and whether it's being met in empowering or depleting ways.

When the Need for Self is Driving Your Life

If this is one of your top needs, you may notice these patterns:

- A constant drive to perform, lead, or be acknowledged
- Sensitivity to criticism or feeling unseen
- Overworking to prove yourself
- People-pleasing to earn approval

- Comparing yourself to others and coming up short
- Struggling with imposter syndrome or perfectionism
- Defining your worth by how much you do, not who you are

When unmet, this need can spiral into intense self-doubt, victimhood, or even thoughts of worthlessness. I've seen clients push themselves into burnout or sabotage meaningful opportunities simply because they didn't believe they were enough. This is why developing a strong, loving relationship with yourself isn't just important, it's essential.

Practical Questions to Explore

➢ Where do I feel most proud of who I am?

➢ Where am I over-performing or seeking approval to feel enough?

➢ Do I know who I am outside of roles like parent, partner, or professional?

➢ What limiting beliefs do I carry about my worth?

➢ What would shift if I chose to believe "I matter just as I am"?

Simple Ways to Meet Your Need for Self

- Write a "wins list" each week and celebrate every small or big success
- Set one boundary that affirms your worth and energy
- Do something you're naturally good at
- Reconnect with your "why" or mission
- Look in the mirror and say one kind thing to yourself each day
- Acknowledge yourself out loud: "I'm proud of…" or "I'm learning to…"
- Wear something that makes you feel uniquely YOU

- Let yourself be seen and share something honest with someone you trust.
- Create a ritual for self-honor: a reflection walk, a gratitude note to yourself, or a solo celebration.

How Self Shows Up in the Roots

Health: Feeling confident and proud of your body and choices
Family: Honoring your individuality within the family system
Relationships: Asserting boundaries, being seen and respected
Career: Expressing your talents and being recognized for your value
Friends: Showing up authentically and sharing your true Self

Closing Thought

You are not here to prove yourself. You are here to *be* yourself. Your worth is not earned through effort, it's remembered through awareness. When you meet the need for Self from within, you stop chasing significance and begin living it. And that's when your presence becomes magnetic, not because you're trying, but because you're standing fully in your truth.

Next up, Intimacy…

CHAPTER 15

NEED 4: INTIMACY

Connection That Begins Within

Humans are wired for connection. We crave closeness, warmth, and a sense of belonging. At its core, Intimacy means truly knowing and being known—being seen for who we are and feeling safe in that space. While Intimacy is often associated with romantic or sexual relationships, it extends far beyond that.

We can experience deep Intimacy with friends, family, mentors, communities, and most importantly, with ourselves. Intimacy is about vulnerability, trust, and authentic connection. It's about the emotional closeness that nourishes us, whether that comes from a conversation with a loved one, a quiet moment of self-reflection, or the tender presence of someone who sees us clearly.

The Many Facets of Intimacy

You don't need to be in a romantic relationship to experience Intimacy. In fact, being single can be a powerful time to deepen your relationship with yourself, explore your emotional needs, and build fulfilling connections in other areas of life. Friendships and familial relationships can also be intimate.

While sexual intimacy can be one form of closeness, it's not a substitute for emotional intimacy, and confusing the two can leave us feeling even more isolated.

Without Intimacy, we can feel disconnected, unseen, or misunderstood. While some people naturally prioritize intimacy, others may avoid it due to fear of rejection, past wounds, or difficulty trusting. Learning to foster Intimacy in healthy ways—both with ourselves and others—is essential to feeling loved, valued, and emotionally fulfilled.

Intimacy represents our innate human need to connect deeply, emotionally, and meaningfully. It's a core part of how we experience love, belonging, and mutual understanding. While some dependency is natural and even healthy, there's a delicate balance. When our need for Intimacy becomes entangled with fear, control, or over-attachment, it can veer into codependency.

People with an acute need for Intimacy often serve as the glue in their relationships and communities. They're the trusted confidantes, the peacemakers, the ones who create safe emotional space for others to be real. They're able to express vulnerability and often invite it in return. These individuals are driven by a desire to love and be loved, and sometimes, it even shows up on the outside. I've had friends with the word love tattooed visibly on their bodies, a bold and beautiful symbol of how deeply Intimacy matters to them.

The shadow side of this need can show up when others don't reciprocate. If someone craves deep connection, constant emotional walls or avoidance from others can cause frustration and self-doubt. Then remember this: you can invite Intimacy but never demand it. You can offer it, but you can't force it.

A powerful way to reframe Intimacy comes from a phrase popularized by psychotherapist and relationship expert Esther Perel, who describes Intimacy as "into-me-see." It reflects the essence of what so many of us are truly craving: to be seen and accepted not only in our strengths but in our vulnerabilities. One of my coaches, Iris Benrubi, beautifully expanded on this idea, breaking it into two reflections: "into-me-I-see"—representing Intimacy with oneself—and "into-me-you-see," which reflects the courage to let others in. Together, they offer a powerful invitation: be willing to see yourself fully, and then offer others the same open-hearted visibility.

A Case of Emotional Intimacy: Nate's Story

Nate was a successful engineer raised in a tight-knit traditional family. His mother was strong-willed and dominant, shaping a household where expectations were clear: marry young, have children, and climb the ladder of conventional success. Nate followed the rules on the surface, but inside, he felt trapped.

He longed for deep connection, but also feared it. His childhood taught him that closeness came with strings—expectations, enmeshment, and loss of autonomy. His parents even attempted to arrange a marriage, which he flat-out refused.

In his adult life, Nate pursued sexual relationships that lacked depth. He called himself a "lone wolf" and proudly identified as a "sigma male," claiming he didn't need anyone. "My career and family are enough," he'd say. But the truth was, he was lonely.

Over eight years, he maintained an on-again, off-again connection with a woman he admired. She was emotionally intelligent, grounded, and kind. Each time she moved toward deeper emotional intimacy, he'd ghost her, sometimes for months, only to resurface again when the loneliness returned.

In coaching, Nate began unpacking the real reasons behind his avoidance. He admitted he feared being controlled, feared losing his freedom, even feared having to compromise his late-night workouts or sleep schedule. What if intimacy meant giving up who he was?

What changed was this: he learned real intimacy doesn't demand that you disappear. It asks you to *show up*. To be honest about what you need, what you fear, and who you are. Nate is still learning. But now, he understands intimacy isn't a trap, it's a choice. A courageous one. And that genuine connection can enhance freedom, not erase it.

From Surface to Soul

When our need for Intimacy is met in healthy ways, we feel emotionally safe, supported, and loved. We're able to be ourselves and allow others to do the same. We open up. We soften. We connect.

Here's what healthy Intimacy provides:

- **Emotional Well-being**: Reduces stress and anxiety through connection
- **Belonging:** Creates a sense of being part of something greater
- **Authenticity:** Encourages vulnerability and truth-telling
- **Resilience:** Helps us process emotions and challenges with support
- **Spiritual Connection:** Deepens our relationship with ourselves and others

Without Intimacy, we feel disconnected. Even when surrounded by people, we might feel emotionally alone, unseen, or misunderstood.

The Light and Shadow Sides of Intimacy

When Intimacy is a Strength:

- Builds emotional safety in relationships
- Encourages authentic communication and mutual trust
- Allows others to feel deeply seen and accepted
- Creates a container for healing, growth, and compassion
- Fosters closeness without codependence

When Intimacy Becomes a Block:

- Can become enmeshed, overly dependent, or clingy

- May lead to fear of abandonment or rejection
- Can cause emotional overwhelm if boundaries are unclear
- Leads to resentment if vulnerability isn't reciprocated
- Might confuse physical closeness with emotional depth

One of the most painful patterns I've seen is when people crave Intimacy but push it away out of fear. They want closeness but feel unsafe when it's offered. Or they settle for surface-level relationships that don't nourish them, just to avoid being alone. Others may confuse sex with Intimacy, believing that physical closeness equals emotional connection—when, in reality, Intimacy requires emotional vulnerability, not just physical contact.

True Intimacy also means developing a deep, compassionate relationship with yourself and being honest about your needs, loving your imperfections, and offering yourself the same care and presence you long for from others. Whether or not you're in a relationship, your need for Intimacy is valid. You deserve to feel connected, emotionally nourished, and truly seen. And those feelings can begin with you.

Code Words

Listen closely to your language, the words others use. These are emotional clues that point to a need for deeper connection:

Connection / Closeness / Bonding: Desire for emotional linking

Vulnerability / Openness: Willingness to be seen and heard

Affection / Tenderness / Warmth: Craving for care and closeness

Belonging / Togetherness / Unity: Need to be included or part of something

Companionship / Support / Friendship: Longing for consistent presence

Love / Passion / Desire: Emotional or romantic closeness

Trust / Understanding / Rapport: Craving safety in being real

Loneliness / Isolation / Disconnection: Signals of unmet Intimacy

These words reflect where Intimacy is either flourishing or where it's being missed, avoided, or denied.

When the Need for Intimacy is Driving Your Life

When Intimacy is a top need, you may notice:

- A deep longing to feel seen, understood, or emotionally close
- Patterns of people-pleasing or self-abandonment to avoid disconnection
- Staying in unbalanced relationships just to avoid loneliness
- Fear of emotional exposure, even when craving connection
- Pursuing sex or flirtation to meet the emotional need for Intimacy
- Over-giving in friendships or partnerships without receiving the same depth in return

This need is beautiful and sensitive. It requires trust, time, and safe containers. But most importantly, it begins with one essential relationship: *the one you have with yourself.*

Practical Questions to Explore

➢ Do I feel emotionally safe and seen in my closest relationships?

➢ Am I willing to be vulnerable or do I guard my heart to protect myself?

➢ How do I define Intimacy and what does it look like in my life now?

➢ Where am I confusing physical closeness with emotional connection?

➢ Am I longing for others to see me while hiding my truest self?

Simple Ways to Meet Your Need for Intimacy

- Call a friend and have a real, vulnerable conversation
- Write yourself a letter from your most loving, accepting self
- Journal honestly about what you're feeling without censoring
- Practice "into-me-I-see" by noticing your own inner world with compassion
- Hug someone for over 20 seconds (it activates oxytocin)
- Let someone know what they mean to you—out loud
- Schedule quality time with a loved one and put your phone away
- Spend quiet time in nature to reconnect with your spiritual intimacy
- Try mirror work by looking into your own eyes with softness

How Intimacy Shows Up in the Roots

Health: Creating a compassionate relationship with your body

Family: Sharing openly and feeling emotionally close

Relationships: Being vulnerable, emotionally available, and fully seen

Career: Building trusting mentorships or authentic collaborations

Friends: One-on-one time, deep conversations, emotional safety

Closing Thoughts

True intimacy begins not with another person, but within. The more you connect with your own emotions, needs, and truths, the more capable you become of offering and receiving deep love.

Let yourself be seen, not just the polished parts, but the real ones. You are worthy of love...not someday, not when you're "better," but right now. Just as you are.

Later in this book, you'll explore the Intimacy Ladder, a powerful tool to help you identify your current level of emotional closeness and grow it intentionally. Whether you're seeking deeper intimacy with yourself, a partner, or others in your life, this ladder offers a step-by-step guide to build connection safely and meaningfully. For now, just know this: wherever you are, it's a valid starting point. Intimacy is always possible.

Up next, we'll explore your need for Growth, the desire to expand beyond your current limits and become who you're meant to be.

CHAPTER 16

NEED 5: GROWTH

The Drive to Evolve and Expand

G rowth is what keeps us moving forward. It's the part of us that yearns to become more than we were yesterday—to learn, heal, stretch, and rise. It's the fire behind progress and the quiet whisper that says, *"There's more for you."*

Growth isn't just about goals or personal development, it's about evolution. Becoming more fully yourself. Expanding beyond past limitations. Reaching for potential you haven't yet touched.

And for some of us, Growth is more than a season, it's a lifestyle. A spiritual posture. A way of being in the world.

Yet, when the pursuit of Growth becomes relentless, it can mask a deeper feeling of never being enough. You might think: "I just need to read one more thing…take one more course…listen to one more podcast…" until it becomes more about consuming information than actually living it.

It's also common for Growth-oriented people to feel hesitant about starting something new until they've achieved a certain level of mastery or certification. The belief might be: "I can't begin until I've learned more." While this mindset honors integrity, it can delay progress or feed perfectionism.

Growth to Evolve

Growth is a dance between expansion and integration. Sometimes, the most profound progress happens through reflection, rest, and trust in what you already know.

When we stop growing, we shrink. Even if life is "fine," without a sense of movement, we begin to feel stagnant, uninspired, or stuck. Meeting your need for Growth keeps your spirit alive.

Here's why Growth is so essential:

Purpose: It gives you a reason to show up and keep going

Resilience: Learning helps you adapt to change and bounce back from setbacks

Empowerment: Each small step builds confidence and agency

Creativity: Personal evolution unlocks new ideas, visions, and possibilities

Fulfillment: Progress, no matter how small, feels good and fuels momentum

Growth doesn't always mean adding more. Sometimes it means going deeper. Sitting still. Listening inwardly. Integration is just as important as acquisition.

The Light and Shadow Sides of Growth

When Growth is a Strength:

- Creates lifelong learners with vision and passion
- Inspires reinvention, exploration, and self-awareness
- Keeps life engaging and dynamic
- Prevents emotional stagnation or complacency
- Empowers people to evolve through adversity

When Growth Becomes a Block:

- Fuels the feeling of never being enough or Imposter Syndrome

- Leads to constant striving or over-consumption of self-help
- May cause burnout from always chasing the next thing
- Can delay action with "I need to learn more first" syndrome
- Creates impatience with others who grow at a different pace

One client shared: "I realized I was always in intake mode—learning, listening, reading—but never integrating. It was like I was trying to grow so fast, I forgot to just be with myself."

Another client, Maya, had been single for over a decade. She'd always say she wanted a relationship, yet it remained on the back burner as something she'd "get to" after earning her degree or finishing a course. She believed intimacy would distract her from her growth. Her days were full of podcasts, classes, and journaling. But one day, she realized that deep personal growth also happens *in* relationship, through reflection, shared vulnerability, and navigating partnership dynamics. It opened a new door for her, one she'd unknowingly closed. And when she walked through it, she didn't stop growing. She grew in an entirely new way.

If you're constantly learning and rarely resting, your Growth may tip into overdrive. The answer isn't to stop growing. It's to grow with intention, not anxiety.

Code Words

These terms often appear when the need to stretch, evolve, or expand is active:

Learning / Discovery / Curiosity: Seeking insight and new knowledge

Progress / Expansion / Momentum: Wanting to move forward

Advancement / Achievement / Mastery: Craving skill-building or next-level living

Transformation / Evolution / Breakthrough: Longing for change or healing

Empowerment / Realization / Awareness: Owning your journey and potential

Challenge / Growth Edge / Stretch: Embracing discomfort for the sake of expansion

Purpose / Vision / Calling: Wanting life to mean something more

When you notice these words in your thoughts or conversations, it's likely this need is asking for attention.

When the Need for Growth is Driving Your Life

If this is one of your top needs, you may notice:

- A constant craving for the next course, book, coach, or breakthrough
- Frustration with anything that feels stagnant or too easy
- Struggling to rest because you associate stillness with laziness
- Feeling like you're behind if you're not improving fast enough
- Pushing others to grow when they may not be ready
- Delaying action until you feel "more qualified" or "better prepared"

This need often shows up in people who are deeply passionate, mission-driven, and spiritually awake. But without integration, Growth becomes performance.

True Growth asks: "Can you honor how far you've come and keep going?"

Practical Questions to Explore

➢ What does Growth look like for me right now? (More? Less? Different?)

➢ Am I chasing Growth to feel worthy or because I'm inspired?

➢ Where am I still waiting to be *"ready"* when I could just begin?

➢ What have I learned lately that I haven't fully applied?

➢ What would it feel like to grow gently instead of urgently?

Simple Ways to Meet Your Need for Growth

- Learn one new thing each week—just for fun
- Revisit old lessons and reflect on how you've changed
- Set one micro-goal that feels exciting but doable
- Take a risk or say yes to something that stretches you
- Pause your intake and let your soul digest what you've learned
- Celebrate a recent challenge you overcame
- Ask yourself, *"What's one way I've grown in the last six months?"*
- Try a new perspective, not just a new skill
- Give yourself permission to evolve without rushing

How Growth Shows Up in the Roots

Health: Learning about nutrition, movement, or body wisdom

Family: Healing patterns or evolving family dynamics

Relationships: Expanding communication and emotional intelligence

Career: Pursuing skills, leadership, or meaningful challenges

Friends: Choosing friends who inspire you to evolve and expand

Closing Thoughts

Growth is sacred. It doesn't have to be exhausting. You're allowed to rise slowly, gently, in your own rhythm. You're allowed to celebrate how far you've come, even as you reach for more.

This need isn't about becoming someone else. It's about becoming more of who you already are. And as we grow, we often reach a point where personal development alone isn't enough. We crave something deeper, something beyond ourselves. That's where Transcendence begins.

CHAPTER 17

NEED 6: TRANSCENDENCE

Giving Beyond Yourself

A t a certain point in life, our internal questions shift.

We stop asking, *"What do I want to get?"* and start asking, *"What am I here to give?"*

That's the essence of Transcendence: the need to connect to something greater than yourself, whether it's service, purpose, community, or the divine. It's the desire to make a difference, leave a legacy, and know that your presence matters in a wider story.

This isn't about ego. It's about expansion. Transcendence takes you beyond your personal needs and anchors you in meaning.

While personal growth, achievement, and self-worth are essential, Transcendence takes fulfillment to another level. It's service without expectation, giving for the sake of impact, and aligning with a higher purpose. True Transcendence isn't about getting credit; it's about creating ripples of positive change, whether anyone sees them.

It's important to acknowledge that the need for Transcendence often intertwines with the need for significance. Making a difference can also make us feel important. But when we're rooted in true service, the ego loosens its grip. It's no longer about how important we are; it's about the lives we touch.

When people move into a stage of life where Transcendence becomes a driving need, something remarkable happens: the other needs align, too. The search for self-worth feels grounded. Growth becomes more meaningful. Variety emerges through new ways of contributing. Even connection deepens, because Transcendence draws people together through shared values and purpose.

I've experienced this shift. Earlier in life, many of my decisions were driven by Self, Growth, and Security…sometimes in healthy ways, sometimes not. When I began leading from a desire to help others— truly help them—everything changed. I felt more whole, more grounded, and more connected. It was as if the other needs were getting met at a higher level simply because I had shifted my focus from *"me"* to *"we."*

Transcendence Through Spiritual Practice

Transcendence is the need to feel part of something greater than ourselves, a connection to the sacred, the infinite, or the deeply meaningful. This doesn't have to be religious. For some, Transcendence is found in prayer or devotion to God/Goddess. For others, it may arise during a silent walk in the woods, gazing at a night sky, feeling the breath during meditation, or being moved to tears by a piece of music. What matters most is the experience of going beyond the ego, touching something timeless and vast.

Spirituality, in its many forms, is one of the most powerful ways we meet this need. Whether through mindfulness practices, spiritual study, communal worship, or daily rituals of gratitude and reverence, these experiences help us zoom out from our problems and anchor into a greater sense of purpose. They remind us we are not alone, not broken, and not defined by what we do. Instead, we can look at who we are at our core.

An artist I worked with shared that despite her achievements, she always felt like something was missing. When she began practicing a daily morning meditation and lighting a candle to set an intention, she found a sense of peace she had never experienced in years of striving.

She saw her challenges not as punishments, but as invitations to align with something deeper. Her art became more soulful. Her relationships softened. And slowly, she stopped chasing success and started creating from a place of devotion.

Another client found Transcendence not through spiritual practice, but through service. After losing her job and feeling directionless, she began volunteering at a local animal rescue center. She told me, "Showing up for those animals made me feel useful again. It reminded me I still had something to give." That connection to beings who couldn't repay her was healing in a way that achievement never had been.

We also feel Transcendence when parenting, mentoring, creating legacy work, or supporting someone in crisis. It's in the quiet acts of generosity that go unnoticed. It's in the ways we show up when no one is watching.

The Gifts of Sacred Work

When we meet our need for Transcendence, we stop feeling like we're just surviving. We begin living from a place of purpose and peace. Even when life is hard, we can find fulfillment in knowing we're part of something bigger.

Here's what Transcendence gives us:

- **Purpose:** A deep sense of direction and meaning
- **Legacy:** The ability to impact others long after we're gone
- **Humility:** Relief from self-obsession and over-identification with success or failure
- **Spiritual Connection:** A feeling of oneness with nature, the universe, or the divine
- **Healing:** By giving to others, we often restore something inside ourselves

Transcendence isn't always loud or public. Sometimes, it's quiet, like a small act of kindness no one sees, or a prayer whispered in the dark. But it's always powerful.

The Light & Shadow Sides of Transcendence

When Transcendence is a Strength:

- Inspires generosity, purpose, and a legacy mindset
- Encourages contribution without expectation
- Deepens spiritual and emotional fulfillment
- Connects people to community, mission, or collective healing
- Helps you find meaning even in difficult circumstances

When Transcendence Becomes a Block:

- Can morph into martyrdom or self-sacrifice
- May lead to burnout when you give beyond your capacity
- Can blur healthy boundaries in the name of "service"
- May feed an ego-driven need to be "the helper" or "the healer"
- Might suppress personal needs in the pursuit of higher ones

When this need is distorted, it can show up as performative altruism or spiritual bypassing—using service or "purpose" to avoid dealing with your own pain. True Transcendence doesn't ignore the self. It includes the self, and expands beyond it with love.

Code Words

Watch for these phrases when the need to serve, uplift, or expand beyond personal limitations is calling:

Purpose / Mission / Calling: Longing for meaningful impact

Service / Contribution / Giving: Wanting to offer something beyond yourself

Legacy / Influence / Impact: Desiring to leave something behind

Spiritual / Sacred / Divine: Craving connection to something eternal

Healing / Mentoring / Guiding: Wanting to support others' journeys

Vision / Change / Empowerment: Hoping to uplift a person or system

Meaning / Fulfillment / Devotion: Seeking soulful satisfaction

Oneness / Belonging / Collective: Feeling part of humanity, nature, or spirit

These words often come with goosebumps. Or tears. Or stillness. They reflect the soul's need to *serve something more.*

When the Need for Transcendence is Driving Your Life

You may notice:

- A strong pull to create something that outlives you
- A deep desire to help others through teaching, caregiving, art, or service
- A search for spiritual connection, meaning, or divine presence
- Disinterest in purely material goals because you want your life to matter
- A tendency to feel unfulfilled by surface-level success
- A longing to uplift, inspire, or heal, sometimes at your own expense

Some people experience Transcendence through spirituality. Others find it in parenting, mentoring, volunteering, creating, or caring for animals. What matters is not what you do, but that you feel like your life contributes to something greater.

Practical Questions to Explore

➤ What lights me up beyond achievement or status?

➤ Where in my life do I already make a difference, even in small ways?

➤ What "greater good" do I feel most connected to?

➤ What legacy do I want to leave behind energetically, emotionally, or creatively?

➤ What small act of love or contribution can I offer today?

Simple Ways to Meet Your Need for Transcendence

- Practice a daily gratitude ritual or prayer
- Volunteer for a cause that matters to you
- Mentor someone who's just beginning the path you've walked
- Contribute anonymously and give without recognition
- Create something that expresses your truth or inspires others
- Write down the values you want to pass on
- Meditate on your connection to the earth, others, or spirit
- Help someone in need, expecting nothing in return
- Light a candle and set an intention for the collective

How Transcendence Shows Up in the Roots

Health: Using your wellness journey to inspire others

Family: Contributing to legacy, shared purpose, or spiritual connection

Relationships: Experiencing unconditional love or soul connection

Career: Making a difference through your work or service

Friends: Supporting community, belonging, or collective growth

Closing Thoughts

You're here for more than survival. You're here to love, to serve, to shine, to lift others as you rise. Transcendence doesn't require perfection. It simply asks that you show up. In your own way. In your own time.

Let your life echo beyond your actions. Not for applause. Because you are part of something sacred.

CHAPTER 18

APPLYING HUMAN NEEDS

Strengthen Your Roots

O nce you understand the six human needs, you can begin applying them to each of your root areas to get unstuck and create lasting change. Many people remain in unfulfilling cycles simply because they are unconsciously meeting their needs in low-quality ways that don't truly serve them.

The key to transformation is recognizing how you're meeting your needs right now, and finding more aligned, sustainable alternatives. These subtle shifts can create profound ripple effects across your entire life.

To make this real, meet Sophia, a successful, driven professional whose story might sound familiar.

Sophia's Story: When High Achievement Comes at a Hidden Cost

Sophia is a marketing executive in her late 30s. On paper, she has it all: financial security, a powerful role, and a polished reputation. But behind the scenes, she feels drained, disconnected, and stuck in a cycle she doesn't know how to break.

She works over 40 hours a week, skips workouts, rarely sees friends, and suffers from chronic anxiety and fatigue. Whenever someone expresses concern, she brushes it off with:

"I'll slow down after this project." "This is what success looks like." "I should just be grateful for the work."

But deep down, Sophia knows something's not right. Even in her free time, she's trying to do the "right" things, like volunteering at a crisis nursery. "I feel like I should be fulfilled," she said during one of our coaching sessions, "but I just feel disappointed."

When I asked her to explore that more, she admitted something surprising: "I thought helping babies would fill me up. But honestly, I feel lonely. I wanted to be part of a team as passionate as I am, but I usually work alone when I show up. I don't feel like I belong to anything, even though I know the cause is important."

Her story reveals a truth many of us experience: meeting needs in ways that check the box logically doesn't always land emotionally.

Step 1: Identifying the Needs Driving the Pattern

Sophia was trying to meet her six human needs—just in ways that weren't truly serving her. Here's what we uncovered:

- **Security**: She overworked to feel financially and professionally secure, even though it was costing her health and peace of mind.
- **Self**: Her career gave her significance, and it became her primary source of identity and worth.
- **Variety**: She used the fast pace of her job to feel stimulated, yet had little room for joyful novelty elsewhere.
- **Intimacy**: She longed for connection, but avoided closeness—too "busy" for friends, and too emotionally guarded at work.
- **Growth**: She was advancing professionally, but neglecting emotional and personal growth.
- **Transcendence**: She hoped volunteering would give her a sense of purpose, and discovered she was craving belonging, not just impact.

Her disappointment made sense. She wasn't just showing up to help babies. She was seeking a sacred community and didn't find one.

Step 2: Recognizing the Cost of the Current Pattern

Sophia realized she was paying a hidden price for success. The very things she used to meet her needs—constant achievement, independence, perfectionism—were also what kept her isolated and exhausted.

She was trying to meet her need for transcendence through service, but it backfired because it lacked the emotional intimacy and shared purpose she craved. "It doesn't feel meaningful when I'm just doing it alone," she said. "I thought I needed to give back...but what I really needed was connection with other adults."

Step 3: Conditioning a New Pattern

Once Sophia saw the actual need behind her disappointment, she made bold changes. Instead of quitting the nursery, she stepped in more deeply. She volunteered to organize events and recruit other volunteers, transforming her role from lone helper to community builder.

Simultaneously, she made space in other areas of life.

- **Redefined Success**: She expanded her definition to include wellness, friendships, and joy—not just titles and outcomes.
- **Set Boundaries**: No emails after 7 p.m. No weekend work unless urgent.
- **Scheduled Connection**: Weekly walks with a friend. One creative date per month.
- **Rebuilt Variety**: She swapped adrenaline for dance classes, travel, and spontaneous time.
- **Sought True Contribution**: Mentorship became her outlet for meaningful impact with connection.

She stopped trying to *earn* her worth through work and started living in alignment with what actually made her feel whole.

Step 4: Results & Transformation

Over time, Sophia came back to life. Her health improved. Her nervous system calmed. She started laughing again—deep belly laughs with old friends and new teammates. Her confidence grew, not just because she was succeeding, but because she finally felt seen and connected.

She still performs at a high level. But now, it's from a place of grounded wholeness, not burnout.

Key Takeaway: Transformation Is About Alignment

Sophia's story is a reminder that getting unstuck isn't about doing more; it's about meeting your needs in ways that actually nourish you. You don't have to abandon your ambition to live with purpose. You just have to realign the way you pursue it.

So ask yourself:

> ➢ In which root areas am I meeting my needs in ways that keep me stuck?

> ➢ Where am I overcompensating in one root while neglecting another?

> ➢ What small shift could help me feel more balanced, connected, and fulfilled?

Your life's roots are unfixed. You can strengthen them at any time by making intentional, aligned choices that meet your needs in empowering ways. This is the bridge between knowing your needs…and rising to meet them.

Now let's apply what you learned about the human needs to your Life Root System in the following Needs Evaluation section.

CHAPTER 19

NEEDS EVALUATION

Assess Your Life Root System

You've learned about the Life Root System and Six Human Needs. Now, let's put them together and apply the knowledge to your own life with a Needs Evaluation. Take a moment to assess how well your current situation is fulfilling your human needs. Using a scale of 1 to 10 (1 = not fulfilled at all, 10 = completely fulfilled), rate your current experience in the following areas:

Health

Security: How stable and secure do you feel in this area of your life?   _____ (1-10)

Variety: Are you experiencing enough excitement, change, and new experiences?   _____ (1-10)

Self: Do you feel a strong sense of self-worth and confidence?   _____ (1-10)

Intimacy: How connected do you feel in your relationships?   _____ (1-10)

Growth: Are you learning, expanding, and improving in meaningful ways?   _____ (1-10)

Transcendence: Do you feel a sense of purpose beyond yourself?   _____ (1-10)

Calculate the average score for this root area: **_____ (1-10)**

Family

Security: How stable and secure do you feel in this area of
your life? _____ (1-10)

Variety: Are you experiencing enough excitement, change,
and new experiences? _____ (1-10)

Self: Do you feel a strong sense of self-worth and
confidence? _____ (1-10)

Intimacy: How connected do you feel in your
relationships? _____ (1-10)

Growth: Are you learning, expanding, and improving in
meaningful ways? _____ (1-10)

Transcendence: Do you feel a sense of purpose beyond
yourself? _____ (1-10)

Calculate the average score for this root area: **_____ (1-10)**

Relationships

Security: How stable and secure do you feel in this area of
your life? _____ (1-10)

Variety: Are you experiencing enough excitement, change,
and new experiences? _____ (1-10)

Self: Do you feel a strong sense of self-worth and
confidence? _____ (1-10)

Intimacy: How connected do you feel in your
relationships? _____ (1-10)

Growth: Are you learning, expanding, and improving in
meaningful ways? _____ (1-10)

Transcendence: Do you feel a sense of purpose beyond
yourself? _____ (1-10)

Calculate the average score for this root area: **_____ (1-10)**

Career

Security: How stable and secure do you feel in this area of
your life? _____ (1-10)

Variety: Are you experiencing enough excitement, change,
and new experiences? _____ (1-10)

Self: Do you feel a strong sense of self-worth and
confidence? _____ (1-10)

Intimacy: How connected do you feel in your
relationships? _____ (1-10)

Growth: Are you learning, expanding, and improving in
meaningful ways? _____ (1-10)

Transcendence: Do you feel a sense of purpose beyond
yourself? _____ (1-10)

Calculate the average score for this root area: _____ **(1-10)**

Friends

Security: How stable and secure do you feel in this area of
your life? _____ (1-10)

Variety: Are you experiencing enough excitement, change,
and new experiences? _____ (1-10)

Self: Do you feel a strong sense of self-worth and
confidence? _____ (1-10)

Intimacy: How connected do you feel in your
relationships? _____ (1-10)

Growth: Are you learning, expanding, and improving in
meaningful ways? _____ (1-10)

Transcendence: Do you feel a sense of purpose beyond
yourself? _____ (1-10)

Calculate the average score for this root area: _____ **(1-10)**

Root-to-Rise Reflection Exercise: Identifying & Strengthening Your Weakest Root

Now that you've explored and evaluated the Life Root System, it's time to assess where you currently stand and create a plan for growth. This exercise will help you identify which root needs the most attention and how to shift from low-quality patterns to healthier, more fulfilling strategies.

Step 1: Identify Your Weakest Root

Look at the five roots, and answer:

> ➤ Which root feels weakest right now and got the lowest score?

> ➤ Where do I feel the most imbalance, stress, or dissatisfaction?

> ➤ Is there a specific root that drains my energy or feels neglected?

Step 2: Recognize How You're Meeting Your Needs

We all meet our six human needs, and sometimes, we do so in ways that don't serve our highest good.

> ➤ How have I been meeting my needs in this weak root?

> ➤ Am I relying on unhealthy coping mechanisms (overworking, numbing, avoiding, self-sabotage)?

> ➤ Am I sacrificing my needs to meet the needs of others?

Step 3: Shift to High-Quality Patterns

The goal is to elevate how you meet your needs in this root by choosing healthier, more sustainable strategies.

> What are two to three higher-quality ways I can start meeting these needs in a healthier way?

> How can I improve this area in a way that supports my well-being rather than drains it?

> What boundaries, habits, or mindset shifts would help me create lasting balance?

Step 4: Take Action

Small, intentional steps lead to big transformations. Instead of waiting for change, commit to one actionable step today.

> What is one change I can make this week to break an unhealthy cycle?

> Can I schedule time for self-care, set a boundary, reach out to a friend, or adjust my mindset?

> What is one thing I can do differently...starting now?

Tip: Write down your commitment and set a reminder to check in with yourself at the end of the week and to do this exercise quarterly (or as often as you want). Transformation happens when awareness leads to action.

Challenge: Don't just think about it—do it. Growth starts with a single decision.

> Which root will I strengthen today?

If you like to journal and fill out worksheets, you may consider using the *Root-to-Rise Companion Workbook* as an additional tool to help you map out your unique root system and track how your needs are being met over time.

Turning Insight Into Action: What to Do With Your Needs Evaluation Results

By now, you've inspected how your six core emotional needs are being met—or not—across the five root areas of your life. This kind of self-awareness is incredibly powerful. It reveals where you feel grounded and supported, and where you may crave more fulfillment, connection, or peace. But insight alone doesn't change your life. Action does.

This section is here to help you translate awareness into movement. Not to overwhelm you with a massive to-do list, it's to gently invite you to meaningful, manageable next steps.

Start Here

Look at your lowest-scoring root:

➤ Which life area feels the most out of alignment or emotionally undernourished?

Identify the unmet needs in that root:

➤ Was it Security? Intimacy? Growth? Recognizing this will help focus energy in the right direction.

Ask yourself these coaching questions:

➤ What small shift could support this need in this area?

➤ What have I been tolerating that no longer serves me?

➤ Who or what might support me as I create change here?

Quick Examples

Low Security in Career? You might update your resume, ask for support, or explore more stable opportunities that align with your values.

Low Intimacy in Relationships? You might open a deeper conversation with a loved one, or practice self-compassion to rebuild emotional trust.

Low Growth in Health? You might try something new, such as a different style of movement, a new recipe, or a mindset shift about what health means now.

Looking Back to Taproots

As you explore actions to support your needs, remember your Taproot, the deep source of strength and meaning you already identified earlier in this journey. When you act from that place of grounded purpose, even slight changes become powerful. Your Taproot is the anchor that fuels your growth and helps you stay centered as you move forward.

Closing Thoughts

This reflection isn't about judging where you are, it's about honoring what you need. When you assess your roots, you create the opportunity to realign with what matters most. Every insight you've gained here is a seed. And with intention, those seeds can grow into stronger foundations, deeper connections, and a more fulfilling life.

Let's continue by exploring how to integrate these insights into a realignment plan—one that helps you rise, rooted in what truly nourishes you.

CHAPTER 20

THE POWER OF HUMAN NEEDS

Summary

T ake a deep breath. You've just uncovered one of the most powerful tools for self-awareness and transformation. Understanding human needs isn't just a mental exercise. It's a mirror. A map. A compassionate way to decode why you do what you do, and, more importantly, how to shift what's not working.

If you had any lightbulb moments while reading, that's your subconscious recognizing a truth it was waiting to hear. Maybe you realized you've been clinging to security so tightly that you've resisted the very changes that would help you grow. Maybe you saw how your desire for intimacy caused you to override your own boundaries—or how your drive for significance keeps you chasing validation instead of peace. Whatever surfaced, this is your moment to reclaim your power.

The Foundation of the
Root-to-Rise Framework

[Refer to the *Root-to-Rise* Infographic for a visual representation of this framework, which illustrates how the roots and rise elements interact.]

Human needs psychology—developed by thought leaders like Abraham Maslow, Tony Robbins, and Cloe Madanes—teaches that every person is driven by six fundamental needs. I've adapted these into the *Root-to-Rise* Framework to help you identify how these needs shape your life and how to meet them in ways that support your growth, not sabotage it.

Security: The need for stability, safety, and comfort

Variety: The need for excitement, change, and new experiences

Self: The need to feel important, valued, and unique

Intimacy: The need for deep connection with yourself and others

Growth: The need for progress, learning, and personal evolution

Transcendence: The need to contribute beyond yourself and align with a greater purpose

One or more of these needs influence every decision you make, whether conscious or unconscious. Sometimes we meet them in healthy, empowering ways. Other times, we meet them in ways that keep us stuck, burned out, or unfulfilled.

What This Awareness Gives You

- **Greater Self-Awareness:** You now have a deeper lens for understanding yourself. If you're wondering why you feel stuck, identify which need is underfed or out of balance and address it.

- **Healthier Relationships:** Knowing that everyone is simply trying to meet their needs creates space for empathy, deeper communication, and connection without blame.

- **Stronger Leadership & Influence:** Whether you're leading a team, raising a child, or guiding a friend, understanding core needs helps you inspire and support others more effectively.

- **More Fulfilling Choices:** When you align your decisions with your genuine needs—not just fear or habit—you live from intention, not reaction.

- **A Life That Feels Like Yours:** Meeting your needs in balanced, conscious ways helps you create a life that feels grounded, alive, and truly worth living.

How Needs Show Up in the Roots

It's important to understand how the six core human needs intertwine with your root areas—they are woven through every part of your life. These needs shape your decisions, behaviors, emotional states, and priorities in each root area: Health, Family, Relationships, Career, and Friends.

Every need shows up in every root area, but not always in the same way or with the same intensity. For example, your need for security might be the most dominant in your health or career roots, while your need for intimacy might be more active in your romantic and family relationships.

This next section will help you explore each root area of your life more deeply—not just in isolation, but through the lens of your core needs. When a root is strong, it's because your needs are being met in healthy, sustainable ways. When a root is weak, it's often because one or more needs are being neglected, unmet, or met in unhealthy ways. This list previews how needs can show how up in each Root area:

Health

Security: routines, insurance, safety
Variety: workouts, new health habits
Self: body image, control, achievement
Intimacy: self-love, emotional wellness
Growth: healing, education, personal goals
Transcendence: becoming a health advocate or role model

Family

Security: stability, legacy, loyalty
Variety: evolving roles, holiday rituals
Self: recognition within family system
Intimacy: connection, unconditional love
Growth: healing ancestral patterns
Transcendence: caregiving, generational impact

Relationships

Security: trust and loyalty

Variety: spontaneity and excitement

Self: feeling valued and chosen

Intimacy: vulnerability, emotional connection

Growth: personal evolution within the relationship

Transcendence: shared mission, partnership impact

Career

Security: income, consistency

Variety: creativity, innovation

Self: status, performance, identity

Intimacy: mentorship, collaboration

Growth: skills, leadership, challenge

Transcendence: mission, service, legacy impact

Friends

Security: being supported

Variety: shared experiences, fun

Self: feeling seen and accepted

Intimacy: honesty, loyalty, belonging

Growth: learning from peers

Transcendence: collective action, uplifting others

As you move into the next chapters, keep this lens in mind. You're not just reflecting on life categories, you're learning how to meet your needs in ways that build strong, nourishing roots.

That's what allows you to rise.

Your Next Step: Becoming the Architect of Your Life

Now that you understand the actual reasons behind your behaviors, you have a choice: you can continue to react from old patterns. Or you can start intentionally designing your life, one rooted in awareness and built on a foundation that can support the life you want to create.

The *Root-to-Rise* method is here to help you do just that. We'll take this understanding of your needs, clear the obstacles in your way, and give you tools to rise to your purpose, your potential, and your joy. This is the beginning of a new way of living, one where your needs can work together in harmony. This is your moment. You've done the inner excavation. Now it's time to assess, plan, and build for your rise.

ROOT-TO-RISE INFOGRAPHIC
PHASE ONE: ROOTS

HUMAN NEEDS

 Transcendence

- Moving past the self to serve others
- Connecting to higher purpose
- Contribution
- Sharing
- Service
- Providing

 Growth

- Growing
- Pulsating energy
- Progress
- Learning
- Feeling momentum
- Advancing
- Breaking free

 Intimacy

- Nurturing
- Valuing relationships
- Belonging
- Feeling passion
- Having desire
- Striving for unity
- Togetherness

 Self

- Self-esteem
- Self-worth
- Significance
- Importance
- Pride
- Importance
- Perfection

 Variety

- Change
- Transitions
- Storms
- Challenges
- Trauma/Crisis
- Chaos
- Variety
- New/Different
- Spice of Life
- Surprise
- Fear

 Security

- Certainty
- Safety
- Rootedness
- Grounded
- Comfort
- Stability
- Predictability
- Protection
- Commitment

LIFE ROOT SYSTEM

HEALTH/FITNESS
- Nutrition
- Food/Beverage
- Supplements
- Fitness/Exercise
- Massage/Body Work
- Wellness vs. Illness

FAMILY
- Parents
- Caregivers
- Siblings
- Partner
- In-laws
- Children
- Chosen

RELATIONSHIPS
- Self
- Romantic Partner
- Commitment
- Chemistry
- Compatibility
- Communication

CAREER
- Time & Money
- Contribution
- Heart-based/Passion vs Corporate
- Hobbies/Craft
- Who you are:
- Strengths/Weaknesses
- Leader vs. Worker
- Visionary vs. Operational
- Analytical/Data-minded

FRIENDS
- Introvert v. Extrovert Needs
- Who are they?
- Values alignment
- Reflection of you
- What do you offer?
- What do they offer?
- Elevate
- Support
- Experience

TAP ROOT
What feeds your soul deeply?

ROOTS

www.glowliving.com
#glowliving
#roottorise
#lovelife

© All Rights Reserved. Glow Living/Glow Marketing LLC 2025

GLOWLIVING
love life

Part Three

CLEARING

*Freeing Yourself from
Life's Obstacles*

Want to go deeper with this work? A companion workbook is in the works to help you integrate, reflect, and take aligned action. Visit GlowLiving.com to learn more and stay updated.

CHAPTER 21

CLEARING THE WAY

Releasing What No Longer Serves You

S ometimes we don't need a new plan, we need to clear what's in the way of the one we already have. The Clearing part of your *Root-to-Rise* journey is all about that: *creating space*. It's the emotional, mental, and energetic weeding that prepares the soil so your life can grow toward your purpose.

But before we talk about what to do, let's acknowledge what it feels like to be stuck.

Stuckness is heavy. It can feel like mental fog or emotional mud. You try to move forward, but something grabs at your heels. You make a little progress, then get pulled back into self-doubt, fear, or the same old patterns. It's frustrating, disorienting, and sometimes quietly heartbreaking. Especially if you've been doing the work—reading the books, journaling, going to therapy—but nothing's really changing.

So many of us are stuck not because we're lazy or broken, but because we're still carrying things we were never meant to hold. Old beliefs. Outdated identities. Unprocessed pain. Protective habits that once helped us survive, but now quietly sabotage our growth. Like tangled weeds, they wrap around our roots and choke the life out of our potential.

Clearing isn't about fixing yourself. It's about making space for who you're becoming.

The Nature of Emotional Weeds

Weeds don't grow overnight. They take root slowly, often invisible, and they thrive in neglect. Emotional weeds are the same. They show up as thought patterns like *"I'm not good enough,"* or habits like people-pleasing, perfectionism, or procrastination. Weeds can also grow from grief we didn't fully process, or the identity we've outgrown but still cling to because it feels safe.

The more we try to rise without tending to our root system, the more we feel resistance. That resistance isn't failure; it's feedback. It's your soul saying, *"There's something here that needs your attention."*

Why You Might Feel Stuck

You might be stuck because you're trying to grow in a direction that no longer fits who you are. Or because you're still holding a version of yourself you've already outgrown. You might be stuck because you're overwhelmed by clutter, by expectation, by emotions you don't know how to process.

And sometimes, you're stuck because your nervous system is still responding to a past version of reality. It learned to play small, stay safe, and avoid risk. Even if your life is different now, those protective patterns don't update automatically. That's not your fault. It's something you can lovingly work with and shift.

Clearing Is a Practice

Just like a real garden, your inner landscape needs regular clearing. Not just once during a big life change, but again and again as you evolve. Think of this process as sacred maintenance, a way of honoring your growth by making room for it.

This chapter marks the beginning of a new phase in your journey: the phase of letting go, breaking cycles, and making space for your next season. Over the next few chapters, you'll uncover and release what's no longer serving you—mental clutter, fear-based habits, old beliefs, and emotional tension—so you can create space for clarity, alignment, and momentum.

But first, we start with awareness. Not judgment. Not blame. Just awareness.

The moment you can name what's in your way, you loosen its grip.

From Awareness to Ownership

Awareness is the spark. Ownership is the shift.

When you move from asking, "Why am I like this?" to "What do I need now?" you reclaim your power. When you can say, "This belief once protected me, but I'm ready for something new," you rise.

This phase isn't about changing everything overnight. It's about identifying one pattern, one belief, one root that's tangled, and gently clearing it. You don't have to do it all today. You just have to begin. Let's clear the way.

Reflection Prompts: Beginning Your Clearing

You don't have to have all the answers. But you need to ask the right questions.

- ➢ What is staying stuck protecting me from?
- ➢ What is it costing me emotionally, creatively, spiritually?
- ➢ If nothing changes, how will I feel in one year? Five years? Twenty?
- ➢ What pattern in my life have I outgrown?
- ➢ What might I need to release in order to rise?

Clearing Practice: A Shift Begins

Next time you notice yourself feeling stuck or circling the same pattern, try this:

- **Interrupt the loop:** Stand up, shake your body, take a deep breath, or say aloud: "This pattern ends now. I choose differently."

- **Take one small, messy step:** Action doesn't have to be perfect to be powerful.

- **Reconnect with your why:** Why does this matter to me? What do I want instead of this pattern?

You don't have to change everything today. But you can begin clearing the way.

CHAPTER 22

FEAR-BASED RESISTANCE

Releasing the Fear Beneath Your Patterns

I f clearing is the process of making space, then resistance is what fills that space when fear is still in the driver's seat. And resistance wears many disguises: perfectionism, procrastination, low standards, inconsistency, overthinking, avoidance. These patterns might look different on the surface, but underneath, they're all rooted in fear.

Fear of failure. Fear of success. Fear of being seen. Fear of judgment. Fear of getting it wrong or not being enough.

Resistance isn't laziness. It's a protective mechanism. It's your nervous system saying, *"Let's not move forward until we're absolutely sure it's safe."*

Most resistance doesn't show up as loud panic. It whispers. It seduces. It tells you to wait until you're ready. Until you're more confident. Until the conditions are perfect. Until someone else goes first.

It says:

"Let me just tweak this one more time."

"I'll start tomorrow."

"What if I mess it up?"

"Who am I to do this anyway?"

And the more you listen, the more stuck you become.

The Many Faces of Resistance

Perfectionism says, *"If it's not flawless, it's not worth doing."* It masquerades as high standards but often leads to paralysis. It disconnects you from joy, experimentation, and growth. It's often self-abandonment—shrinking to be palatable, or contorting to gain approval. But perfectionism isn't protection, it's a prison.

Procrastination says, *"I'll feel more ready later."* It soothes your anxiety in the short term while quietly reinforcing fear in the long run. What you delay today becomes heavier tomorrow. Procrastination is not laziness, it's often a freeze response, especially when you're overwhelmed or afraid to get it wrong.

Inconsistency says, *"I can't stay focused."* But often, inconsistency isn't about discipline; it's about emotional fatigue. It's the push-pull of wanting something and fearing what might happen if you actually get it. Burnout, shame, and fear of success all contribute to the pattern.

Worry says, *"What if it goes wrong?"* It disguises itself as preparation, but really, it's mental clutter. Worry keeps you in a loop of imagined failure rather than grounded action. It often points to a deep desire for control, stability, or safety.

These are normal. All of them are human. And they do not have to run the show.

⬦ For expanded versions of these topics and deeper coaching insights, visit GlowLiving.com.

The Fear Beneath the Pattern

Let's go deeper.

- Perfectionism is often driven by the fear of not being good enough.
- Procrastination can stem from the fear of failure or success.

- Inconsistency may reflect a fear of commitment or losing freedom.

- Worry can be a byproduct of unhealed trauma, or unmet needs for safety and control.

When you recognize the need beneath the behavior, you can begin meeting it in a healthier way.

The Inner Critic vs. the Wise Self

One reason fear-based resistance is so sticky is because it's fueled by an inner voice that sounds convincing.

The Inner Critic says:

You're going to mess this up."
"You're behind."
"Everyone else has it together."

The Wise Self says:

"You're allowed to be learning."
"You don't have to go fast to be making progress."
"Your pace is still forward."

The Inner Critic thinks fear is useful. The Wise Self knows courage is more honest. It's up to you to choose which voice you respond to.

Sometimes, the Inner Critic is actually your inner child, scared and trying to stay safe. When resistance arises, try speaking directly to that part of you. Say: *"You're safe now. I've got you. You don't have to carry this alone anymore."* This kind of reassurance helps you shift out of fear and back into your grounded self.

From Resistance to Momentum

So how do you shift?

1. Interrupt the Pattern

Fear lives in loops. Interrupting the loop helps your brain see an alternative path. Stand up. Breathe deeply. Shake your body. Change your environment. Say aloud: *"This pattern ends now. I choose differently."*

2. Reconnect with Your Why

Stuckness often comes from disconnection.

Remember your Taproots and ask:

➤ What do I want right now?

➤ Why does it matter?

➤ What will it cost me to stay stuck?

Reconnecting to your why activates emotional momentum.

3. Take One Imperfect Action

Let go of flawless. Let go of ready. Progress begins with a small, brave step.

Start messy. Set a timer for 15 minutes and just begin. Pick one option instead of over-analyzing five. Do the thing badly on purpose, just to prove it won't break you.

You don't need to feel fully confident to move forward. You just need to move. And when your fear voice kicks in, try anchoring into a new narrative. Here are a couple of mantras that help rewire the moment:

- *Momentum over mastery.*
- *Progress over perfection.*

Say them out loud. Write them down. Let them become the soundtrack that drowns out your inner critic.

4. Expect Resistance, and Move Anyway

Growth is not about being fearless. It's about being willing. When fear shows up, it means you're getting closer to something meaningful.

Try asking:

> ➤ What is this resistance trying to protect me from?
> ➤ What is it costing me?
> ➤ Who would I be without this fear?

Let your next move come from love, not fear.

5. Ask for Support

Fear shrinks in the presence of connection. Whether it's a coach, therapist, friend, or sacred community. Share your truth with someone who can hold space for your becoming.

You Don't Have to Be Ready, Just Willing

Readiness is a myth. No one ever feels 100% ready to rise. You just need a little courage, one decision, and the willingness to move forward...even with shaky hands. You are not behind. You are not failing. Let resistance be a doorway, not a dead end.

Fear Reframed

There's a powerful reframe for fear that's worth remembering:

**F.E.A.R.: Forget Everything And Run →
Face Everything And Rise**

Fear will always be a part of being human. But you don't have to let it define your story. Whether your faith is spiritual or practical—faith in yourself, in your support system, or in the next step—you are not meant to live in the shadow of what-ifs.

The next chapter will help you go even deeper into the unconscious beliefs that keep you stuck and small. Let's keep clearing.

CHAPTER 23

MENTAL CLUTTER &

EMOTIONAL OVERLOAD

Clearing the Space Between Chaos and Clarity

D isorganization isn't just about messy spaces; it's about mental clutter, decision fatigue, and the quiet erosion of self-trust. It's the stress of missed deadlines, the anxiety of forgetting something important, the shame of a to-do list that never ends. And over time, this overwhelm doesn't just affect your outer world, it seeps into your sense of self.

Disorganization is not a character flaw. It's a symptom. A coping strategy. A signal that something deeper is asking to be seen. Maybe it's burnout. Maybe it's emotional overload. Maybe it's the absence of a system that truly works for the way your brain is wired.

When Outer Chaos Reflects
Inner Overwhelm

A cluttered environment often mirrors a cluttered mind. That pile of papers, the overflowing inbox, the chaotic schedule all whisper, *"You're behind. You'll never catch up."* This external noise reinforces internal narratives of inadequacy, and soon, you're not just surrounded by clutter, you *become* it. Foggy. Frazzled. Frustrated.

You may find yourself:

- Starting projects but rarely finishing them
- Spending more time managing chaos than making progress
- Feeling like rest is impossible because the mental load never stops
- Sabotaging goals, not because you don't care, because the path feels too overwhelming to even begin

You're Not Lazy, You're Overloaded

Disorganization isn't about a lack of discipline. It often stems from emotional fatigue, neurodivergence, chronic stress, or the belief that structure equals rigidity. But structure doesn't have to be suffocating. When aligned with your energy and goals, it becomes supportive like scaffolding for your growth.

Getting organized isn't about being perfect. It's about creating ease. It's about removing friction so your energy can go toward the things that matter most. It's not about color-coded systems (unless you love them). It's about finding what works for *you*.

When Structure Becomes a Cage

On the flip side, some people respond to overwhelm by gripping tightly to control. They over-schedule, obsess over routines, or turn organization into perfectionism. While this can create a sense of safety, it may also breed anxiety, rigidity, or even relationship strain.

True organization isn't about micromanaging every detail. It's about creating enough structure to feel grounded, without choking off spontaneity, creativity, or connection. Ask yourself: "Am I using structure to support my peace, or to soothe my fear of losing control?"

Case Study: Daniel's Transformation from Chaos to Clarity

Daniel, a 33-year-old professional, struggled with chronic disorganization. Missed deadlines, forgotten commitments, constant clutter all chipped away at his self-worth. He wasn't lazy, he was overwhelmed. His cluttered environment drained his focus, strained his relationships, and made his dreams feel out of reach.

His turning point came when he stopped blaming himself and started building simple, compassionate systems:

- A digital calendar and reminders to stay on track each day
- Daily task lists to reduce mental strain
- Decluttering his desk and inbox to lower baseline stress
- Breaking projects into small, manageable chunks
- Getting support from a mentor who helped him stay on track

Daniel didn't change overnight. But with time, the results were undeniable. He became more reliable, focused, and fulfilled—not because he worked harder, but because he created space to work smarter. He stopped seeing organization as a burden and started seeing it as self-respect.

Emotional Overload: The Hidden Obstacle

Sometimes, it's not physical clutter that blocks us, it's the emotional kind. Mental overload, unresolved decisions, unspoken worries, and energetic leaks all contribute to a state of inner chaos.

If you feel you're always *"on,"* juggling too much, or one small task away from snapping, it's time to clear your emotional cache. Ask yourself:

➤ What am I holding onto that I haven't processed?

➤ What expectations am I trying to meet that no longer serve me?

➤ What's the one boundary I need to set to reclaim my peace?

Clearing isn't just about what you throw away, it's about what you *choose* to make room for.

Tools to Lighten the Load

1. The Dump & Sort Journal Practice

When your brain is buzzing with unfinished tasks, open loops, or worries, take 10 minutes to spill it all onto paper. Don't edit. Don't organize. Just release. Then:

- Highlight what's urgent
- Delegate what's not yours to carry
- Delete what doesn't matter
- Schedule what needs attention

2. Digital Declutter

Your inbox, desktop, and phone notifications contribute to constant cognitive strain. Set aside time to:

- Unsubscribe from unnecessary emails
- Create folders for active projects
- Use Do Not Disturb when you need focused time

3. Calendar Hygiene

If your schedule controls you, take it back:

- Color-code root-based priorities (Health, Career, Relationships, etc.)
- Block time for transition and rest
- Say no to what drains you, yes to what fuels you

4. The One-Drawer Rule

When overwhelmed, don't organize your whole life. Start with one drawer. One folder. One list. Every act of clearing is a signal to your brain: *I'm moving forward.*

And remember the words of my dear friend Cynthia Smith: "*Stop trying to boil the ocean.*" Translation? You don't have to fix everything at once. Just start with one clear, intentional step. That's how transformation begins.

From Awareness to Ownership

Clutter—mental, emotional, or physical—isn't the enemy. It's information. It shows you where you've outgrown old ways of functioning. The goal isn't to eliminate chaos entirely. It's creating just enough order that your energy flows with ease. And when that happens, everything changes. You stop spinning. You start moving. You find your rhythm.

Reflection Prompts

- ➤ What part of my life feels the most chaotic right now?
- ➤ What's one system or habit that could bring more ease into that area?
- ➤ What clutter (physical or emotional) am I ready to release?
- ➤ Where have I confused "*structure*" with "*restriction*" and how can I reclaim it as support?

Getting organized is not about being rigid. It's about reclaiming your power. Every cleared space, every clarified task, every boundary you hold is an act of freedom. It says:

"I choose clarity over chaos. I choose flow over friction.
I choose to make space for my rise."

CHAPTER 24

REWRITING THE SCRIPT

A New Narrative for Healing and Emotional Freedom

L imiting beliefs are like invisible chains. They hold us back from reaching our full potential, often without us even realizing it. These deeply ingrained thoughts shape how we see ourselves, others, and the world around us. Whether they stem from childhood experiences, societal conditioning, or past disappointments, they create mental roadblocks that keep us stuck, shrinking, or sabotaging what we truly want.

At their core, limiting beliefs are survival strategies. They may have once helped you cope, avoid pain, or stay safe in uncertain situations. But what once protected you may now be what's preventing you from expanding.

What's the Story You've Been Living By?

If you've ever caught yourself thinking, *"I'm not good enough," "I don't have what it takes,"* or *"It's too late for me,"* you're not alone. These thoughts are common, and they are not facts. They're just stories. And like any story, they can be rewritten.

Every choice we make—whether it's what we eat, how we engage in relationships, or how we respond to stress—is driven by underlying needs. When those needs are unmet, we often default to behaviors that bring temporary relief, even if they hold us back long term. These are the patterns we must gently, courageously unravel.

Patterns Are Clues, Not Character Flaws

Your patterns are not proof of your failure. They're reflections of your need for safety, belonging, love, significance, or growth.

Some of the most common ways people meet their needs in unhealthy ways include:

- Emotional eating or food obsession
- Repeated procrastination or perfectionism
- Relationship sabotage or romantic affairs
- Chronic overworking or people-pleasing
- Social comparison and online validation

At first glance, these behaviors may seem unrelated. But at the root, they serve the same purpose: to soothe discomfort and meet emotional needs in the only way you knew how.

The goal is to understand what need they were trying to meet, not to judge these patterns, and find a better way.

Jack's Story:
From Bad Luck to Breakthrough

Jack, a 32-year-old account executive, believed bad luck followed him like a shadow. A series of traffic stops. A spilled coffee. A job opportunity that slipped away. He didn't see these as everyday mishaps. He saw them as confirmation: "This is just my life. Things don't work out for me."

His self-talk was steeped in defeat. "Of course this would happen to me," he'd mutter, barely noticing the things that *did* go right. It wasn't just a mindset, it became a lens that distorted how he saw himself, others, and the world. He stopped applying for new jobs. He turned down dates. He skipped social events. Why try, he reasoned, when bad luck would just strike again?

Over time, this belief isolated him. Friends noticed him withdrawing. His work suffered. And inside, he felt helpless and anxious, like he was just waiting for the next thing to go wrong.

Through coaching, Jack finally questioned the story he'd been telling himself. He traced it back to his childhood, where frequent moves and unreliable parenting had left him bracing for instability. Believing he was unlucky gave him a strange sense of control. If everything was doomed anyway, at least he wouldn't be surprised.

But what began as protection had turned into paralysis.

We worked on shifting both his mindset and his emotional state. He started tracking what went well, including small wins, like a kind text from a friend or a creative breakthrough. He practiced gratitude each night and adjusted his posture to stand more open and grounded. These weren't just mindset hacks, they were nervous system resets.

As his state changed, so did his story. He applied for jobs again, this time with presence and confidence. He said yes to a hiking group invite. He even booked a solo trip, something he never would've risked before. And when things inevitably didn't go perfectly? He didn't spiral. He adapted.

Jack didn't just stop believing he was unlucky. He started believing in himself. And that changed everything.

Jack's belief was about unluckiness, but it could just as easily have been about unworthiness, failure, or not being enough. The core message is this: it's not the belief itself that defines you, but what you do with it. No matter what story has been keeping you stuck, breaking free is the same.

Why State Matters When Rewriting Beliefs

You can't change a belief while stuck in the same emotional state that created it. That's why mindset shifts alone rarely stick. To rewrite your inner narrative, you also have to shift how you feel physically, mentally, and emotionally. That's where The Triad comes in.

Later in this book, we'll explore the Triad in depth, a framework that helps you shift your emotional state by adjusting your body, focus, and inner meaning. But here's a preview:

Physiology (Body): How are you breathing, moving, carrying yourself? Slumped posture reinforces self-doubt. Movement opens emotional flow.

Focus (Mind): What are you paying attention to? When you fixate on failure, your mind will keep feeding you more of it.

Meaning (Spirit): What story are you telling yourself? *"I'm broken"* vs. *"I'm healing"* creates very different emotions and outcomes.

Your emotional state influences your beliefs. And when you learn to shift your state, you create space for new beliefs to grow.

From Awareness to Rewrite

Here's what's most important to remember: You are not your patterns. You are not your past.

You are a storyteller. And you can become the author of a new narrative. Every belief can be rewritten. Every pattern can be reshaped. Every moment is a blank page.

You don't need to have it all figured out. You just need to take the pen back into your own hand and begin again, one word, one truth, one brave choice at a time.

Reflection Prompts: Rewriting the Script

1. Identify the Pattern

> ➤ What's one behavior or habit that's keeps me stuck? What need is it helping me meet (e.g., safety, connection, self-worth)?

2. Trace the Story

> ➤ What is the core belief behind this behavior? Where did this belief come from? How has it shaped my life?

3. Interrupt the Loop

> ➤ What can I do differently next time the pattern shows up? How can I interrupt it physically, mentally, or emotionally?

4. Rewrite the Narrative

> ➤ Create an empowering version of the old belief.

Even a small shift in language can unlock a powerful emotional change. Try rewriting an old belief like this:

Old: *"I'm not lovable."* → New: *"I am worthy of love just as I am."*

Old: *"I'll always fail."* → New: *"I am learning, growing, and getting stronger."*

5. Meet the Need in a New Way

> ➤ What's one healthy, conscious way to meet the underlying need?

Here are a few ideas to get you started, depending on which need is most active for you right now:

Intimacy → Call a trusted friend

Self → Reflect on recent wins or service to others

Security → Create a simple plan and stick to it for 3 days

6. Reassure Your Inner Child

Imagine your younger self—the one who first felt this pain.

➢ What does that part of me need to hear today? Write it down. Speak it aloud. Honor the longing with compassion.

This chapter is your invitation to step off the hamster wheel of self-sabotage and into a new story. One where you no longer need to chase love, success, or fulfillment through temporary highs or external fixes. You now have the tools to meet your needs in ways that uplift, rather than drain you.

You don't have to earn your worth. You just have to remember it. And from that place, your rise begins.

CHAPTER 25

HIDDEN EMOTIONAL TRAPS

Freeing Yourself From Internal Conflict

H ave you ever felt emotionally stuck, where no matter what you choose, it feels like the wrong decision? That sense of paralysis—where your heart pulls one way, your mind another, and fear circles like a storm—can feel suffocating. These are hidden emotional traps: internal conflicts that make even small decisions feel like life-altering gambles.

They don't always look like dramatic life choices. Sometimes, they sound like:

"If I speak up, I'll seem difficult. If I stay silent, I'll betray myself."

"If I slow down, I'm lazy. If I push forward, I'm burned out."

"If I leave, I'll regret it. If I stay, I'll resent it."

These moments often signal something deeper: a conflict between emotional needs. Security vs. Growth. Connection vs. Authenticity. Approval vs. Freedom. When all paths feel risky, fear convinces us the safest option is to freeze. That freeze—the internal stalemate—can quietly drain your energy, your self-trust, and your clarity.

The Too Much / Not Enough Trap

This emotional trap is one of the most common, especially for women and high achievers. You fear being too much: too emotional, too ambitious, too loud. But you also fear not being enough: not smart enough, not beautiful enough, not worthy. So you toggle between shrinking and striving, never quite feeling at home in your own skin.

This trap keeps you second-guessing, filtering yourself, and overthinking how others perceive you. The way out isn't about proving anything. It's about reclaiming your wholeness.

The Self vs. Others Trap

This trap shows up when you've spent so long caring for others that you've forgotten how to care for yourself. You want rest, but fear being seen as selfish. You need boundaries, but feel guilty about enforcing them. You've learned to meet everyone's needs, except your own.

Eventually, your well runs dry. You give until you're exhausted, then wonder why you feel resentful. The truth? You're allowed to need space. You're allowed to say no. You're allowed to belong to yourself.

The Success vs. Fulfillment Trap

You've built the life you were told to want in a job, a relationship, maybe a family. On the outside, it looks good. But inside, something feels off. You're checking the boxes but feel like a stranger to yourself.

This trap is subtle, but powerful. You fear leaving what you've built, but staying feels like a soul-deep compromise. The path forward isn't about blowing up your life. It's about listening to the quiet voice that says, *"There's more."*

Double Binds: When Staying Feels Safer Than Choosing

Now let's look at the most paralyzing trap of all: the double bind. It's the classic *"damned if you do, damned if you don't"* dilemma. No matter what choice you make, it feels like there will be pain, regret, or loss.

The tricky thing about double binds is that they often stem from a fear of the future:

"What if I make the wrong choice?"
"What if I regret it?"
"What if things get worse?"

This fear keeps us frozen, hoping the situation will resolve itself. But in reality, not deciding is still a decision—a decision to stay stuck.

Double binds often show up as:

- **Career Trap:** Your job is unfulfilling, but leaving feels risky. Stay, and you're unhappy. Leave, and you fear instability.

- **Relationship Dilemma:** You love someone but feel unmet. Stay and sacrifice yourself? Leave and face heartbreak?

- **Work-Life Struggle:** Career vs. family. Achievement vs. presence. Guilt, no matter what you choose.

- **Societal Pressure:** Especially for women: Be nurturing, but not too soft. Be bold, but not too assertive.

- **Masculine Identity Conflict:** Especially for men: Be strong and stoic, but also emotionally available. Provide financially, but be present at home. Express vulnerability, but not "too much." The result? Many men suppress emotional needs to maintain an image, leading to disconnection and internalized pressure.

These are not small conflicts. They live in your nervous system and show up as anxiety, procrastination, fatigue, or disconnection.

Let's look at how these emotional traps play out in real life. The following stories show what happens when people get stuck between competing needs and what it takes to break free. Each one highlights a different kind of inner conflict, from romantic turmoil to career guilt to emotional coping. As you read, consider which parts feel familiar in your own life.

Case Study 1: Frank
The Cost of Avoiding the Truth

Frank came to me deep in a double bind. He'd been married for over a decade with two young kids and a stable life. On the surface, things looked solid. But underneath, he was unraveling. His marriage had become emotionally flat, and instead of facing it directly, he began an affair with a young exotic dancer.

He felt embarrassed. "It's such a cliché," he said. "But I haven't felt this alive in years." The attention, the thrill, the secrecy—it pulled him in. But so did the shame. He felt stuck between two painful options: stay in a marriage where he felt invisible but had kids to consider, or continue an affair that betrayed his values and integrity.

Through the coaching process, I helped Frank map his emotional needs using the same Needs Evaluation included in this book. That's when the pattern became clear.

His marriage offered him Security including routine, shared parenting, a steady home. Yet it lacked Variety, passion, and emotional connection. His affair gave him Variety in spades including adventure, novelty, sexual energy, yet came with zero grounding or stability. By having both, Frank was unintentionally trying to meet opposing needs, but in ways that couldn't coexist. He felt torn in half, emotionally exhausted, and unable to move forward.

His breakthrough came when he realized the affair wasn't just about lust or fantasy. It was about unmet needs. "I wasn't trying to be reckless," he said. "I was trying to feel alive again." That self-compassion cracked the shame cycle open. He ended the affair. And not long after, he left the marriage, not to pursue his affair partner, but to finally stop avoiding the deeper truth: he needed a life that aligned with his core needs in healthy, sustainable ways.

Over time, Frank rebuilt. He did the hard emotional work, developed clarity about his values, and later met someone with whom he could create a relationship that honored both stability and passion.

What once felt like an impossible trap became the turning point for a more authentic life.

Case Study 2: Camila
Breaking the Double Bind

Camila, 36, felt torn between her thriving career and being a present mom. When she focused on work, guilt consumed her. When she slowed down for family, she feared becoming irrelevant professionally. Her heart was in both places, and it broke trying to choose.

How Camila broke free:

- **Clarity Through Self-Reflection:** She identified her true values and stopped seeing it as an either/or decision.
- **Open Communication:** She negotiated flexible work hours and asked for help at home.
- **Releasing Guilt:** She let go of the myth that being divided meant being deficient.
- **Self-Care & Adaptability:** Some seasons required more work; others, more family. She flowed with the rhythm instead of fighting it.

Camila used her Needs Evaluation to continually check which area of life needed more care. She stopped trying to win at all roles and focused on being present, honest, and supported. That was her freedom.

Case Study 3: Alice
Emotional Coping with Food

At 42, Alice used food as emotional armor. She hated being obese, but food felt like her only source of comfort. Whenever stress, loneliness, or overwhelm hit, she turned to eating—not from hunger, but to soothe the pain. Through reflection, she recognized that food wasn't just fuel. It was her strategy.

Eating met multiple emotional needs:

- **Security** through comfort food
- **Variety** in trying new tastes
- **Self** through indulgence and self-soothing
- **Intimacy** through shared meals or eating alone to feel emotionally safe

This insight was her turning point. Food wasn't the real problem, it was how she had learned to cope. What once helped her survive now kept her stuck.

When Alice started identifying new ways to meet those same needs, her life changed. She got:

- **Security** through grounding routines and rest
- **Variety** through new hobbies and spontaneous adventures
- **Self** through affirmations, therapy, exercise and honoring her body
- **Intimacy** through real emotional connection, not just shared calories

As she built a life that nourished her on a deeper level, her relationship with food shifted. She no longer relied on it to feel whole. She lost most of the excess weight gradually, under medical supervision. More importantly, she shed the belief that she couldn't cope without food.

Now, when she reaches for comfort food out of habit, she pauses. She remembers her Taproot, the part of her that craves vitality, self-respect, and love, and chooses a different form of nourishment.

How to Break Free

Double binds are not dead ends. They are invitations to rise.

Step 1: Identify the Trap

- ➢ What are the two conflicting options?
- ➢ What is the perceived cost of each?

➤ What am I really afraid of?

Step 2: Challenge the Fear

➤ Are both stories true?

➤ Have I survived worse?

➤ What would I tell a friend in my shoes?

Step 3: Shift the Frame

Instead of either/or, ask:

➤ What would honoring both look like?

➤ What does my highest self need most right now?

➤ If fear weren't in charge, what would I choose?

Step 4: Take One Step

➤ What's one small action I can take to move out of this trap?

➤ What would courage look like today?

➤ Who can support me?

A Higher Vantage Point

At the base of a mountain, all trails look steep. But as you climb, the path becomes clearer. What once felt like an impossible choice can, from a higher perspective, reveal options you couldn't see before.

You don't have to figure it all out today. You just have to move. One step. One boundary. One truth spoken. That's how the fog lifts.

You're not trapped. You're being invited to rise.

CHAPTER 26

FOUNDATION OF SELF-RESPECT

From Not Enough to Just Right

"I'm enough."

"I value myself."

"I love who I am."

"I'm worthy."

"I'm awesome!"

W ouldn't it be amazing if these statements always rang true in our hearts without hesitation? If we could walk through life fully believing in our worth—no second-guessing, no shrinking, no doubting?

Unfortunately, many of us struggle with what I call *"Not-Enough Syndrome."* It creeps in as a quiet, insidious voice whispering in response to an idea, opportunity, or challenge:

"You're not qualified enough."

"You're not smart enough."

"You're not attractive enough."

These thoughts become so ingrained—so automatic—that we barely notice them. Yet they hold immense power. They keep us playing small, settling for less, and lowering our standards in life, work, and relationships.

If you've ever felt like you weren't "good enough" to go after what you really want, let's get to the root of that belief and start rewriting the narrative.

Why We Question Our Worth

Before you get frustrated with yourself for struggling with self-worth, let's clear one thing up: that nagging voice in your head isn't trying to sabotage you, it's trying to *protect* you. It's your primitive brain at work.

The logic goes like this:

"If you don't try, you can't fail."
"If you don't put yourself out there, you can't get rejected."
"If you stay small, you won't get hurt."

That's survival-mode thinking, not expansion-mode thinking.

This instinct served our ancestors well, protecting them from danger and exile. But in today's world, staying small doesn't keep us safe, it keeps us stuck.

The Primitive Brain & How It Holds Us Back

The primitive brain governs our fight, flight, or freeze response. It's why we hesitate, overthink, and talk ourselves out of taking action.

The moment we consider doing something bold such as starting a business, applying for a leadership position, setting boundaries in a relationship, our brain sounds the alarm:

"Too risky."
"What if you fail?"
"You'll embarrass yourself."

The result? We freeze. We second-guess. We shrink. Yet growth never happens inside the comfort zone. Recognizing that not every thought is true is a game-changer. Just because you feel you're not enough doesn't mean that you aren't.

Tuning Out the Noise

The world doesn't always make self-worth easy. Social media, advertising, and cultural expectations bombard us with messages about who we should be, what we should look like, and how we should define success. If your confidence takes a hit from comparison or pressure, it's time to disconnect from the noise and turn inward.

Instead of waiting for the world to validate your worth, start telling yourself: *"I am worthy. I am enough. I bring value to the world just by being me."* It may feel awkward at first, but rewriting your inner dialogue is how you break free from years of conditioning.

The Power of Self-Talk

"Words are things, I'm convinced. You must be careful about the words you use or the words you allow to be used in your house."

—Maya Angelou

Your self-talk—the mental conversation you have every day—can either lift you up or tear you down.

Empowering Self-Talk:

"I am capable."

"I can do this."

"I am worthy of success."

Self-Sabotaging Talk:

"I always mess things up."

"I'll never be good enough."

"I don't deserve this."

Our thoughts → shape our emotions → shape our actions → shape our reality. Want to change your life? Start by changing your inner dialogue.

Case Study: Emily:
The Journey to Self-Worth

Emily, 54, had spent most of her life questioning her value. On the outside, she appeared competent and kind—a reliable employee, a supportive friend. But inside, a different story played on repeat:

"I'm not good enough."

"I'll never be successful."

"No one really values me unless I'm doing something for them."

She stayed in jobs where she was overlooked, friendships where she gave more than she got, and relationships where she accepted less than she deserved. Even receiving compliments made her uncomfortable.

The turning point came in a work meeting. Someone else—less experienced, less prepared—was praised for an idea she had shared the week prior. She smiled and said nothing. But inside, something cracked.

That night, she wrote in her journal for two hours. It wasn't about the meeting; it was about a lifetime of staying small. From there, she made a quiet vow: *"No more shrinking."*

She began journaling her thoughts, working with a therapist, and challenging her inner critic. She adopted the mantra:

"I am capable. I am worthy. I do not need to earn love or respect."

She spoke up in meetings, applied for a leadership role, and gradually surrounded herself with people who mirrored her growth. It didn't happen overnight, but over time, Emily stopped looking outward for permission to feel valuable. She owned her worth, from the inside out.

Exercise: Rewriting Your Inner Dialogue

Step 1: Identify the Limiting Beliefs

I'm not _____ enough.

I'm not _____ enough.

I'm not _____ enough.

Step 2: Flip the Script

I am _____.

I am _____.

I am _____.

Step 3: Make It Real

- Say it aloud in the mirror
- Write it on sticky notes
- Set phone reminders
- Use mantras during breathwork, walks, and transitions

Affirmation requires repetition. Repetition builds belief. Belief fuels change.

Standards: Stop Settling

Low standards convince us to tolerate the unacceptable—stagnant relationships, soul-draining jobs, and patterns that keep us small. Every time you settle, you reinforce the belief: *"This is all I get."*

Why do we settle?

- Lack of confidence
- Fear of disappointment
- Scarcity thinking
- Childhood conditioning
- Subconscious patterns

You don't need permission to want more. You don't have to earn your worth. You are not here to settle. You are here to rise.

The Secret to Raising Standards: Shift Your State

Your moment-to-moment state—how you carry your body, what you focus on, and the meaning you assign to your experiences—shapes your standards.

This is a concept we'll explore more fully later in the book, but for now, think of it this way:

- **Body:** Breathe deeper. Stand taller. Move with intention.
- **Mind:** Focus on what's possible, not just what's missing.
- **Spirit:** Speak with clarity. *"I choose"* is more powerful than *"I'll try."*

Even small shifts in how you think, move, and speak to yourself can raise the bar for how you live.

Case Study: James The Power of One Decision

James, 63, had been in the same construction job for two decades. The pay was steady, but his soul was stagnant. His romantic relationship had become more transactional than connective. He wanted to cut back on work to explore the world, and she was a homebody. He told himself it was "fine."

But one day, after a buddy told him about an adventure trip he'd recently taken, James whispered to himself in his parked car: *"I'm not happy. And I haven't been for a long time."*

Instead of dismissing the moment, he let it in. Then he made a choice to stop settling. He started walking each morning to clear his mind. He made a vision board and travel bucket list. He spoke to his partner with honesty. He eventually left both the job and the relationship, not from recklessness, but from clarity.

James went on to consult part-time and volunteer internationally building homes for families in need. He built a life that feels like his. He finally believed he deserved one.

They Have to Want It More Than You Do

Have you ever done more for someone than they're doing for themselves? Then you've felt the slow leak of over-functioning.

For years, I poured myself into helping people who weren't truly helping themselves—giving advice no one followed, stepping in before others had even asked for help, picking up slack in relationships, work, and family. Underneath it all was something I hadn't fully admitted: *I was trying to prove my worth by being needed.*

One day, after burning out from yet another situation where I was carrying 80% of the weight, I had a wake-up moment. I realized supporting people is noble, but carrying them is not only exhausting, it's disabling.

This is the perfect time to remember The 51% Rule.

They have to want it more than you do.

That means:

Don't work harder on someone's life than they do. Don't carry more emotional weight than they're willing to hold. Don't give 100% in relationships where someone's giving 20%.

You *can* support someone, but carry them is draining, and it disables them.

Everyone must be responsible for *at least* 51% of their own life. That still leaves 49% room for love, support, and presence, which is more than enough. Support doesn't mean doing the work for them. It means walking beside them while they lead.

If you're stuck in patterns of over-giving, over-functioning, or over-responsibility, this rule can become a lifeline. It's not about withholding love; it's about protecting your energy so you can love without losing yourself. It can show up in a variety of situations, including:

- You're raising kids while supporting an aging parent.
- You're managing a business while carrying the emotional labor at home.
- You're constantly fixing, advising, or rescuing while putting your own dreams on hold.

Behind the hustle? A fear of being "too much" or "not enough." A belief that worth must be earned.

Keep in mind that boundaries aren't selfish, they're sacred. They teach people how to respect your time, energy, and value.

You Are Not Here to Carry People You're Here to Inspire Them

Let people carry their own weight. Let them rise to their own potential. You are not anyone's emotional life raft.

The quality of your life rises to match the standards you set for yourself.

Choose your worth. Choose your energy. Choose yourself. And anything that doesn't rise to meet you? Let it go.

CHAPTER 27

CLEARING THE PATH

The *Root-to-Rise* journey isn't just about pushing forward; it's about clearing space for growth. You've bravely confronted what's been weighing you down, shining a light on obstacles, limiting beliefs, and patterns that have kept you stuck. Maybe not every challenge in this section applies directly to you, but the ones that do likely spark powerful insights and shifts.

Pause for a moment and reflect:

> ➤ What resonated most deeply with me?

> ➤ Which patterns, fears, or roadblocks did I recognize within myself?

> ➤ How does it feel to see what's been holding me back?

Here's something I want you to really hear: *you can't unsee what you now know. Awareness itself is transformational. Once you've named an obstacle, it loses much of its power over you.*

You're no longer controlled by unconscious patterns; instead, you're actively choosing your next steps. That's a breakthrough. Celebrate it!

To recap some key lessons from this section:

- Limiting beliefs are just stories you've learned. They aren't permanent, and you have the power to rewrite them.

- Double binds lose their strength when you find clarity and reframe your options to honor your true needs.

- Your self-worth shapes every choice you make; reinforcing your own value helps you confidently build the life you want.

- Raising your standards means choosing not to settle for less than you deserve. It's about aligning your life with your true potential.

- Healthy boundaries empower you and the surrounding people, allowing each person to take responsibility and grow.

- Organizing your time and space creates clarity and reduces stress, so you can focus on what matters most.

- Embracing imperfection lets you take meaningful action instead of staying frozen by unrealistic expectations

- Worry and fear diminish when you replace them with trust, presence, and purposeful action.

- Commitment and consistency build the momentum needed to sustain long-term growth and real progress.

- Procrastination loses its hold when you choose action over perfection, even small, imperfect steps matter.

You now have a foundation. You have tools and insights that will support you as we move into deeper, equally important territory—learning how to navigate the powerful emotions that accompany change, loss, and uncertainty. Managing your emotions, processing hard experiences, and cultivating resilience are critical steps in rising toward a life you love.

Clear the Way, Rise Stronger

Use this quick-reference guide to stay grounded and keep clearing your path forward.

1. Pattern Awareness

☑   I've identified one recurring pattern that no longer serves me.

☑ I've explored where it came from and how it may have helped me cope.

☑ I've named the core need this pattern has been trying to meet.

2. Reframe Limiting Beliefs

☑ I've challenged one belief that has kept me stuck or small.

☑ I've rewritten it into a more empowering truth.

☑ I've practiced this new belief through language, focus, and movement (The Triad).

3. Break Free from Double Binds

☑ I've named a situation where I felt *"damned if I do, damned if I don't."*

☑ I've reframed it as a decision about alignment, not fear.

☑ I've made or committed to making a choice that honors my true needs.

4. Raise My Standards & Boundaries

☑ I've named one area where I've been settling.

☑ I've defined what a higher standard looks like in that area.

☑ I've communicated or enforced at least one healthy boundary.

5. Take Consistent, Imperfect Action

☑ I've taken one aligned step, even if small.

☑ I've committed to progress over perfection.

☑ I've chosen a support system or accountability practice to keep me going.

As you continue your journey, be mindful that obstacles don't always show up in obvious ways. Sometimes they're subtle patterns woven into the fabric of daily life like people-pleasing, overthinking, emotional numbing, or comparing yourself to others. You may cling to old identities, loyalties, or stories that no longer serve you, simply because they've become familiar.

While this section has explored some of the most common internal blocks, it's important to stay curious about the unique ways resistance can show up for you. Keep listening inwardly.

Clearing is not about judging yourself, it's about becoming aware, so you can choose differently. You are not your patterns. And every time you notice one, you're one step closer to freedom.

Cleared & Ready to Rise

You've done the inner work. You've explored your roots, reclaimed your needs, and cleared what no longer serves you. Now, it's time to rise with intention, clarity, and the courage to live the life that's truly yours.

The next phase of your *Root-to-Rise* journey is Phase II: Resilience, which is about emotional mastery and weathering the elements, the most difficult times in life.

You'll discover how to face challenges without losing yourself, move through pain instead of avoiding it, and strengthen your emotional core so you can weather life's inevitable storms. Because before you rise, you must root yourself deeply in resilience.

Let's dive in and learn how to navigate the rich emotional landscape of life masterfully, transforming even your toughest moments into meaningful opportunities for growth.

ROOT-TO-RISE INFOGRAPHIC

PHASE ONE: ROOTS

HUMAN NEEDS

 **Transcendence**

- Moving past the self to serve others
- Connecting to higher purpose
- Contribution
- Sharing
- Service
- Providing

 **Growth**

- Growing
- Pulsating energy
- Progress
- Learning
- Feeling momentum
- Advancing
- Breaking free

 **Intimacy**

- Nurturing
- Valuing relationships
- Belonging
- Feeling passion
- Having desire
- Striving for unity
- Togetherness

 Self

- Self-esteem
- Self-worth
- Significance
- Importance
- Pride
- Importance
- Perfection

 **Variety**

- Change
- Transitions
- Storms
- Challenges
- Trauma/Crisis
- Chaos
- Variety
- New/Different
- Spice of Life
- Surprise
- Fear

  Security

- Certainty
- Safety
- Rootedness
- Grounded
- Comfort
- Stability
- Predictability
- Protection
- Commitment

CLEARING OBSTACLES

- Nourishing Needy Roots
- Honoring Driving Needs
- Pain Points
- Getting Unstuck
- Fears & Limiting Beliefs
- Double Binds
- Leveraging you Tap Root

LIFE ROOT SYSTEM

HEALTH/FITNESS

- Nutrition
- Food/Beverage
- Supplements
- Fitness/Exercise
- Massage/Body Work
- Wellness vs. Illness

FAMILY

- Parents
- Caregivers
- Siblings
- Partner
- In-laws
- Children
- Chosen

RELATIONSHIPS

- Self
- Romantic Partner
- Commitment
- Chemistry
- Compatibility
- Communication

CAREER

- Time & Money
- Contribution
- Heart-based/ Passion vs Corporate
- Hobbies/Craft
- Who you are:
  - Strengths/ Weaknesses
  - Leader vs. Worker
  - Visionary vs. Operational
  - Analytical/ Data-minded

FRIENDS

- Introvert v. Extrovert Needs
- Who are they?
- Reflection of you
- What do you offer?
- What do they offer?
- Elevate
- Support
- Experience

www.glowliving.com
#glowliving
#roottorise
#lovelife

TAP ROOT
What feeds your soul deeply?

ROOTS

GLOWLIVING
love life

© All Rights Reserved. Glow Living/Glow Marketing LLC 2025

PHASE II:
RESILIENCE

Part One

EMOTIONS

CHAPTER 28

NAVIGATING EMOTIONS

Riding Life's Waves with Grace

Gracefully surfing the waves of our emotions can be challenging, especially when those waves become intense or unpredictable. But here's the good news: *when we nurture a strong, balanced root system, we create the inner stability that anchors us during emotional storms.* That stability gives us the confidence and safety to let emotions move through us without drowning in them.

Healthy emotional navigation isn't about avoiding feelings or rushing to fix them. It's about understanding our emotional responses and using them as guides to uncover beliefs, desires, fears, and inner truths. Emotions are messengers. When you learn to decode what they're really saying, they become a guidance system, helping you recognize what aligns with your values and where you're being called to grow.

This emotional navigation goes beyond noticing feelings. It involves understanding, managing, and responding to both your own emotions and those of others in a constructive, grounded way. Let's explore the essential tools that support this kind of resilience, clarity, and connection.

Tools for Emotional Awareness & Resilience

- **Emotional Awareness**: Everything starts here. Naming what you feel—whether it's joy, anxiety, anger, or numbness—gives you power. Clarity brings choice, and choice creates freedom.

- **Emotional Intelligence**: Beyond naming feelings, emotional intelligence helps you understand what they mean and manage them effectively. It also includes tuning into the emotions of others to deepen connection and trust.

- **Emotional Regulation**: When emotions intensify, regulation helps you pause before reacting. It's the space between the trigger and your response. With practice, this becomes a superpower.

- **Healthy Expression**: Emotions need to be expressed, not suppressed or exploded. Speaking your truth clearly and respectfully invites others to meet you where you are.

- **Empathy**: Empathy is emotional presence. It's sitting with someone in their experience and saying, *"You're not alone."* Often, that's all someone really needs.

- **Problem Solving**: Emotional distress sometimes arises from unresolved issues. When you address the root causes—conflict, miscommunication, unmet needs—you release unnecessary emotional weight.

- **Self-Care**: Your emotional self needs care, not just crisis management. Whether it's journaling, movement, meditation, rest, or time in nature, self-care replenishes the emotional reserves needed for resilience.

- **Asking for Support**: You don't have to process everything alone. Coaching, therapy, or trusted friends can help you see what you can't yet. Seeking help isn't weakness; it's wisdom.

The Real-Time Reset:
The Triad Framework

Of all the tools I use to regulate emotions, The Triad is the one I return to again and again, especially in moments of overwhelm, conflict, or self-doubt.

I first learned this during my Robbins-Madanes Training, where it was taught as a foundational framework for shifting your emotional state. The concept is simple but powerful: three forces create every emotion you experience, whether you're aware of them or not.

The Three Elements of The Triad:

- **Physiology (Body)**: How are you breathing? What's your posture? Are your muscles tense or relaxed? The way you hold your body sends instant signals to your nervous system, either reinforcing the stress response or guiding you back to safety.

- **Focus (Mind)**: What are you paying attention to? Are you zoomed in on a problem or widening your lens to see the full picture? Your focus acts like a flashlight. Whatever you shine it on gets bigger. Change your focus, and you change the emotional weight of the moment.

- **Meaning (Spirit)**: What story are you telling yourself about what's happening? Are you interpreting a delay as failure, or as redirection? The meaning we attach to our experiences is where emotions are born. Change the story, and you shift the emotion.

Note: In the Robbins-Madanes model, this third element is called *Language*. I've adapted it as *Meaning* in the *Root-to-Rise* Framework because it goes deeper—beyond words to the spiritual interpretation you assign to your experiences. Meaning honors not just how you speak about your life, but what you believe about it.

A Real-Life Example

I once sat in a meeting where a colleague unexpectedly dismissed an idea I'd been nurturing for weeks. I felt my chest tighten, my breath grow shallow. My thoughts started spiraling: *"They don't respect me. I always have to prove myself. Maybe I'm not cut out for this."*

I wanted to shut down, and I caught myself.

I stepped outside and used The Triad:

- **Physiology**: I shook out my arms, took ten deep belly breaths, and stood taller.
- **Focus**: I reminded myself of the projects I'd led successfully just the week before.
- **Meaning**: Instead of seeing the comment as rejection, I reframed it as a request for alignment and clarity.

I returned more grounded, spoke with confidence, and the conversation moved forward with mutual respect. That's the power of this tool. It brings you back to yourself.

Daily Integration: The Centered Mindset Shift

Once you understand The Triad, the next step is using it intentionally throughout your day. I call this practice the Centered Mindset Shift, the art of realigning with your inner balance moment by moment.

This isn't about waiting for emotions to pass or hoping the outside world will change. It's about reclaiming your power through small but powerful shifts in your body, mind, and spirit.

Think of The Triad like a triangle: strong, balanced, and stable. Each side supports your emotional state and your ability to respond with intention.

Physiology (Body): Move to Shift

Your body is always communicating. Between meetings, stretch your spine. After a hard conversation, shake it out or take a walk. If you're anxious, breathe slowly and deeply. If you're sad, try standing tall and opening your chest. Movement sends your nervous system a new signal: *I'm safe. I'm here. I've got this.*

Focus (Mind): Direct Your Attention

Where attention goes, emotion follows. Your brain is wired to spot problems. It's how it keeps you alive. But you don't have to stay stuck in the stress loop. Ask yourself:

- ➢ What else is true?
- ➢ What's going well?
- ➢ What do I feel grateful for?

Practices like morning intentions, gratitude journaling, or even a mindful pause in traffic can redirect your emotional trajectory.

Meaning (Spirit): Reframe the Story

When something doesn't go your way, pause and ask: What story am I telling myself about this? Is it empowering or limiting? The meanings you assign shape your experience, however they're not permanent. You can choose to tell yourself a new, more empowering story at any time.

This is where your true power lies. And it's why, in *Root-to-Rise*, I replaced *Language* with *Meaning*. It's not just how you speak, it's what you believe.

Reclaiming Your Center

You won't always feel balanced, and that's okay. The Triad isn't a rule. It's a reset.

When emotions feel overwhelming, check in:

- **Body**: What's my posture, breath, and energy level right now?
- **Mind**: What am I focusing on? Is it helpful or harmful?
- **Spirit**: What meaning am I assigning to this moment?

Then shift just one. And watch how the others follow.

Emotional mastery isn't about controlling every feeling. It's about staying connected to yourself in the midst of them. It's about knowing how to return—again and again—to your grounded, powerful, centered self.

From Storm to Stillness

Emotional highs and lows are part of being human. We can't always control what arises, but we can choose how we meet it.

When fear or frustration surge, we can resist and suppress, or greet them with curiosity and compassion.

Ask:

➢ What is this feeling trying to teach me?

➢ What need is unmet right now?

➢ What part of me is asking for care or truth?

This is the essence of emotional resilience; knowing how to return to calm.

Let your emotions move through you, not define you. You are not your emotions. You are the one observing them. And when you meet them with presence, even the wildest waves will eventually settle into stillness, and so will you.

CHAPTER 29

BREAKING DEPRESSIVE
PATTERNS

Taking Your Power Back

N ow that you understand how emotions guide your life, let's explore what happens when those feelings grow heavy— when sadness lingers, and joy feels just out of reach.

Depression is one of the hardest emotional states we face. It can leave us feeling trapped, overwhelmed by sadness, and uncertain of how to find our way out. Sometimes, depression rolls in gently, like a rising tide, slowly filling us with a heaviness we can't quite pinpoint. Other times, it crashes suddenly, leaving us disoriented, disconnected, or numb.

For many of us, feeling deeply is uncomfortable, so we retreat into emotional numbness or disconnection. We might even wonder why we can't cry, even though we "should" feel sad or upset.

✦ Important note: This chapter offers supportive tools rooted in coaching and self-awareness. It is not a substitute for therapy, medical treatment, or professional mental health care. If you're experiencing persistent or severe depression, please reach out to a licensed therapist or doctor. Help is available—and you are not alone.

When I Realized I Was Doing Depression

I first experienced depression as a teenager. I believed it was something that happened to me, an external force beyond my control. Years later, during my coach training, I was introduced to The Triad, and it changed everything. You learned about it in the previous chapters. It's the idea that our body, our focus, and the meaning we assign to our experiences shape our emotional state.

For me, this realization was freeing. It showed me that depression wasn't just happening to me. I was unconsciously taking part in it. And once I saw that, I had a way to shift it.

This insight didn't blame me, it freed me. The Triad showed me that depression can emerge not only from circumstances, but from the way we use our body, direct our attention, and interpret our experiences (through the meaning we assign to them). Once I saw this, I had a way to shift out of it.

The Message Behind Depressive Feelings

Depressive emotions often carry an important message. They're not just symptoms, they're signals. When depression arises, it's often trying to show us that something needs attention physically, mentally, emotionally, or spiritually.

Let's break down how The Triad influences depressive patterns and how you can interrupt them in real time.

When Sadness Lingers: Using The Triad to Shift Depressive Patterns

1. Physiology (Body)

Your physical state deeply affects your emotions. Medical conditions, chronic illness, lack of sleep, or poor nutrition all impact mood, and even your posture, breathing, and movement patterns matter.

I noticed my depressive pattern usually began with a physical withdrawal. I'd curl up, hunch over, lower my gaze, slow my breathing, and place my hand on my forehead—subtly disconnecting from the world. I later learned this is common. Our bodies signal defeat long before our minds catch up.

The shift: Now, when I notice this happening, I act fast. I stand tall, go outside, lift my gaze to the sky, stretch my arms upward, and place my hands in the "how wonderful" mudra, a symbol of gratitude and openness.

That simple shift doesn't erase the sadness, but it does open the door to release and recalibration. It helps tears come when they need to, and helps energy return when I'm ready.

The lesson: *Change your body, change your emotions.*

2. Focus (Mind)

Even after changing your body, depressive feelings can linger—especially if your thoughts stay stuck in grief, loss, or *"what's wrong."* But instead of bypassing your emotions, the goal is to move through them with awareness.

My mantra here is:

"FEEL + DEAL = HEAL"

Yes, feel the emotion. Let the tears come. Name the fear. Sit with the pain. Then ask yourself:

> ➤ What is this feeling trying to show me?
>
> ➤ What's the lesson, or even the gift, in this?
>
> ➤ What can I be grateful for, even now?

Gratitude is one of the most powerful antidotes to depression. That's why I recommend keeping a dedicated journal to remind yourself of what's still good, even when everything feels heavy. Revisit these entries during darker days. They become lifelines of hope and strength.

3. Meaning (Spirit)

Meaning is where depression often roots deepest. When we're in pain, our inner dialogue can become harsh, critical, or hopeless. Over time, these messages become internal mantras:

"I'm not good enough."

"No one cares."

"Things will never change."

Tony Robbins calls these internal scripts "in-CANT-ations"—disempowering beliefs that keep us trapped. The solution? Rewire them with "in-CAN-tations"—empowering mantras that support your healing.

Here's how to shift the narrative:

Step 1: Catch the limiting belief

"I'm not attractive enough. No one will ever truly love me."

Step 2: Thank the thought for trying to protect you

"I see you're trying to keep me from getting hurt, but I'm ready for real connection now."

Step 3: Choose a new mantra

"I am beautiful inside and out, and worthy of authentic, lasting love."

Practice it daily. Write it down. Say it out loud. Post it on your mirror. Over time, you'll believe it.

If you've been practicing The Triad to navigate day-to-day emotional shifts, this chapter invites you to apply it in a more sustained and compassionate way, especially when sadness lingers.

Your Toolkit for Breaking Depressive Patterns

Here's how you can begin using The Triad to create change immediately:

Physiology (Body)

- Identify the signs. How does your body change when depression starts? (Slouching, stillness, low energy?)
- Create a shift plan. Write down three simple actions that energize you. (Stretch. Walk. Dance. Look up at the sky.)

Focus (Mind)

- Journaling: What recent thoughts or situations have weighed you down? Get them on paper.
- Gratitude anchors: List five people, moments, or memories you're thankful for—and why.
- Seek the hidden gift: Choose a challenge you've faced recently. Ask, *"What did this teach me?"*

Meaning (Spirit)

- **Reframe a thought:** Catch one limiting belief today and rewrite it.
- Write a mantra: Choose an empowering statement and repeat it three times a day.
- **Practice it daily:** Create reminders on your phone, in your planner, or on your mirror.

Holistic Integration

Let's check in:

- ➤ Which part of your Triad needs attention right now— your body, your focus, or your inner story? Identify one area and then list two simple actions to strengthen it.
- ➤ Support system mapping: Who can you call when things feel dark? List three people and write exactly how you'll reach out for support when needed.

Holistic Healing & Professional Support

Depression is complex—physically, emotionally, and spiritually. The tools in this chapter support emotional awareness and everyday empowerment, but they are *not a replacement for clinical treatment.*

If you're experiencing persistent or intense depression, please consult a licensed therapist, counselor, or medical professional. There is no shame in needing help; only strength in asking for it.

By consciously shifting your physiology, adjusting your focus, and empowering your inner narrative, you reclaim control over your emotional well-being. You are stronger and more capable than you realize. You can reshape your emotional patterns and regain joy.

Final Reflection

Breaking depressive patterns is possible when you realize you're not just a victim of emotions. You're also a participant in how they form. And you have tools to shift them.

By adjusting your body, refocusing your mind, and choosing more empowering meanings, you heal from the inside out.

Emotional mastery isn't about perfection. It's about presence. Compassion. Practice. And the courage to take one small step at a time. You are stronger than you think. Joy can return. And when it does, it won't just be relief, it will be resilience you've earned.

You are not broken. You are not alone.

ENERGY ARROWS

The Invisible Forces Shaping Our Connections

W e often underestimate how powerful we really are, and how much our moods, emotions, and energy influence the people around us. Every moment, whether we realize it, we're sending out energy arrows, emotional signals that affect others for better or worse.

What are Energy Arrows?

Energy arrows are the emotional frequencies we emit through our body language, tone of voice, facial expressions, and presence. They're not visible, but they're profoundly felt. Think of them as unseen arrows of energy that either uplift and invite others in, or create tension, confusion, or distance.

Imagine this: You're in a great mood, feeling light and optimistic, when you encounter someone clearly upset. As they vent, their frustration fills the space. Without meaning to, your body tenses, your chest tightens, and your mood shifts negatively. That's the impact of their energy arrows.

Now flip the scenario. You walk into a room radiating joy, smiling at strangers, holding doors open, offering warmth. People smile back. Some seem drawn to you. That's your positive energy in action.

We are always broadcasting. And the more conscious we become of that, the more intentional we can be with the energy we offer and receive.

Take a moment to reflect:

> ➤ How do my energy arrows impact others?

> ➤ Do I lift people up, or unknowingly bring them down?

> ➤ How do I respond when someone sends negativity my way?

If you don't have strong emotional boundaries, it's easy to absorb the energy of others. You might start your day feeling grounded, only to feel heavy after a tense conversation or emotional exchange. This is where awareness becomes power.

Protecting Your Energy

While we can't control other people's emotional states, we can protect our own energy from being overwhelmed or hijacked. Here are a few practical tools:

1. Visualizations for Energy Protection

The Shield: Envision a glowing shield around your body that deflects negative energy like a force field. Let what doesn't serve you bounce off and dissolve.

The Energy Basket: Imagine holding a basket in front of you. When someone speaks with emotional charge, their words land in the basket, not in your heart. You can listen without absorbing their emotions if you visualize their energy (or words) going into the basket.

2. Conscious Communication

Mirror Their Words: Reflect what you hear: *"It sounds like you're feeling really overwhelmed."* This helps others feel seen and lowers emotional intensity.

Validate Without Absorbing: Saying *"I can understand why you'd feel that way"* affirms their experience without requiring your agreement. It's about acknowledging their perspective, not adopting it.

Empathize and Redirect: Once someone feels heard, they may be more open to a shift in energy. With sensitivity, you can offer a personal story or insight that gently introduces a new perspective—ideally one that fosters connection and calm.

> ✦ **Important Note:** Resist the urge to fix their problem unless they explicitly ask for advice. Instead, ask for permission before offering input: *"Would you be open to hearing something that helped me in a similar situation?"*

When someone is emotionally charged, they may not be in a place to receive guidance. The most impactful time to share is when they are open and ready.

3. The Triad & Energy Arrows

If you're tense, hunched over, focused on stress, and spinning a fear-based narrative, your arrows will reflect that. But if you stand tall, breathe deeply, speak with warmth, and choose empowering thoughts, your arrows will carry strength, calm, and clarity.

This is why self-regulation is an act of love, not just for yourself, but for everyone around you.

4. Energy Awareness in Daily Life

Pay attention to how your energy moves throughout the day:

➢ Who energizes me? Who drains me?

➢ What kind of energy do I bring into a room?

➢ Am I absorbing others' moods or letting them pass through?

Just because someone sends a negative arrow doesn't mean you have to catch it.

The Key Aspects of Energy Arrows

Direction: Energy moves toward others and affects them.

Type of Energy: Joy uplifts. Tension repels.

Intensity: A whisper of anxiety differs from a storm of rage.

Conversion: Energy is transferable and can shift. Calm can cool chaos. Love can soften grief.

What Kind of Arrows Are You Sending?

You're always communicating, whether through words, body language, or emotional tone. Even in silence, you're speaking energetically. So ask yourself:

> ➤ What energy do I want to send today?

> ➤ How do I want people to feel in my presence?

By becoming more intentional with your energy arrows—both the ones you send and the ones you receive—you step into your power as a conscious creator of connection, compassion, and joy.

When to Reset Your Energy Arrows

We all have moments when our energy gets thrown off, such as after a tense conversation, during a stressful commute, or simply when we wake up feeling "off." In those moments, it's easy to unconsciously broadcast stress, irritability, or shutdown energy to everyone around us.

Consider this: *you have the power to shift your state, and your impact, in under a minute.*

Use this quick Arrow Reset any time you feel yourself absorbing someone else's emotions, spiraling into negativity, or just wanting to show up with more intention. It's a simple but powerful way to reclaim your energy and choose what you're sending out into the world.

Arrow Reset in 60 Seconds

Notice: Pause and name the energy you're emitting (tense, flat, light, etc.).

Breathe: Three deep breaths with the exhale extending longer to signal calm.

Shift Focus: Ask: "What's one empowering thought I can focus on right now?"

Choose a New Arrow: Set an intention: *"I'm sending grounded warmth,"* or *"I bring ease into this space."*

Even the smallest shift in your energy can change the surrounding atmosphere. When you reset your arrows with intention, you don't just protect your peace, you become a source of calm, clarity, and connection for everyone you encounter.

Energy Is Contagious

Every emotion you carry becomes part of the emotional environment you live in and create for others. Your presence is your power. Choose to radiate something worth catching.

CHAPTER 31

HAPPY DANCE

Celebrating the Rise Within

W hen was the last time you did a happy dance? I mean, really let loose, moved your body with zero inhibitions, and allowed joy to take over—no overthinking, no worrying about what others might think, just pure celebration?

A happy dance isn't just a silly gesture; it's a metaphor and a powerful expression of joy. It's spontaneous, uninhibited, and completely yours. Whether it's a little wiggle of excitement, a victory shuffle, or a full-blown dance party in your kitchen, a happy dance is more than movement, it's a statement that says, I feel good, and I'm not afraid to show it!

Here's the thing: if you haven't done a happy dance in a while, you might be unknowingly limiting your joy.

Why We Hold Back Our Happiness

If the idea of breaking into a happy dance feels foreign or even uncomfortable, it's worth exploring why. We don't always realize the subtle ways we suppress joy, but often, it comes down to two big factors:

1. Your Environment and Relationships

➢ Who are you spending most of your time with?

➤ Do you feel free to be fully happy around them, or do you unconsciously tone it down?

For example, if your partner, family member, or close friend is struggling—maybe with an illness, stress, or personal hardship—you may feel guilty about expressing too much happiness. You might think, How can I be joyful when they're in pain?

But suppressing happiness doesn't help them, it only drains you. What if, instead, you talked to them about it? What if you agree to consciously allow space for joy, even amidst difficulty?

Sometimes, we create cycles where both people avoid expressing joy out of sensitivity for the other. Instead of lifting each other up, you both end up feeling heavier. Joy is contagious. By allowing yourself to feel it and express it, you may just help them find a little more lightness, too.

2. Not Taking Time to Celebrate Wins

Many of us find ourselves trapped in the endless loop of doing. There's always another task, another goal, another milestone to reach. Our to-do lists can feel never-ending, and when we finally check something off, we barely pause before moving on to the next thing. If you never stop to celebrate, you're training yourself to only focus on what's next, instead of what's now.

Ask yourself:

➤ Do I give myself permission to acknowledge my progress?

➤ Do I celebrate the small wins or only the big ones?

➤ Do I wait for someone else to validate my achievements, or do I honor them myself?

If you're constantly moving the goal post, joy will always feel just out of reach. But when you choose to celebrate, even the small things, you create a life filled with more gratitude, fulfillment, and energy.

So go ahead, give yourself a reward when you accomplish something meaningful. It doesn't have to be extravagant. It could be a treat, an hour of relaxation, or a happy dance in your living room.

The more you celebrate, the more momentum you create.

The Science Behind the Happy Dance

A happy dance isn't just a feel-good moment; it's a scientifically backed way to elevate your well-being. When you dance with joy, your body and mind reap the benefits:

- **Boosts Mood:** Dancing releases endorphins, the body's natural mood enhancers, amplifying positive emotions
- **Reduces Stress:** Movement helps release tension and gives your body an outlet to process emotions, reducing anxiety and stress.
- **Increases Energy:** Even a short burst of dancing invigorates you, waking up your body and mind.
- **Improves Physical Health:** Dancing gets your blood flowing, enhances flexibility, and strengthens coordination.
- **Deepens Social Connection:** Dancing with others strengthens bonds and creates shared moments of happiness.
- **Enhances Self-Expression:** Moving your body freely reinforces confidence and authenticity.
- **Promotes Mindfulness:** When you dance, you're fully present—not stuck in past regrets or future worries.
- **Triggers Dopamine Release:** Movement and celebration activate dopamine, the brain's "reward" chemical, reinforcing happiness.

Happiness is something we create. And movement is one of the simplest, most natural ways to generate joy.

Reclaim Your Joy:
Make Happy Dancing a Habit

If it's been a while since you truly let yourself celebrate, here's your invitation to change that.

Step 1: Identify What's Holding You Back

➢ Do I feel self-conscious about expressing happiness?

➢ Am I waiting for permission to celebrate my wins?

➢ Have I been suppressing joy at matching someone else's energy?

Step 2: Give Yourself the Gift of Celebration

Acknowledge your progress. Write down three things you've accomplished recently (big or small).

- Decide on a reward. Pick a way to celebrate yourself that feels good, whether it's a dance, a treat, or a moment of gratitude.
- Make it a ritual. Build intentional moments of celebration into your life. After completing a task, after a workout, after a big (or small) win…happy dance it out!

Step 3: Let Go & Move

Make a happy dance playlist of your favorite songs. Play and move however you feel—no rules, no judgments. Smile. Laugh. Celebrate yourself.

Dance Like No One's Watching

If you take one thing away from this, let it be this: Your joy is not optional. *It's essential.*

Remember, when you shift your body, you shift your state. This is your Triad in action, reclaiming joy through movement.

A happy dance isn't just about movement; it's also about permission. Permission to be light. Permission to express. Permission to fully experience life's beauty in all its little moments. You deserve to celebrate. You deserve to feel good. So the next time happiness bubbles up inside you, don't hold back. Don't stifle it. Don't wait for a "bigger" win. Let it out, move your body, and feel the joy.

And dance.

CHAPTER 32

EMOTIONAL FITNESS FOR RELATIONSHIPS

E motional fitness is the foundation of the relationships we create, the partners we attract, and the depth of intimacy we experience. It's what allows us to show up fully, communicate effectively, and navigate challenges with resilience instead of reaction. The quality of your relationships isn't just about who you're with; it's about *who you are* within them.

The stronger your emotional fitness, the healthier and more fulfilling your relationships will be. Without it, relationships can feel like an emotional rollercoaster—amazing one day, fragile the next—depending on your mood, stress levels, or self-perception. But when you build emotional fitness, you cultivate stability, self-awareness, and the ability to maintain love and connection, even through life's inevitable ups and downs.

What is Emotional Fitness for Relationships?

Emotional fitness means having the self-awareness, resilience, and communication skills to create relationships that thrive. It's about how you regulate emotions, express yourself, and connect with others in a way that fosters understanding, trust, and lasting intimacy. Here are ten steps to emotional fitness in relationships:

1. **Self-Awareness:** Emotional fitness starts with knowing yourself. Recognizing your emotions, triggers, and relationship patterns helps you respond consciously instead of reacting impulsively. The more self-aware you are, the better you can communicate what you need, recognize when you're projecting, and take responsibility for your own emotional state.

2. **Emotional Regulation:** Conflict and stress are inevitable, and emotional fitness gives you the tools to manage them. Instead of lashing out or shutting down, you learn to regulate emotions in a way that allows for healthy communication and problem-solving.

3. **Empathy:** Emotionally fit people don't just understand their own emotions—they also tune in to what others feel. Empathy deepens connection, allowing you to listen with an open heart, validate feelings, and offer support instead of judgment.

4. **Healthy Communication:** Strong relationships are built on open, honest, and respectful communication. Emotional fitness means expressing yourself clearly, listening actively, and avoiding destructive communication patterns like criticism, defensiveness, or stonewalling.

5. **Conflict Resolution:** No relationship is perfect, and emotionally fit people navigate conflict with maturity and self-awareness. They seek solutions, compromise where needed, and repair connection instead of escalating tension.

6. **Boundaries:** Emotionally fit people respect their own limits and the limits of others. They don't overextend themselves to please people, nor do they tolerate toxic behavior. Boundaries create relationships that feel safe, balanced, and mutually respectful.

7. **Resilience:** Life brings challenges including job losses, family stress, personal struggles. Emotional fitness gives you the resilience to weather storms without breaking your relationships in the process.

8. **Positive Mindset:** A mindset of gratitude and optimism helps you focus on what's right in your relationships instead of obsessing over

imperfections. Emotional fitness includes choosing to nurture appreciation over criticism.

9. **Adaptability:** Relationships evolve, and emotionally fit people embrace change. They grow alongside their partners and adapt to life's transitions with grace instead of resistance.

10. **Self-Care:** Taking care of your emotional well-being isn't selfish, it's necessary. Emotional fitness means making space for your own needs, self-reflection, and personal growth so you can show up as the best version of yourself in your relationships.

My Journey:
From Emotional Instability to Strength

I didn't always have emotional fitness. In my younger years, I struggled with depression, self-doubt, and feelings of unworthiness. As a result, I attracted relationships that reflected exactly where I was emotionally, and with partners who couldn't fully meet my needs because I wasn't meeting my own.

My relationships felt unstable. One moment filled with connection, the next with uncertainty. When I felt good, the relationship thrived. But when I spiraled into self-doubt, everything felt like it was falling apart. My emotions dictated my relationships, and that instability created cycles of fear, frustration, and unmet expectations.

What I finally learned was that no partner, no external validation, and no amount of love from others could fill the void I felt inside. I had to start by deeply loving and accepting myself.

Now, looking back at all the validation I received over the years—the affection, the praise, the love—I realize it was never enough because I wasn't feeling it from the inside. But that's no longer the case. Today, I know how to ground myself, nurture myself, and reconnect with myself in healthy ways. It can be hard to do in the face of a conflict, and I'm not always good at it. However, I always strive to show up in my relationships with more love, presence, and stability than ever before.

Building Emotional Fitness: The Triad in Action

If you feel like emotional fitness is out of reach for you, I invite you to reconsider. The shift can happen faster than you think. It starts with awareness, and it speeds up when you apply The Triad:

1. **Physiology (Body):** How we treat our bodies directly affects our emotional fitness. Are you moving, eating well, and practicing physical self-care? Exercise, sleep, and nutrition all play a role in emotional stability. When you take care of your body, you naturally build resilience to stress and emotional fluctuations.

2. **Focus (Mind):** Where you direct your attention shapes your emotional state. Do you focus on what's wrong in your relationships, or do you train your mind to notice what's right? If your thought patterns are consistently negative, your emotions will follow. Learning to redirect focus toward gratitude, solutions, and positive outcomes is a key part of emotional fitness.

3. **Meaning (Spirit):** The way you interpret experiences determines your emotional response. Do you assign negative meanings to things that happen, or do you reframe challenges as opportunities for growth? If your inner dialogue is filled with self-doubt, criticism, or victimhood, it will show up in your relationships. Changing your self-talk, and the meaning you give to experiences, is one of the fastest ways to shift your emotional state.

Putting Emotional Fitness Into Action

Want to strengthen your emotional fitness? Here's where to start:

- **Self-Check:** Reflect on how emotionally fit you feel right now. Which areas do you need to work on most: self-awareness, emotional regulation, communication, boundaries?

- **Commit to Self-Care:** Choose one way to support your emotional well-being today, whether it's exercise, journaling, therapy, or meditation.

- **Reframe Your Thoughts:** Catch yourself when you slip into negative thought loops. Ask, "How can I see this differently?"

- **Practice Emotional Regulation:** The next time you feel triggered in a relationship, pause. Take a deep breath. Choose a response instead of a reaction.

- **Strengthen Your Boundaries:** Identify one place in your life where you need stronger boundaries and commit to holding them.

In every relationship, Energy Arrows are constantly at play between partners, friends, colleagues, and family. When emotions run high, your energy can unconsciously spike outward through tone of voice, body language, or reactive behavior, and affect the other person's nervous system. Similarly, you can absorb others' energy arrows, especially if you're highly empathetic or sensitive. Developing emotional fitness means learning to regulate the direction and intensity of your energy so that you stay grounded, even when others aren't. By managing your own energy first—through breath, posture, focus, or intentional pauses—you create a space for healthier communication, deeper connection, and mutual respect. You stop throwing arrows and start offering your presence.

Love Starts Within

If your relationships have felt unstable, frustrating, or unfulfilling, don't just look at the other person. Look at yourself. Your emotional fitness determines the health of your relationships, and when you strengthen it, everything shifts. Perfection isn't the goal; awareness is. Growth begins with taking responsibility for your emotions, your actions, and the energy you bring into every interaction. The deeper you love, respect, and trust yourself, the deeper you'll love, respect, and trust others. This is your invitation to level up your emotional fitness.

Why Joy is an Essential Part of Emotional Fitness

Emotional fitness isn't just about navigating conflict, setting boundaries, or staying grounded through challenges. It's also about our capacity to experience, and express, joy.

In fact, joy is one of the most powerful ways we connect with ourselves and others. It fuels resilience, deepens relationships, and reminds us of what's worth fighting for. But often, especially in emotionally intense relationships, we forget to celebrate. We forget to play. We forget to dance. And we forget to invite others to dance with us.

That's where the happy dance comes in, not as a cute idea, but as a practice of emotional liberation. A reclaiming of joy as a radical act of self-care, connection, and freedom. Because when we allow our joy to spill out—and invite others to share in it—we create moments of real emotional intimacy, built not from struggle, but from shared celebration.

Reflection: Checking In with Yourself

As you reflect on your emotional fitness, take a moment to gently check in:

➤ How have my past emotional patterns shaped my relationships, both the ones I've nurtured and the ones that struggled?

➤ Where can I offer myself compassion for the ways I've shown up in the past, knowing I did the best I could with the tools I had?

➤ How does it feel to know I have the power to grow, to choose differently, and to strengthen my foundation moving forward?

You are not defined by who you were; you are empowered by who you are becoming.

Now, what's your favorite song to dance to? Put it on.

CHAPTER 33

EMOTIONAL GUIDANCE SYSTEM

A Compass Within

I f you've ever felt like your emotions are "too much" or wished you could just turn them off, you're not alone. Our emotions are not the problem, they're the compass. They don't show up to derail us; they show up to redirect us.

When you feel joy, love, or peace, your emotions are telling you: This is aligned. When you feel anger, sadness, or anxiety, your emotions are saying: Something's off. That doesn't mean you're broken. It means something within you needs attention.

Your feelings are feedback. They guide you back to your center when you've drifted.

Earlier, we explored how to shift your emotional state using The Triad—changing your physiology, focus, and meaning. We've also looked at what happens when sadness lingers and how energy moves through your system. Now, let's zoom out and remember that every emotion has a place in your inner landscape.

Rather than seeing emotions as good or bad, you can see them on a spectrum, from constricted to expansive, heavy to light, reactive to peaceful. The goal isn't to leap from despair to joy overnight. It's to reach for the next best feeling, even if that's simply going from overwhelmed to neutral.

This is what I call emotional guidance: the subtle shifts that help you climb your way toward alignment, one rung at a time. The more you listen, the faster you catch yourself and recalibrate.

Instead of asking, *"Why am I feeling this?"* try asking:

➤ What is this emotion pointing to?

➤ What need might be unmet right now?

➤ What shift could bring relief or clarity?

When you meet yourself with compassion and curiosity, your emotions lose their charge. They become teachers, not threats.

You don't need to stay in low-vibe states to prove anything or push through. You're allowed to shift. You're allowed to rise.

Reflection Prompt

Think about an emotion that's been dominant for you lately.

➤ What is it trying to show me?

➤ If it had a voice, what would it say I need more—or less—of right now?

Affirmation

As you close this section, take a breath and let these words land in your heart:

I trust my emotions to guide me, not define me. I honor every feeling as a messenger, and I meet each one with compassion. With every breath, I return to my center, and from this place, I rise.

ROOT-TO-RISE INFOGRAPHIC
PHASE TWO: RESILIENCE

HUMAN NEEDS

 **Transcendence**

- Moving past the self to serve others
- Connecting to higher purpose
- Contribution
- Sharing
- Service
- Providing

 Growth

- Growing
- Pulsating energy
- Progress
- Learning
- Feeling momentum
- Advancing
- Breaking free

 Intimacy

- Nurturing
- Valuing relationships
- Belonging
- Feeling passion
- Having desire
- Striving for unity
- Togetherness

 Self

- Self-esteem
- Self-worth
- Significance
- Importance
- Pride
- Importance
- Perfection

 Variety

- Change
- Transitions
- Storms
- Challenges
- Trauma/Crisis
- Chaos
- Variety
- New/Different
- Spice of Life
- Surprise
- Fear

  Security

- Certainty
- Safety
- Rootedness
- Grounded
- Comfort
- Stability
- Predictability
- Protection
- Commitment

FOCUS MIND / MEANING SPIRIT / PHYSIOLOGY BODY

RESILIENCE

NAVIGATING EMOTIONS

Triad:
- Body/Mind/Spirit
- Physiology/Focus/Meaning

CLEARING OBSTACLES

- Nourishing Needy Roots
- Honoring Driving Needs
- Pain Points
- Getting Unstuck
- Fears & Limiting Beliefs
- Double Binds
- Leveraging you Tap Root

LIFE ROOT SYSTEM

HEALTH/FITNESS
- Nutrition
- Food/Beverage
- Supplements
- Fitness/Exercise
- Massage/Body Work
- Wellness vs. Illness

FAMILY
- Parents
- Caregivers
- Siblings
- Partner
- In-laws
- Children
- Chosen

RELATIONSHIPS
- Self
- Romantic Partner
- Commitment
- Chemistry
- Compatibility
- Communication

CAREER
- Time & Money
- Contribution
- Heart-based/Passion vs Corporate
- Hobbies/Craft
- Who you are:
  - Strengths/Weaknesses
  - Leader vs. Worker
  - Visionary vs. Operational
  - Analytical/Data-minded

FRIENDS
- Introvert v. Extrovert Needs
- Who are they? Values alignment
- Reflection of you
- What do you offer?
- What do they offer?
- Elevate
- Support
- Experience

TAP ROOT
What feeds your soul deeply?

ROOTS

www.glowliving.com
#glowliving
#roottorise
#lovelife

 GLOWLIVING
love life

© All Rights Reserved. Glow Living/Glow Marketing LLC 2025

Part Two

ELEMENTS

CHAPTER 34

WITHSTANDING THE ELEMENTS

Building Resilience Through Life's Hardest Seasons

W hat do you do when life breaks your heart? When everything you counted on falls away? These aren't theoretical questions, they're real, human experiences. We all face them.

The storms of life don't ask if we're ready, they arrive uninvited. And what if the hardest seasons of your life could also be the most transformative?

Even when we feel steady and secure, life can throw curveballs that test our resilience and shake our foundations. While these moments can feel disorienting and painful, they are also some of the greatest opportunities for growth, transformation, and self-discovery.

This section of *Root-to-Rise* explores the art of enduring life's most difficult seasons, not just surviving them, but emerging stronger, wiser, and more grounded.

Storms will come. The question is: *how will you navigate them?*

We'll take a deep dive into five of life's most challenging experiences:

- **Winds of Change (Transitions):** The slow or sudden transitions that shift the ground beneath our feet including career pivots, relationship endings, unexpected life turns.

These seasons of change can feel disorienting, but they also offer an invitation to reimagine who you are becoming.

- **Storms (Crisis):** The crises that strike without warning, testing our emotional, financial, and physical strength. Whether it's illness, betrayal, or unexpected upheaval, storms demand that we find stability—not after the chaos, but within it.

- **Crashing Waves (Grief & Loss):** The deeply human experience of mourning someone, something, or some part of yourself that once defined you. Grief, though searing, can deepen our capacity for love, compassion, and the tender courage it takes to begin again.

- **Stress:** The daily pressures that, if left unchecked, can accumulate into burnout, anxiety, and overwhelm. Learning to manage stress is essential for preserving your energy and gaining clarity.

- **Letting Go & Forgiveness:** The sacred act of releasing resentment, attachments, and old identities toward others, yourself, and the past. True freedom doesn't come from holding on tighter; it comes from surrendering with grace and creating space for healing, growth, and new beginnings.

These turbulent seasons of life can feel isolating, but they are also times when profound transformation is possible.

When everything is stripped away—your old identity, your sense of control, your comfort zone—you rebuild in alignment with your deepest truths and highest potential.

While we don't choose many of the storms we face, we do get to choose how we respond.

This section is about equipping you with tools, strategies, and mindset shifts to help you move through life's hardest moments with grace and strength. You'll learn how to stay grounded, ask for what you need, and find stability even when everything around you feels uncertain.

If you are currently navigating one of life's storms, be gentle with yourself as you read this. Take what resonates, apply what helps, and most importantly, trust that this season is shaping you into an even stronger version of yourself. No storm lasts forever, and neither will this moment in your life. It's not just about enduring. It's about rising.

You've already done powerful work strengthening your emotional roots. Now, you're ready to test them in the real storms of life. Change, crisis, grief, stress, forgiveness, and letting go will challenge every part of who you are, and they will also reveal a deeper strength you didn't know you had.

You are not the same person who started this journey. You are grounded. You are growing.

Now, let's step into the Winds of Change, and learn how to rise through every season of life.

CHAPTER 35

WINDS OF CHANGE

Navigating Life's Transitions

C hange is inevitable. Sometimes we welcome it. Sometimes it blindsides us. But no matter how it arrives, change asks us to move, to stretch, to grow.

The Winds of Change show up in countless ways: a career shift, a divorce, an unexpected move, a new stage of life, a change in identity or calling. Even positive transitions—falling in love, achieving success, becoming a parent—require us to let go of what was and step into what's next.

Change unsettles our roots. It stirs up uncertainty, grief, excitement, and fear…sometimes all at once. But it also offers a sacred opportunity: the chance to decide consciously who you want to become.

In *Root-to-Rise*, we don't just endure change. We work with it. We root deeper into what matters most and rise into our next chapter with intention and strength.

Why Change Feels So Hard

Change challenges one of our deepest human needs: Security. When life shifts unexpectedly, the mind naturally clings to what feels familiar, even if that familiarity no longer serves us.

You might find yourself grieving a life you thought you'd have. You might feel adrift without the routines, relationships, or identity that once grounded you. You might wonder: *"If I'm not who I was before, then who am I now?"*

These feelings are normal. They aren't signs that you're broken. They are signs you're evolving.

Real growth rarely feels comfortable in the beginning. It asks us to stand in uncertainty long enough to find new strength. A strength we never would have discovered without being pushed beyond what we knew.

Navigating Change with Resilience

In times of transition, it's essential to ground yourself intentionally. Here are a few ways to do that:

1. Anchor to Your Core Values: When everything around you is shifting, your values become your compass. Rooting into what matters most gives you clarity when the path ahead looks unclear. Ask yourself:

➤ What are my top three core values?

➤ How can I let these values guide my next steps?

2. Honor What You're Leaving Behind: Transitions involve loss, even when we're stepping into something better. It's important to grieve the old chapter before fully embracing the new. Gratitude and grief can coexist. Reflect on:

➤ What am I releasing as I move forward?

➤ What did this chapter of my life give me I can carry with gratitude?

3. Focus on What Remains Steady: In every season of upheaval, some things remain: your skills, your character, your experiences, your relationships, your resilience. Naming these anchors helps restore a sense of safety.

Answer:

> ➢ What is still true about me, no matter what changes?

> ➢ What roots are still strongly rooted during this change?

> ➢ What resources and strengths am I bringing into this next chapter?

4. Reframe Fear as Excitement: Fear and excitement are chemically similar in the body. Changing your internal language from *"I'm scared"* to *"I'm stepping into something new"* can calm your nervous system and open you to possibility.

Try saying to yourself: *"This isn't fear. This is the energy of transformation." "I'm allowed to be both scared and brave."*

5. Stay Open to Who You're Becoming: The most powerful gift of change is the opportunity to realign your life with your evolving truth. Who you were yesterday does not define who you must be tomorrow. Ask:

> ➢ Who am I becoming through this transition?

> ➢ What possibilities excite or inspire me, even if they scare me a little?

6. When Change Feels Like Loss: Sometimes, change feels less like a new beginning and more like an unwanted ending. Divorce. Estrangement. Loss of a career. An empty home after the kids leave.

In these seasons, remember:

Your grief is valid.

Your fear is understandable.

Your worth does not depend on any role, job, or relationship.

You are whole, even when everything around you is shifting.

Give yourself permission to mourn what was, and slowly, patiently, turn your heart toward what might be.

Your Roots Will Hold

In the middle of a life transition, it can feel like the ground is crumbling beneath you. Your roots are stronger than you think. You can stay grounded, even as the winds howl. You have the strength to rebuild, even when the old structures fall. You have the wisdom to rise, even when you can't yet see what you're rising into.

Trust yourself. Great transformations and extraordinary lives arise from seasons of change.

Reflection Prompts: Embracing Winds of Change

➢ What changes am I currently navigating (big or small)?

➢ What emotions are coming up for me around this change?

➢ Where can I offer myself more compassion during this transition?

➢ What strengths have past life transitions revealed in me?

➢ What new dreams or possibilities are calling to me now?

Final Thoughts

Change doesn't come to destroy you, it comes to awaken you. You are allowed to grieve, to stumble, to question, and to hope. You are allowed to rebuild at your own pace. You are allowed to rise.

And you will.

Change often arrives gradually, like a shifting wind. But sometimes, it strikes like a sudden storm, upending everything at once. In the next chapter, we'll explore how to stay grounded when life's storms come fast, hard, and without warning. Now, let's explore how to stay grounded when life's challenges hit with full force.

CHAPTER 36

STORMS OF LIFE

Strength in the Midst of Crisis

S torms, whether sudden or slow-moving, can test our limits in ways we never expected. These moments come in many forms: personal or family emergencies, financial hardship, unexpected illnesses, career setbacks, or crises that shake your world in ways you never saw coming. Unlike the Winds of Change, which bring transitions we can often expect, storms hit hard and fast. They force us into survival mode, making it difficult to think clearly or trust that we'll make it through. But no storm lasts forever.

Finding Stability When Life Feels Unsteady

During turbulent times, the instinct to retreat, isolate, or shut down can be strong. But weathering life's storms requires the opposite such as reaching out, leaning into support, and staying rooted in what keeps you strong.

Here are some key strategies to anchor yourself during a storm:

- Reach out for support. You don't have to do this alone. Seek help from friends, family, a mentor, or professional services. Let people show up for you.

- Prioritize self-care. Even amid crisis, minor acts of self-care matter. Sleep, movement, nutrition, and mindfulness can keep your nervous system from becoming overwhelmed.

- Take things one step at a time. The full path ahead may feel overwhelming. Just focus on the next right step. Then the next.

- Control what you can, release what you can't. Some things are out of your hands. Shift your energy toward what's within your power.

- Remind yourself: *"This will pass."* The storm may be strong, but so are you. Every difficult moment you've survived before has led you here.

These strategies don't eliminate the storm, but they help you find your footing when everything feels like it's shifting beneath you.

Storms can sometimes trigger deep emotional pain, anxiety, depression, or trauma responses that feel too overwhelming to navigate alone. Reaching out to a therapist, counselor, coach, or crisis support service can provide essential tools and emotional safety during your healing process. Asking for professional help isn't a sign of weakness, it's a powerful act of self-respect and courage.

Personal Story:
Weathering the Financial Storm

Storms don't always come as one major event. Sometimes, they unfold over time, forcing us to navigate ongoing uncertainty. One of the most challenging aspects of being self-employed is the financial rollercoaster with seasons of abundance followed by dry spells. When you rely on your own time, energy, and ability to secure work, any disruption to that rhythm can feel like a crisis.

For me, that storm came when my stepmom was battling breast cancer. As a marketing consultant and coach, my income depended entirely on my ability to take on and manage clients. When she needed support, I made the choice to step away from work to be there for her and my dad. I had to put my business on hold, and with that came a wave of financial uncertainty.

As a mom, I had real financial responsibilities, and for the first time in my life, I applied for Medicare because healthcare in California was so expensive. It was a humbling experience. Having always relied on my ability to generate income, I suddenly found myself in a position where I needed financial help. But it was necessary. I couldn't focus on work and caregiving, so I had to make the decision that felt right for my family.

During this time, I leaned into trust and the belief that when I was ready to rebuild, opportunities would come. After my stepmom passed away and I moved through the most intense waves of grief, I had to step back into work and reestablish my financial footing. I didn't want to ask my dad for financial support while he was also grieving so I focused on what I could control: reconnecting with my network, reaching out to potential clients, and trusting that I could rebuild.

And I did. Looking back, this period in my life reinforced one of the most important lessons about weathering financial storms:

- Sometimes, survival mode is necessary, and there is no shame in doing what you need to do to get through it.
- There will be times when you have to lean on safety nets— whether that's assistance programs, community support, or lowering your expenses.
- There will be times when your career is not the top priority because something greater requires your attention.
- And there will be times when you must trust in your own resilience, even when you can't see how things will turn out.

If you are in a season of financial uncertainty, remind yourself:

- You are not failing, you are adapting.
- You can rebuild, even if it takes time.
- Security comes in many forms. Find where your stability lies, even if it's not financial at the moment.
- This storm will not last forever.

If you're in the midst of survival mode, know that it's okay to pause, breathe, and focus only on what's necessary. Healing doesn't happen on a schedule, and strength doesn't mean rushing through the pain.

When There's One Storm After Another

Some seasons of life bring not just one storm, but wave after wave of challenges. Just as you regain your footing, another setback knocks you down. If you find yourself in this space, remember:

- You are allowed to pause. If you're in a period of crisis, give yourself permission to stop pushing forward at full speed. Survival mode is not the time to take on unnecessary burdens or make decisions that require in-depth analysis.

- You don't have to have all the answers today. The future may feel uncertain, but clarity will come as you keep moving forward, step by step. Sometimes, waiting to make important decisions will allow them to come when there is more clarity.

- You are not alone. Even if it feels like no one understands what you're going through, there is support available. Reach out, even when it's hard.

- You are stronger than you think. Every challenge you've faced before has prepared you for this moment. Trust in your resilience.

- Your experience will make you relatable to others and potentially provide insights that can help them when going through something similar.

No storm lasts forever. And when the skies clear, you will emerge— stronger, wiser, and ready to rise. Storms can shake your world, but they do not have to break you. They are the ultimate tests of resilience, but they are also opportunities to realign with what truly matters. As you move through your own storms, lean into your support system, prioritize your well-being, and trust that you have the strength to weather whatever comes your way.

Reflection Prompts:
Weathering Life's Storms

➢ What storm am I currently moving through or still healing from?

➢ Where am I stronger today because of past storms I've survived?

➢ What anchors can I rely on when life feels uncertain?

➢ Who can I reach out to for support when I need it most?

➢ What small act of self-care or courage can I take today to steady myself?

Some storms pass quickly, but others leave lasting imprints on our hearts. Your strength is permanent.

You are not stuck in this moment. You are becoming the stronger, wiser, more radiant version of yourself. One that will be more relatable and empathetic as a result of your experience.

Next, we'll explore how to navigate the deep waters of grief, and find healing through them.

CHAPTER 37

CRASHING WAVES

Grief & Loss

G rief is one of the deepest and most universal human experiences. It can be the loss of a loved one or it can also be the loss of a relationship, a job, a dream, a phase of life, or even a version of yourself. Loss takes many forms, and all are valid.

What makes grief so challenging is that it doesn't follow a predictable or linear path. The five stages—denial, anger, bargaining, depression, and acceptance—aren't a checklist to complete. They're a framework to help us understand the waves of emotions we may experience. Some days, acceptance feels within reach. Other days, the weight of loss pulls us back into sorrow, longing, or even anger. Grief isn't something we "get over." It's something we learn to carry.

What's important to remember is that grief, as painful as it is, is also a testament to love. We grieve deeply because we loved deeply. And though loss changes the shape of that love, it doesn't erase it.

A Personal Story: Grieving Without Goodbye

One of the hardest aspects of grief is when we don't get the closure we seek. My best friend of 40 years ended her life, and I didn't get a chance to say goodbye. Instead, I got a call from her phone. It wasn't her. It was her cousin, letting me know she had made the decision to end her suffering.

It was heartbreaking to learn the extent of her pain and isolation. Over the years, she had discussed Death with Dignity and had even asked if I'd be there for her. But in the end, she chose not to include me. That choice hurt, and yet it was also a relief. I was willing to be there for her, but the thought of witnessing her departure felt unbearably heavy.

After she passed, I kept waiting for a letter or card—something to explain her ultimate choice in her own words. But it never came. Eventually, I created my form of closure. I gathered old cards, photos, and gifts she had given me over the years and assembled an altar in her honor. As I looked at it, I realized she had left me something after all. Her words, her love, her memories—they were all there. Through them, I could see both her struggle and her devotion. And though I wished I could have changed her outcome, I honored her decision with empathy rather than just pain.

One of those gifts was a super-soft purple blanket with the word *Sister* on it. On the days when I miss her most, I wrap myself in that blanket and let it hold me. This small but powerful reminder shows me that her love still envelops me, even though she is no longer physically here.

Her passing reinforced something grief often teaches us: not every loss comes with an answer. Sometimes, we have to find our own way to integrate the absence and to honor the love that remains, even when someone is gone. Others may experience grief in the form of estrangement, where there's still hope but no contact.

The Complex Nature of Grief

Grief isn't just about death. It can also be the loss of a marriage, a friendship, a home, or even an identity. Sometimes, we grieve transitions we chose, like leaving a city we love for a new opportunity, or letting go of a dream that no longer fits. Other times, life forces grief upon us, reshaping our world without our consent.

What makes grief so challenging is that it's unpredictable. Some days, you may feel okay. Other days, the weight of loss blindsides you. That's normal. Healing doesn't happen on a schedule, and there is no "right way" to grieve.

One thing that helps is understanding that grief isn't just about pain, it's about adaptation. It's learning how to live in a world that has changed. We create new ways to honor our losses while still moving forward.

Ways to Support Yourself Through Grief

Acknowledge what you're feeling. Suppressing grief only prolongs the process. Allow yourself to sit with your emotions without judgment or pressure to feel a certain way. Seek connection through a trusted friend, a support group, or a professional therapist or coach who can help you hold space for the complicated emotions that arise.

While grief can feel isolating, you don't have to navigate it alone. Find your own form of closure, whether that's creating an altar, writing a letter, or engaging in a ritual that feels meaningful to you. You can powerfully move forward by honoring what was lost. Most importantly, give yourself grace. There is no timeline for grief. Some days will feel heavier than others, and that's okay. And people will understand. Grief isn't about "moving on," it's about integrating loss into your life in a way that allows you to carry it while still continuing on your path.

Exercise: Writing a Letter to Your Loss

One way to process grief is through writing. Try writing a letter to the person (or thing) you lost. Express what you didn't get to say. Acknowledge what you miss. Share the ways they've shaped you. If it feels right, write a response from their perspective offering the words of love or comfort you wish you had heard. Not all grief comes with the closure we desire. But that doesn't mean we can't create our own meaning from it.

Reflection Prompts: Embracing and Healing Grief

> ➢ What (or who) am I grieving right now?

> ➢ What emotions have surfaced most strongly during this process?

> ➢ What memories or moments am I most grateful for from what I've lost?

> ➢ In what ways can I honor the love, the dreams, or the chapter that has ended?

> ➢ Where in my life can I allow myself more gentleness and grace as I heal?

> ➢ Who can I reach out to for support such as a friend, a counselor, or a professional who can walk with me through this season?

> ➢ What small act of remembrance or ritual would feel comforting to create in honor of what was lost?

Love Doesn't End with Loss

Another way to keep someone's memory alive is to consciously carry forward the best parts of who they were. When my friend Chris passed away unexpectedly, I realized one of the most beautiful ways I could honor him was to embody the generosity he was known for. Chris was the person who went the extra mile to make people feel special. He'd rent the limo, tip for the better table, buy the souvenirs, or send a thoughtful gift if you couldn't be there. In remembering him, I asked myself, "How can I show up in the world with that same spirit?"

Now, when I take a moment to create a meaningful experience for someone else, I do it with him in mind. In this way, his presence lives on, not just in memory, but in action. This form of tribute is powerful. It turns loss into legacy and allows us to integrate what we cherished about someone into who we continue to become.

Though it may not feel like it now, your heart will expand again. The depth of your grief reflects the depth of your love, and that love still exists, even in their absence. You will carry them with you in the way you speak their name, in the way you live your life, and in the way you cherish the memories they left behind.

Closing Thoughts

Grief is hard, unpredictable, and deeply personal. And it is also an invitation to honor, to remember, and to continue loving, even after loss.

Though it may not always feel like it, love continues to surround you with your memories, your growth, and the quiet strength within you.

Be gentle with yourself. You are stronger than you know.

CHAPTER 38

PRESSURE SYSTEMS

Turning Stress into Strength

S tress isn't just an inconvenience, it's a silent thief of joy, energy, and well-being. It infiltrates our minds, wears down our bodies, and, if left unchecked, can lead to emotional burnout and even chronic illness.

We hear it all the time, "stress is a killer." But what does that really mean? It means that stress, when prolonged, creates a state of "dis-ease" in the body. If we don't take action, it could lead to serious illness.

I'll never forget what my dear friend Brenda told me before she passed away from leukemia. She believed that stress had played a major role in her illness. She had ignored the warning signs—overwhelm, exhaustion, emotional strain—believing that she could push through without making changes. By the time she realized the toll it had taken, it was too late. She believed that "dis-ease" with life is responsible for disease in the body.

Her words became a wake-up call for me. Stress isn't just about feeling frazzled, it can affect your longevity, your health, and your happiness. So I practice what a friend calls "radical self-care" which involved firm boundaries and conscious choices that protect my mental and physical health. Not as an indulgence, but as a necessity. Because if we don't take care of ourselves, we can't show up fully for the people and things we love.

Stress doesn't have to control you. There are ways to break the cycle, shift your energy, and reclaim your peace. And one of the most powerful tools we can use? Gratitude.

Recognizing the Signs of Chronic Stress

You may already experience the effects of stress without realizing it. Pay attention if you've been experiencing prolonged periods with any of these symptoms:

- Frequent headaches or muscle tension
- Fatigue or trouble sleeping
- Digestive issues or appetite changes
- Feeling overwhelmed, irritable, or emotionally numb
- Low motivation or lack of joy
- Depression, anxiety, or social withdrawal

If you're noticing these signs, take it as a serious signal that your body is out of balance. Stress doesn't just go away on its own. You have to actively shift it. And the first step is awareness.

The Triad: A Tool for Stress Management

One of the most powerful ways I combat stress is by using The Triad—a practice that helps shift my mental and emotional state in real time. Whenever I feel overwhelmed, I take a nature walk, using this time to check in with the three key aspects of The Triad:

Physiology: *What am I doing with my body?*

Am I tense, shallow-breathing, or locked in stress? Moving in nature immediately shifts my state—exercise, fresh air, and the simple act of walking all help lower stress hormones and boost my mood.

Focus: *What am I fixating on?*

If I'm spiraling about my to-do list or feeling like I'm not good enough, I step back into observer-mode. I acknowledge these thoughts, but I don't let them take over.

Meaning: *What story am I telling myself?*

Am I framing my stress as proof that I'm failing? Instead, I reframe my perspective: "I have a lot on my plate because I'm building something meaningful. I can handle this one step at a time."

At the end of my walk, I stop at a massive tree—my Guardian Oak—and place my hand on its mossy branch. Sometimes, I listen for wisdom. Sometimes, I simply say thank you. And without fail, I leave with a clearer mind and a lighter heart. This practice has given me some of my greatest insights, even inspiring blogs and sections of this very book. The wisdom is always there. We just have to create space to hear it.

Strategies for Stress Reduction

1. **Prioritize Radical Self-Care:** Self-care isn't just about bubble baths and spa days. It's about setting boundaries, creating space to rest, and treating yourself with compassion. If you're in a stressful season, prioritize the basics:

   - Get enough sleep
   - Nourish your body with healthy food
   - Move daily (even a short walk counts)
   - Unplug from screens and social media
   - Carve out time for hobbies, connection, and relaxation

2. **Say NO & Protect Your Energy:** One of the biggest causes of stress is overcommitment. If you're constantly saying yes to everything and everyone, it's time to re-evaluate.

   - Set clear boundaries to protect your time and energy.
   - Don't feel guilty for saying no because your well-being matters.

- Identify energy-draining relationships. It's okay to distance yourself from people who add to your stress.

3. Move Your Body: Stress lives in the body, so one of the best ways to release it is through movement.

- Stretch, dance, go for a walk, do yoga. Just move.
- Exercise releases endorphins and lowers cortisol.
- Physical activity helps shift you from a fight-or-flight state to a place of calm.

4. Connect & Express: You don't have to carry stress alone. Talk about it.

- Call a friend, therapist, or coach.
- Journal your thoughts to get them out of your head and onto paper.
- Lean into community and let people support you.

Stress thrives in silence. Break the cycle by reaching out.

If your stress feels overwhelming or persistent, don't hesitate to seek professional support. Therapists, counselors, and coaches can offer tools, perspective, and a safe space to help you heal.

The Transformative Power of Gratitude

If stress is a thief, gratitude is a healer and a powerful form of magic. Gratitude can shift energy, transform emotions, and rewire the way we experience life. When we cultivate gratitude, we're not just thinking positive thoughts. We're tapping into a frequency of abundance, presence, and joy. Gratitude is alchemy. It has the power to transmute pain into wisdom, loss into appreciation, and even anger into peace. It's one of the few emotions that can override stress and negativity in an instant.

Gratitude as an Antidote to Anger

Anger is a stormy emotion. It's wild, consuming, and often destructive. While anger has its place and can serve as a signal that something isn't right, staying in a state of prolonged anger can be toxic. Gratitude is one of the most powerful ways to diffuse anger. When you consciously shift your focus from frustration to appreciation, you disrupt the emotional charge of anger.

Next time you feel resentment or irritation creeping in, pause and ask:

> ➤ What can I be grateful for at this moment?

> ➤ Is there a lesson hidden within this challenge?

> ➤ What is this anger teaching me about what I value?

When you redirect your focus to gratitude, it doesn't mean ignoring or suppressing your emotions. It means choosing to respond rather than react. Gratitude reminds you of your power, your presence, and your ability to rise above negativity.

Journal Prompt: Gratitude & The Triad

Use these prompts to check in with yourself and shift your state:

> ➤ **Physiology:** What are you doing with your body when you feel stressed or overwhelmed? How can you shift it in a way that supports you?

> ➤ **Focus:** What are you focusing on? Are you fixating on problems, or are you acknowledging what's working?

> ➤ **Meaning:** What story are you telling yourself? How can you reframe it in a way that feels empowering?

> ➤ **Gratitude:** What are three things you're grateful for today?

Write your answers down., reflect, and let gratitude work its magic.

Standing Strong During High Pressure Systems

Change is inevitable, but so is your ability to adapt. Stress is real, but it doesn't have to control you. Gratitude doesn't erase pain, but it shifts your perspective. Letting go creates space for new beginnings. You are more resilient than you realize. Every storm you've faced has prepared you for the next.

Trust your roots. They will hold you steady. Even during the storm, your roots are holding. You are stronger than you know, steadier than you feel, and braver than you believe. Take it one breath, one step, one moment at a time.

You are rising, even now.

CHAPTER 39

RELEASING TO RISE

Freeing Yourself by Letting Go

T hroughout this section, we've explored how to withstand the elements including navigating the winds of change, weathering life's storms, moving through grief, breaking free from stress, and unlocking the power of gratitude. Now, as we close this part of the journey, it's time to talk about one of the most profound acts of resilience: *letting go*.

True resilience isn't about holding onto everything. It's about knowing what to release so you can move forward with strength and clarity.

When Holding On Becomes a Hidden Habit

Letting go sounds simple. But if you've ever tried to release a grudge, a belief, or a version of yourself, you know it's not. That's because we don't hold on just to suffer. We hold on because, on some level, it's meeting a need.

Maybe you cling to a toxic relationship because it gives you a sense of security, even if it's chaotic. Maybe you revisit old failures because they justify a belief about yourself that feels familiar. Maybe you keep chasing perfection because it makes you feel worthy, even as it exhausts you.

We hold on because part of us believes: *"This protects me."* But over time, the cost adds up.

- Your energy (constantly looping thoughts or emotional reactivity)
- Your peace (anxiety, resentment, fear)
- Your identity (staying stuck in who you were, not who you're becoming)
- Your relationships (projecting past pain into the present)
- Your growth (clinging to old patterns leaves no room for expansion)

And most of all, it costs you your freedom.

A Personal Story: Letting Go in Motherhood

Parenting is one of the most humbling lessons in letting go.

When my son was a baby, I cherished the closeness—those quiet moments of nursing, the way he clung to me, the deep bond that came from being his entire world. But when he began to walk, I had to let go of that baby version of him and embrace the toddler who wanted to explore on his own. It felt like my heart was chasing him at every step.

That pattern repeated through every stage. When he turned sixteen and got his driver's license, I had to literally let him go and watch him drive away, trusting he'd be safe even though worry filled every inch of my body. The physical distance mirrored the emotional one that was growing. He was individuating. Becoming his own person. And I had to honor that, even when it hurt.

Then came the big release go date. He moved away to college at eighteen. I drove away from campus in tears, the silence in the car echoing the silence waiting for me at home. As a single mom, I'd return to an empty house where his energy lingered, then slowly faded—until he returned for a visit and it lit up again. Each goodbye was heartbreaking, yet completely natural.

Letting go didn't mean I loved him less. It meant I loved him enough to allow him to grow and individuate. I let myself feel the sadness, the uncertainty, the loss of a role I had cherished. And through it all, I surrounded myself with support from my boyfriend, my friends, and my own practices of healing. That chapter of motherhood taught me what no book or coach ever could: *letting go is less about release and more about transformation.* And that the only way to the other side of loss, change, or growth is through the heart of it.

Letting go isn't about losing. It's about transforming. It's the space where grief and love meet.

Releasing & Rising

Letting go doesn't mean you erase the past. It means you honor it while making space for what's next. It means:

- Releasing the outdated stories of who you thought you had to be
- Letting go of roles that no longer fit
- Allowing emotions to rise and move through you without judgment
- Trusting that what's meant to stay will stay, and what's meant to change will open new doors

Whether you're letting go of a relationship, a version of yourself, an old identity, or even a dream that's no longer aligned, remember: it's okay to grieve. And don't confuse grief with failure. Often, it's the bravest thing we can do.

Ask yourself:

➢ What am I holding onto that no longer serves me?

➢ What need is this meeting and is there a higher way to meet it?

➢ Who am I becoming if I let this go?

Letting go is sacred work. It doesn't happen all at once. Sometimes, we let go in layers. But every time you release, you rise.

Nature's Wisdom: Letting Go with the Seasons

Nature provides some of the best metaphors for life's transitions. Just as the seasons change, so too do we. And if we align ourselves with nature's rhythms, we can learn how to release what no longer serves us.

Autumn: The Art of Release Trees shed their leaves effortlessly in the fall, trusting that new growth will come when the time is right.

> ➢ What beliefs, habits, or relationships am I ready to release?

Winter: Stillness & Reflection Nature slows down in winter, conserving energy for the growth ahead.

> ➢ How am I giving myself permission to pause, reflect, and prepare for new beginnings?

Spring: New Beginnings Just as flowers bloom, spring reminds us that new opportunities arise when we make space for them.

> ➢ What seeds am I ready to plant?

Summer: Flourishing in Your Fullness This is the season of expansion, joy, and reaping the rewards of your growth.

> ➢ How am I celebrating my growth?

Seasons happen *within* us, not just around us. Letting go creates space for what's next.

Forgiveness: The Emotional Release Valve

Letting go often sounds easier than it feels, especially when what you're holding onto involves people who hurt you, choices you regret, or versions of yourself you haven't yet made peace with. This is where forgiveness becomes essential.

Forgiveness isn't about pretending it didn't hurt or rushing to forget. It's not about excusing the past. It's about giving yourself the freedom to stop carrying it. Think of it as the emotional release valve, a way to let the pressure out so you don't have to live weighed down by anger, guilt, or pain. Forgiveness isn't for them. It's for *you*. It doesn't mean re-opening the door to someone who broke your trust. It means reclaiming your energy from the story that's been replaying in your mind.

You don't have to forgive all at once. Sometimes forgiveness happens in layers. Sometimes, it's simply saying, "I'm open to releasing this" even if you're not ready yet.

Whether it's forgiving someone else or forgiving yourself, it's one of the most transformative ways to lighten your load and create space for something new. Forgiveness is one of the most profound forms of letting go. And like autumn leaves, you can choose to release, not because you no longer care, but because you're ready to grow.

Forgiveness practices:
- Write a letter you never send
- Mirror practice: Look yourself in the eyes and say, "I forgive you"
- Burn ritual: Write down what you're releasing and burn it safely

The Backpack Exercise:
What Are You Ready to Release?

If you've been carrying a heavy emotional load, here's a visualization exercise to help you let go in a way that feels tangible. Picture yourself wearing a backpack. It's filled with everything weighing you down.

Is it stress? Fear? Guilt? A relationship that drains you? A habit that no longer serves you? A limiting belief about yourself?

Feel the weight of it. Notice how it affects your body, your energy, your spirit. Acknowledge that you've been carrying this for a long time. Ask yourself:

➢ Why have I been carrying this?

➢ In what ways has it served me (even if unhealthily)?

➢ What would happen if I put it down?

If any part of your backpack includes pain from a person, a memory, or even your own mistakes, pause and ask:

➢ What would forgiveness look like here?

➢ Am I ready to begin letting this go, one breath at a time?

Now visualize yourself removing the backpack and setting it down. Perhaps you could throw it off a cliff. Maybe you watch it dissolve into light. Or send it to space and have it explode into millions of tiny pieces. Or send it floating away down a river. Breathe deeply. Feel the lightness of releasing this burden. Step forward, unencumbered, ready to embrace what's ahead.

Creating Space for Growth

Letting go isn't just about releasing; it's also about replacing what you've lost with something nourishing. If releasing this baggage leaves a void, fill it with intentional choices:

If you're letting go of stress eating → replace it with mindful movement or healthy activities.

If you're releasing toxic relationships → surround yourself with people who uplift and support you.

If you're dropping self-doubt → actively reaffirm your strengths and accomplishments.

As always, come back to the Triad: Shift your body. Refocus your mind. Reframe your meaning. Let go with intention. Letting go isn't just about removal; it's about elevation.

From Wounds to Wisdom

Letting go—and the forgiveness that often comes with it—is not a finish line. It's a path you walk at your own pace. Some days, you'll feel closer to peace; other days, the old weight may return. That's okay. Healing isn't linear, and neither is becoming whole.

Wherever you are on this journey, you are doing brave, beautiful work. Be patient with your heart. Wrap yourself in grace. And every time you release something that no longer serves you, you rise a little higher into the life you're meant to live.

CHAPTER 40

AFTER THE STORM

What Carries You Forward

L ife has a way of shaking us—sometimes gently, sometimes without mercy. Change, grief, loss, and crisis touch us all, often when we least expect it. This section was about helping you steady yourself when the winds pick up, and the ground feels unsteady. The storm is only part of the story. What matters just as much is what you carry out of it.

Key Takeaways from Withstanding the Elements

As we close this part of the journey, let's reflect on the biggest lessons we've explored:

- **Winds of Change** remind us that while change is inevitable, our ability to adapt is within our control. Instead of fixating on what's lost, we can focus on what remains steady. Identity shifts—whether through divorce, career changes, or life pivots—are opportunities to redefine ourselves with deeper truth and purpose.

- **Storms of Life** teach us that no storm lasts forever, even when it feels like it will. In times of crisis, leaning on your support system is essential. By breaking challenges into small, manageable steps, you can continue moving forward, even when the full path feels overwhelming.

- **Crashing Waves** reminds us that grief is not just about death; it can be the loss of a relationship, a dream, or a version of yourself. There is no "right" way to grieve, and healing happens at your own pace. Honoring what was lost—by carrying forward its lessons and love—becomes part of how we continue to live with an open heart.

- **Pressure Systems** means recognizing that stress is a silent thief of health and happiness—and that radical self-care is not a luxury, it's a necessity. Using The Triad—Physiology, Focus, and Meaning— gives you tools to shift your emotional and mental state, reclaiming peace even amid pressure.

- **Releasing to Rise** explains that letting go is more than surrender, it's a sacred act of transformation. It's where pain becomes wisdom, and what once weighed you down becomes the very thing that lifts you. Releasing outdated roles, relationships, or beliefs is never easy, but it's how we create space for peace, clarity, and growth. Whether it's through grief, forgiveness, or gentle self-compassion, letting go is the alchemy that turns heaviness into lightness, regret into grace, and resistance into resilience.

Key Reminders from the Elements

- Change is inevitable, and how you meet it is a choice.
- Crisis doesn't define you, your response does.
- Grief is not a problem to fix, it's a process to honor.
- Stress is a signal, not a life sentence.
- Letting go and forgiveness aren't signs of weakness, they are signs of powerful self-trust.

Practices That Steady You

You've explored tools like:

- Grounding through breath, ritual, and radical self-care
- Making space for grief instead of pushing it away

- Releasing control and learning to flow with change
- Reframing stress through The Triad and micro-restoration
- Creating resilience through emotional regulation, boundaries, and gratitude

These aren't just ideas. They are *anchors*. They are the roots that will hold you steady when the winds return.

Reflection Prompts

➢ What is one storm I've come through that showed me how strong I am?

➢ What practice or mindset shift helps me stay grounded during change?

➢ What am I still carrying that it's time to release?

Trust Your Roots, Let Yourself Rise

The storms of life don't have to break you. They can soften you, strengthen you, and strip away what no longer serves you…if you let them.

You are not powerless in the face of change. You are not defined by what happens to you; you are defined by how you rise. You can adapt, even when it feels impossible. You have strength within you that you haven't even fully discovered yet. You have the power to release what weighs you down and grow into something entirely new.

Let go. Make space. Trust your roots.

You made it. Now it's time to rise!

Coming Next: Phase III: Rise

In the next part of the journey, we move into Rise: the powerful process of stepping into your authenticity. Authenticity isn't about becoming someone new; it's about stripping away the masks, letting go of external expectations, and embracing the person you were always meant to be.

ROOT-TO-RISE INFOGRAPHIC

PHASE THREE: RISE

RISE

HUMAN NEEDS

Transcendence

- Moving past the self to serve others
- Connecting to higher purpose
- Contribution
- Sharing
- Service
- Providing

Growth

- Growing
- Pulsating energy
- Progress
- Learning
- Feeling momentum
- Advancing
- Breaking free

Intimacy

- Nurturing
- Valuing relationships
- Belonging
- Feeling passion
- Having desire
- Striving for unity
- Togetherness

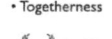
Self

- Self-esteem
- Self-worth
- Significance
- Importance
- Pride
- Importance
- Perfection

Variety

- Change
- Transitions
- Storms
- Challenges
- Trauma/Crisis
- Chaos
- Variety
- New/Different
- Spice of Life
- Surprise
- Fear

Security

- Certainty
- Safety
- Rootedness
- Grounded
- Comfort
- Stability
- Predictability
- Protection
- Commitment

WITHSTANDING THE ELEMENTS

- Winds of Change
- Storms/Upheaval
- Grief & Loss

NAVIGATING EMOTIONS

Triad:
- Body/Mind/Spirit
- Physiology/Focus/Meaning

CLEARING OBSTACLES

- Nourishing Needy Roots
- Honoring Driving Needs
- Pain Points
- Getting Unstuck
- Fears & Limiting Beliefs
- Double Binds
- Leveraging you Tap Root

FOCUS MIND | **MEANING SPIRIT**

PHYSIOLOGY BODY

RESILIENCE

LIFE ROOT SYSTEM

HEALTH/FITNESS	FAMILY	RELATIONSHIPS	CAREER	FRIENDS
• Nutrition	• Parents	• Self	• Time & Money	• Introvert v. Extrovert Needs
• Food/Beverage	• Caregivers	• Romantic Partner	• Contribution	• Who are they?
• Supplements	• Siblings	• Commitment	• Heart-based/ Passion vs Corporate	• Reflection of you
• Fitness/Exercise	• Partner	• Chemistry	• Hobbies/Craft	• What do you offer?
• Massage/Body Work	• In-laws	• Compatibility	• Who you are:	• What do they offer?
• Wellness vs. Illness	• Children	• Communication	• Strengths/ Weaknesses	• Elevate
	• Chosen		• Leader vs. Worker	• Support
			• Visionary vs. Operational	• Experience
			• Analytical/ Data-minded	

www.glowliving.com
#glowliving
#roottorise
#lovelife

TAP ROOT
What feeds your soul deeply?

GLOWLIVING
love life

ROOTS

© All Rights Reserved. Glow Living/Glow Marketing LLC 2025

PHASE III: RISE

Part One

- - -

AUTHENTICITY

- - -

CHAPTER 41

CONNECTING TO AUTHENTICITY

Aligning with Your True Self

A uthenticity is about living in alignment with whom you truly are—your values, desires, and purpose—rather than conforming to external expectations or societal norms. It's about shedding the masks, releasing the roles that don't serve you, and embracing the version of yourself that feels the most honest, free, and fulfilled.

When you live out of alignment with your authentic self, you'll always feel like something is missing. You might have the "perfect" job, the "ideal" relationship, or a life that looks great from the outside, yet inside, you feel disconnected, restless, or even trapped. That's because true fulfillment comes from honoring your own needs, not from checking off boxes created by someone else's definition of success.

This isn't just intuition and research backs it up. A study in the *Journal of Counseling Psychology* found that people who scored higher in authenticity reported greater life satisfaction, self-esteem, and well-being, and lower levels of anxiety and depression (Wood et al., 2008).

In this chapter, we're diving deep into what it means to connect with your authenticity, why it's so essential for your happiness, and how to take the bold steps to claim it.

The Foundations of Authenticity

To live authentically, you have to be deeply in tune with yourself. Here are some of the key aspects of authenticity:

- **Self-Awareness**: Understanding your values, beliefs, passions, strengths, and weaknesses is the first step in aligning with your authentic self.

- **Honesty**: Authenticity requires radical self-honesty. It means acknowledging your true desires, fears, and needs without self-censorship. You can't live authentically if you're not willing to admit your own truth.

- **Living Your Values:** When your actions reflect your deeply held beliefs and principles, you experience greater fulfillment and peace. If something feels "off," ask whether you're living according to your own standards or someone else's.

- **Letting Go of Pretense:** No more performing. Authenticity means the courage to be seen exactly as you are—flaws, quirks, and all.

- **Expressing Your Truth:** Whether through your words, actions, creativity, or personal style, self-expression reinforces your authenticity.

- **Evolving Over Time:** Your authenticity isn't fixed. As you grow and change, so will your expression of who you are. Honor that evolution.

- **Practicing Self-Compassion:** Accepting yourself completely, strengths and imperfections alike, is key.

Here's something that might surprise you: some psychologists argue that there isn't just one "authentic self" waiting to be uncovered, but many parts of us that grow. The idea of a fixed identity can create pressure. Instead, authenticity may look like honoring who you are today while leaving room for who you're still becoming.

Living authentically also requires the courage to stand alone. You may face situations where your truth goes against the grain. Choosing your truth over convenience, even when it's uncomfortable, is what deep alignment looks like.

The Cost of Living Out of Alignment

Many of us take on identities, careers, or roles we believe will earn us acceptance. But when those choices don't reflect our true selves, we feel empty.

Signs of misalignment include:

- Feeling unfulfilled at work or in relationships
- Suppressing your desires to please others
- Persistent stress, anxiety, or a sense that something is "off"

Neuroscience calls this cognitive dissonance, the stress of living in a way that conflicts with your beliefs. Over time, it erodes your energy and self-trust.

Breaking Free from the Fear of Change

Fear is one of the biggest blocks to authenticity—fear of judgment, failure, or disappointing others. But the price of staying inauthentic is too high.

You can't seek approval and authenticity at the same time. Researcher Brené Brown calls this "armoring up," the hiding behind perfectionism or people-pleasing to avoid rejection. True freedom comes from making choices that reflect your real self.

Living authentically may disrupt certain relationships, yet the people who truly love you will support your growth.

Remember, failure isn't getting it wrong. It's refusing to try. Every effort toward authenticity is a win.

Authenticity in Career and Relationships

If your job doesn't excite you, ask if you chose it for passion or validation. If you feel disconnected in relationships, ask whether you're expressing your true needs.

Authenticity isn't selfish. The right people will honor your truth.

You don't need others to change. Just hold your truth, let your values lead, and give others the space to meet you there…or let them go.

Your Truth is Your Power

Authenticity means choosing self-respect over approval, self-honor over avoidance, and growth over comfort.

➢ Who will I be when I stand unapologetically in my truth?

➢ What will I create when I stop seeking permission?

At Glow Living, the logo—a diamond heart—holds deep meaning. It represents that we are all multi-faceted beings, with different sides that shine in different contexts. Just like a diamond reflects light through many angles, we show aspects of ourselves as they feel appropriate to the moment. Some parts of us are ready to be seen in the sun, while others stay in the shadows, not because they're false, but because they're sacred, tender, or still unfolding. Authenticity doesn't mean putting every part of ourselves on display at all times. It means knowing, accepting, and honoring our full selves—and choosing to lead with truth, not performance.

The time to align with your truth is now. Let's step forward together.

Next up: Let's explore the masks we wear, and how to gently take them off.

CHAPTER 42

UNVEILING THE MASKS

Why We're Not Always Authentic

A uthenticity is the foundation of a fulfilling life. It's the courage to be who we truly are, to express ourselves without fear, and to live in alignment with our deepest values. But many of us unknowingly wear masks, the personas shaped by childhood, societal expectations, or the desire to fit in. These masks often feel safer than revealing our true selves, but over time, they create a disconnect that can leave us feeling unfulfilled and out of sync with our own lives.

This chapter is about recognizing the masks we wear, understanding why we created them, and taking steps toward shedding them so we can reclaim our authenticity and live in alignment with who we were always meant to be.

The Shadows of Childhood: How We Learn to Hide Ourselves

Authenticity is natural. We are born knowing exactly who we are. But as we grow, we become shaped, and sometimes distorted, by our environment. Childhood is especially powerful. It's when the need for acceptance and safety becomes so strong that we mold ourselves to get the world's approval.

You may have learned to:

- Be the peacemaker, always avoiding conflict.
- Be the achiever, earning love through success.
- Be the caretaker, ignoring your needs to keep others happy.
- Be the chameleon, adapting to fit into any room but losing your sense of self in the process.

These strategies were smart. They helped you stay safe, gain approval, or avoid punishment. But what once protected you may now be holding you back.

The Cost of Hiding

Wearing a mask might win praise, but it doesn't nourish the soul. Over time, it creates emotional exhaustion. You may feel:

- Disconnected from yourself
- Unseen in your relationships
- Burned out from performing a role
- Unclear about what you actually want

This is your invitation to take the mask off…not all at once, but layer by layer.

Reclaiming the Real You

The first step in shedding your masks is compassionate self-awareness. Ask yourself:

- ➤ What persona do I feel I have to be in order to be accepted?
- ➤ When do I feel most fake or performative?
- ➤ What parts of me have I been hiding to keep others comfortable?

Then begin the process of reintegration; welcoming back the parts of yourself that you've tucked away. The quirky, the bold, the quiet, the messy, the tender. All of you belongs.

Permission to Be Fully You

One of the biggest lies we're taught is that we must choose between being loved and being ourselves. The truth? You can be both. But it starts with giving yourself permission. Say yes to:

- Speaking up, even when your voice shakes.
- Showing up, even if you feel different.
- Saying no, even if others expect yes.
- Living boldly, even if it breaks the mold.

Authenticity is not about perfection. It's about honesty. And your honesty creates space for others to do the same.

Reflection Prompts: Letting Go of the Mask

➢ What masks have I worn to feel safe, successful, or loved?

➢ What am I afraid will happen if I take them off?

➢ What parts of myself am I ready to reclaim?

➢ Who in my life sees the real me, and how can I invite more of that connection?

The more you shed the layers that no longer serve you, the more you align with your truth—and the more powerful, free, and alive you become.

CHAPTER 43

SELF-CONFIDENCE & YOUR WILD SIDE

Are you playing small to fit in? How often do you shrink yourself to make others more comfortable? Maybe you silence your voice in conversations, tone down your excitement, or convince yourself that you should only take up as much space as others allow. But self-confidence isn't about seeking approval, it's about knowing your worth without it.

At our core, we all have a wild, unapologetic energy—a vibrant part of us that is bold, creative, and expressive. Yet many of us have buried this part of ourselves under layers of self-doubt, fear of judgment, and the need for external validation. We trade authenticity for acceptance. We hide our wild side because someone, somewhere, made us feel like it was too much. But the more we suppress who we truly are, the more dissatisfied and disconnected we become.

For many people, confidence hasn't always been safe. You may have been told you were "too much," "too loud," or "not enough" because of your race, gender, sexuality, neurodivergence, or background. If that's true for you, know this: your voice matters. Confidence doesn't mean conforming to someone else's standard. It means standing in your truth, especially when the world hasn't always made space for it.

Why Do We Dim Ourselves?

Parents, teachers, and peers condition us to seek approval from a young age. We learn what behaviors are "acceptable" and what parts of ourselves we must hide. Over time, this conditioning manifests in two primary ways: some seek validation through attention *("Look at me!")*, while others shrink in fear *("Don't look at me.")*. Neither serves us. True confidence doesn't come from chasing approval or fading into the background, it comes from within.

Many of us dim our light for different reasons: fear of judgment or rejection, the desire to be liked, guilt over outgrowing relationships, or the need to match the energy of those around us. Consider this: self-confidence isn't something that's given to you. It's something you reclaim. And it starts with giving yourself permission to be fully, unapologetically you.

Breaking Free From Approval-Seeking

The biggest barrier to confidence is often the stories we tell ourselves. If you've been repeating self-defeating narratives for years, they can feel like absolute truth:

"I'm not smart enough."

"I'm not attractive enough."

"I'm not worthy of what I want."

But these are not facts. They are beliefs…the ones that you have the power to change. Pause and ask yourself:

➢ Where did this belief come from?

➢ Is it helping me or holding me back?

➢ What would my life look like if I stopped believing it?

The moment you recognize that you've been reinforcing limiting beliefs, you gain the power to rewrite them. Instead of waiting for validation, start generating it from within. Instead of looking for permission, give it to yourself.

Embracing Your Wild Side: The Ultimate Confidence Hack

Confidence isn't just about self-assurance; it's about freedom and deciding to stop doubting yourself. It allows full expression without shame, guilt, or hesitation. Your wild side is the unfiltered, instinctual part of you that wants to be seen and heard. It's the part that laughs too loudly, dances freely, expresses passion without holding back, and speaks truth without sugarcoating.

Many of us have tamed, controlled, or hidden this side. We learned that being "too much" made people uncomfortable, so we contained our passions. We felt guilt for shining too brightly in rooms where others were dimming. So we shrink. We suppress our fire. We become smaller versions of ourselves to fit into spaces that were never meant to hold our full light.

But when you embrace your wildness, everything changes. You feel lighter because you're no longer carrying the weight of who you "should" be. You become magnetic, because confidence is contagious. And most importantly, you stop apologizing for taking up space.

How to Cultivate Self-Confidence & Unleash Your Wild Side

When you fully step into yourself, you become a leader—not because you force others to change, but because you give them permission to do the same. In friendships, you set the tone for authenticity, encouraging deeper connections. In relationships, you invite partners into deeper intimacy, free from masks. In personal growth, you create a feedback loop of authenticity, where everyone benefits.

True confidence is about standing fully in yourself because you no longer need to prove anything.

- **Own Your Gifts & Value**: Take inventory of what makes you uniquely you. What strengths, talents, and qualities define you? When you focus on what you bring to the table, confidence naturally follows.

- **Rewrite Your Self-Talk**: Start noticing how you speak to yourself. If your inner dialogue is harsh or limiting, challenge it. Replace *"I can't"* with *"I am more than capable."* Reframe *"I'm not enough"* into *"I am whole as I am."*

- **Do Something Uncomfortable**: Growth lives on the other side of discomfort. Take a bold step. Dance in public, share your voice, say no when you mean it. Each act of courage expands your confidence.

Confidence isn't something you find; it's something you build. And it starts the moment you stop waiting for permission to be yourself. It isn't about being the loudest person in the room or having all the answers. It's about trusting yourself and taking up space without apology. And most importantly, it's the refusal to dim your light for anyone. The world doesn't need another person playing small; it needs more people stepping boldly into their power.

Visualization: Meet Your Wild Self

Find a quiet space. Close your eyes. Picture a version of you who is completely free—uninhibited, playful, bold, radiant.

- ➢ What am I doing?
- ➢ What do I wear?
- ➢ How do I speak?
- ➢ What energy surrounds me?

Let that version of you speak.

- ➢ What do I want to reclaim?

This wild side has always been there. It's just waiting for permission to come alive again.

Confidence Challenge

Pick one small act of boldness, such as:

- Post something vulnerable
- Wear that outfit you love but usually second-guess
- Ask for what you need
- Say no or say yes

Circle one (or create your own) and do it this week. Confidence builds through action.

Remember, confidence isn't just in your mind. It lives in your body too. If you're feeling small or unsure, try shifting your physiology. This comes from The Triad you learned earlier: stand tall, breathe deeply, ground your feet. These subtle changes send powerful messages to your nervous system and help you embody confidence from the inside out.

Awakening Wild Confidence & Inner Joy

You don't need to become someone else to be confident. You only need to remember who you already are.

Confidence isn't about perfection; it's about being fully alive. It's about showing up, speaking up, and trusting that your presence matters.

Let your wildness breathe. Let your true self lead. You were never "too much," you were simply waiting for the right moment to be fully seen. You are already enough. And the moment you own that, everything begins to shift.

As your confidence awakens, so does something else, including the playful, joyful spirit of your Inner Child. This part of you has always been there, quietly waiting to feel safe enough to come out and shine. Now is the time to welcome that light back into your life.

CHAPTER 44

LIGHTENING UP

Reconnecting with Your Inner Child

There comes a point in any healing journey when you're ready to let go of the weight of grief, stress, or self-imposed limitations, and invite joy back in. After a breakup, I found myself in that place. I was tired of over-analyzing and waiting to feel better. I wanted to shift from heaviness to lightness, from survival to presence, from sadness to laughter.

If you've been going through a stressful period, feeling stuck, or weighed down by life's pressures, it might be time to give yourself that same gift—a gift of levity, playfulness, and emotional freedom.

Why the Inner Child Holds the Key

One of the most powerful ways to lighten up is by reconnecting with your Inner Child, the part of you that craves play, creativity, and spontaneity. This part laughs without hesitation, dances without self-consciousness, and finds joy in the simplest things.

When ignored, life can feel like an endless to-do list. But when honored, your Inner Child reconnects you with joy, freedom, and ease.

But this part of you doesn't just hold playfulness. The Inner Child also carries your earliest experiences of fear, unmet needs, and emotional wounds. Many adult struggles stem from unresolved childhood moments where we felt unsafe, unseen, or unheard.

A Personal Story: Reclaiming My Inner Child

For a long time, I used to say I didn't really remember my childhood. When someone asked, I'd draw a blank, and only vague images came to mind. It was as if my Inner Child had tucked herself away, waiting for a safer time to re-emerge.

That began to shift during a powerful session of EMDR (Eye Movement Desensitization and Reprocessing) therapy, a research-backed approach that helps people heal from trauma by reprocessing painful memories. Rather than just talking through past pain, EMDR uses guided bilateral stimulation—like eye movements or tapping—to create new, healing associations in the brain.

During one session, my therapist asked me to recall my earliest memory. At first, nothing came. But then a fragment surfaced: I was about five years old, riding in the back of a police car and staying overnight in a foster home. I later learned it was just one day. In that moment, I didn't know if I'd see my parents again.

That experience had left a hidden imprint. Somewhere deep inside, I had internalized a belief that the world wasn't stable, and that uncertainty might mean abandonment.

Recognizing that belief became a turning point. I began speaking directly to my Inner Child: *"I'm an adult now, and I've got you."* When fear or anxiety crept in, I'd gently reassure, *"We're safe. I've proven I can take care of us. We're loved. We're going to be okay."*

That simple, conscious act of acknowledgment opened a door— not just to healing, but to joy. As my Inner Child felt seen and safe, more memories returned. So did laughter. So did play. Because when our Inner Child feels held, our adult self can finally relax into lightness.

Joy as an Act of Emotional Liberation

Reconnecting with joy is a therapeutic act of emotional freedom. Many of us were taught to suppress joy. Maybe you were told you were *"too loud," "too silly,"* or *"not serious enough."* Over time, joy can feel frivolous—or even unsafe. Something to be earned *after* the work is done.

But here's the thing: joy *is* part of the work. Joy *is* healing.

When you allow yourself to dance in the kitchen, laugh until you snort, paint just for fun, or get silly with someone you trust, you're sending your nervous system a new message:

"It's safe to feel good again."
"It's safe to be light."

Practicing Joy: Tools to Reconnect with Your Inner Child

- Write a letter to your Inner Child: What do they need to hear from you today?

- Do something your younger self would've loved: blow bubbles, color outside the lines, build a fort, sing without caring who hears.

- Create an "Inner Child playlist" of songs that make you smile and happy dance.

- Visualize hugging your younger self. Offer love, safety, and encouragement.

- Play without purpose. Let joy exist without needing to produce anything.

Joy Without Outcome: Creating for the Sake of the Soul

One way I connect with my Inner Child is through crafting and painting. I especially love making jewelry as gifts. At one point, a partner encouraged me to create not just for others, but for myself. At first, it felt indulgent. I was so used to tying creativity to productivity that making something "just because" stirred guilt.

Even now, I sometimes catch myself questioning whether I "should" spend time on joyful expression. But I've learned that art without agenda isn't selfish, it's soul food. It nourishes my spirit. It keeps my Inner Child engaged and alive.

If you find it hard to create just for you, know this: you're not alone. Playful, purposeless creativity is its own form of healing. You don't need permission. The act itself is enough.

Journal Prompts

➤ What did I love doing as a child that I've stopped doing?

➤ What messages did I receive about being playful, loud, or silly?

➤ What would joy look like if I removed the guilt, fear, or shame?

➤ What does my Inner Child need from me today?

Final Reflections

When you reclaim joy, you reclaim a part of yourself that never left…one that's been waiting to be welcomed back. This isn't just about lightening your mood. It's about changing your identity narrative.

It's saying: *"I'm not just here to survive. I'm here to live fully."*

And that begins by letting your Inner Child out to play.

Reclaiming our lightness helps us face change with greater resilience. Now, let's explore how honoring our growth sometimes means standing firm, even when the world around us shifts.

CHAPTER 45

STANDING TRUE

Honoring Growth, Embracing Change

A s you evolve on your journey of self-discovery and personal growth, you may notice that the way you show up in your relationships begins to shift. Some people will embrace and celebrate these changes, while others may feel threatened, resistant, or confused. Managing these transitions with grace and courage is essential to maintaining healthy connections while staying true to yourself.

The Price of Holding Back

Many people suppress their true selves out of fear of judgment, rejection, or losing relationships. But the cost of holding back is often greater than the risk of stepping forward.

Holding back leads to dissatisfaction, regret, and an inner crisis. The longer you deny your authenticity, the greater your discontent will grow. Years from now, you don't want to look back and wish you had been braver in pursuing your truth. Avoiding growth to keep others comfortable often leads to a fractured sense of self, where you feel disconnected from both your desires and your relationships.

You can either live for other people's expectations or you can live for yourself. But you cannot do both.

The Courage to Say No & Setting Boundaries

As you evolve, people may ask you to do things that no longer align with your truth. Saying no can feel daunting, especially when it risks upsetting someone or altering the relationship dynamic. However, standing in your truth is a gift—not just to yourself, but to others.

Setting boundaries is an essential part of honoring your growth. When you uphold your authenticity, you acknowledge your own needs and stop taking responsibility for expectations that compromise who you truly are. You also empower others to grow by modeling self-respect—inviting them to reflect on their own patterns rather than enabling old dynamics.

And while not everyone will adapt to the new version of you, that's okay. Some may struggle with your transformation, not because they don't care, but because they were attached to the version of you that once fit their needs. Their discomfort is not a reflection of your worth. It's simply a part of their journey, not yours.

Life's Three Key Questions

To align with your authenticity, ask yourself:

> ➤ What do I truly want?

> ➤ Why do I want it?

> ➤ What am I willing to do to get it?

Answering these questions requires bravery, because stepping into your truth sometimes means stepping away from relationships, roles, or expectations that no longer fit. But clarity is power. When you know what you want and why, you can move forward with confidence.

These three questions aren't just journal prompts—they're a compass. The answers you uncover can help you set priorities, make aligned decisions, and even map out a life plan that reflects your truth. If you feel stuck, unclear, or off course, return to them. They are a powerful starting point for any transformation.

Still, each question can be surprisingly hard to answer. Figuring out what you truly want in life can be obvious for some people, but for others it may feel elusive or even impossible to define. It often requires digging deep beneath layers of conditioning and being radically honest with yourself in a way you never have before. To uncover your truth, you must set aside the expectations of others and the limiting beliefs that tell you what is or isn't possible. This isn't about what's acceptable or what others think you should want—it's about what your heart and soul are genuinely calling for.

Once you have clarity on what you want, the next step is to explore why. Your "why" is the taproot that anchors your motivation and keeps you grounded when the road ahead becomes uncertain or difficult. When your purpose is tied to something meaningful and authentic, it can sustain you through challenges and help you rise above obstacles that might otherwise derail you.

Finally, you must ask yourself what you're truly willing to do to achieve it. Willingness is the bridge between intention and action. It determines whether your dream remains a vision or becomes reality. Are you willing to return to a beginner's mind, learn new skills, challenge your limiting beliefs, take risks, and embrace change? Many people fall short not because they lack desire, but because they aren't fully willing to do what it takes to grow into the person their dream requires them to become. Your level of willingness reveals how deeply committed you are to your own evolution. It's that commitment that ultimately fuels transformation.

Facing Resistance
A Case Study: Alicia's Transformation

Alicia had spent years as a dedicated stay-at-home mom, always prioritizing the needs of her family over her own. But deep down, she longed for something more—a challenge, a passion that was solely hers. One day, she made a life-changing decision: she committed to bodybuilding.

With unwavering discipline, she transformed her body, built incredible strength, and even started winning competitions. The physical transformation was just the beginning; her confidence soared, and she felt more empowered than ever before.

At the gym, Alicia found a supportive community that celebrated her progress. But at home, it was a different story. Instead of being proud of her dedication and success, Alicia's husband felt threatened by her transformation. He resented the time she spent at the gym, accused her of being selfish, and made her feel guilty for pursuing her goals and spending less time with him and the kids.

Her transformation disrupted his sense of security, making him feel left behind. Despite her best efforts to navigate the tension, the gap between them only grew wider. Ultimately, their marriage ended, not because Alicia had done anything wrong, but because her evolution highlighted her husband's insecurities.

The lesson? Not everyone will rise with you. Growth challenges relationships, and some will thrive while others will fall away. Alicia's story is a reminder that when we step into our fullest selves, we may outgrow certain dynamics and expand beyond what others will accept.

The Sovereign Path: Choosing Authenticity Over Approval

Stepping into your truth comes with risks. You may lose both your old identity and relationships that no longer align with your evolution. While this can be painful, it is also deeply freeing.

Growth requires shedding the version of yourself that was shaped for others' approval. Some relationships will naturally fall away, much like a rocket shedding pieces as it ascends into orbit. This isn't a failure; it's a natural part of transformation.

It's okay to grieve relationships that don't survive your growth. But staying small just to hold on to them is never the answer.

Authenticity asks you to release what no longer fits and make peace with the fact that not everyone will continue with you on this journey.

The path to authenticity is one of courage, self-acceptance, and unwavering commitment to your truth. This is the journey of *Root-to-Rise* where you honor your evolution, embrace your sovereignty, and allow yourself to fully step into the life that was meant for you.

Giving Yourself Permission to Be You

One of the biggest challenges in embracing change is giving yourself permission to prioritize your happiness. Many of us were conditioned to seek external validation before making major decisions. But aligning with your true self means:

- **Acknowledging Your Desires:** You have a right to pursue what makes you happy.

- **Recognizing Your Worthiness:** You don't need permission to live authentically, you are already worthy of it.

- **Inviting Others to Align With You:** Not everyone will, but those who do are your true allies.

Your authenticity is not something you need to justify. You do not need to explain or defend the changes that are right for you. Those who genuinely love you will support your growth.

Some people will support your growth. Some won't. Keep growing anyway. Not everyone walks every season of life with you, and that's okay. The right people will celebrate your authenticity, not fear it. Your growth will call in those who are meant to walk the next chapter of your life with you, and lovingly release those who are not.

The path of *Root-to-Rise* is about standing tall in your truth, honoring your evolution, and rising into the life you were born to live.

As we rise into our truth, our relationships naturally shift too. Let's explore how authenticity can strengthen—or sometimes transform—the friendships we hold dear.

CHAPTER 46

AUTHENTICITY IN FRIENDSHIPS

H ave you ever had a best friend you talked to almost every day, only to find that your connection isn't what it used to be? Maybe life pulled you in different directions, schedules got busier, or circumstances changed. That disconnection can be painful, leaving you wondering where you stand with them, and, honestly, where they stand with you.

Friendships naturally evolve. People enter new relationships, build families, move cities, and take on careers that demand more time and energy. But the real challenge isn't that friendships change, it's that we often fail to communicate those changes. We assume our friends will "just understand" or that things will return to how they were. But when expectations shift without conversation, misunderstandings and hurt feelings can grow in the space where connection used to be.

Authenticity in friendships means showing up honestly and openly, even when things change. It's about having the conversations that prevent unnecessary distance, instead of leaving each other guessing.

Why Friendships Change Over Time

Shared experiences build friendships, and these experiences change as we grow. The version of ourselves that first connected with someone may not be the same version we are today. Without acknowledging that reality and updating the blueprint for the relationship, we set ourselves up for disappointment.

Some of the most common reasons friendships shift:

- **New Romantic Relationship Priorities:** Time once dedicated to friends may now be spent nurturing a partnership.
- **Career & Family Demands:** Juggling responsibilities leaves less space for spontaneous connections.
- **Geographical Distance:** Moving away requires adjusting how we stay in touch.
- **Personal Growth & Change:** One person may grow in ways that no longer align with the friendship dynamic.

The problem isn't that these changes happen, it's that we rarely talk about them. We assume the other person will always understand, or worse, we assume the shift in connection means they no longer care.

If you've ever thought, *"She doesn't make time for me anymore. Maybe I don't matter to her,"* or *"I don't reach out because I don't want to bother her,"* you've already experienced the silent damage unspoken expectations can cause.

The Problem with Unspoken Expectations

Friendship disappointments often stem from expectations that were never communicated.

We assume friendships should remain the same, even as life evolves. We expect a friend to check in, initiate plans, or maintain the same level of emotional investment without ever expressing that need. When they don't, we take it personally, even though they probably have no idea we feel that way.

Unspoken expectations create:

- **Misunderstandings:** One friend assumes the other no longer cares when, in reality, life just got busy.

- **Resentment:** When we feel let down but never express why, bitterness builds.
- **Confusion:** If expectations are unclear, both people may struggle to know what's "normal" now.
- **Missed Opportunities for Reconnection:** When neither person initiates, the friendship fades unnecessarily.

Instead of letting distance create assumptions, we need to have the conversations that bring clarity before silence turns into disconnection.

A Personal Example:
Navigating a Long-Distance Friendship

One of my close friends and I used to see each other almost daily. When she moved to a different city, we still expected to connect frequently, but over time, it became harder to keep up our usual pace. A small child at home often distracted her during our phone calls, making deep conversations difficult.

At first, the disconnect felt frustrating. I could sense that she still wanted to talk every day, but our schedules weren't allowing it. Instead of letting feelings get hurt, we had an honest conversation about the change in patterns. Together, we decided we could call whenever we wanted, but wouldn't expect an immediate response. And, when life got busy, a weekly check-in was enough to keep us feeling connected. By talking about it upfront, we avoided unnecessary frustration. Neither of us took the changes personally, and instead, we redefined what friendship looked like in this new phase of life.

Case Study:
Sarah & Emma's Friendship Shift

Sarah and Emma had been close friends for years, talking daily and spending weekends together. When Sarah entered a serious relationship, her availability changed. However, she never told Emma what to expect.

Emma, feeling the shift, assumed Sarah was losing interest. She felt hurt but didn't want to seem needy, so she pulled back, too. The space between them grew until resentment took hold.

Eventually, they had an open and honest conversation where Sarah explained that, while she still deeply valued Emma, her relationship required more of her time. Emma admitted she had been struggling with the change, but had said nothing. Had they communicated sooner, they could have avoided weeks of unnecessary tension. Instead, their conversation helped them redefine what their friendship could look like in this new chapter of their lives.

The Intimacy Ladder: A Tool for Navigating Changing Friendships

Friendships are not all meant to live on the same level of closeness. Some are your soul-deep daily anchors. Others are more casual or seasonal, but still meaningful. The Intimacy Ladder is a simple way to visualize where your relationships stand right now, and how they might naturally shift over time.

Think of your connections as existing on different rungs of a ladder. The top rungs are reserved for your most emotionally intimate, reciprocal relationships. These are the people you trust fully and turn to regularly as a priority. As you move down the ladder, you'll find friends you still care about, but with less frequency of contact, shared vulnerability, or current alignment.

Rather than assuming the worst when a friendship changes, ask yourself:

➢ Where does this person truly fit in my life right now?

➢ Am I expecting them to stay on a higher rung out of loyalty, guilt, or habit?

➢ Have I communicated my needs or simply hoped they'd "just know"?

➢ What expectations am I holding that haven't been voiced?

For example, someone who was once your go-to for everything might now live in a different state, be raising kids, or navigating a new season of life. That doesn't mean the bond is broken, it may just mean the friendship belongs on a different rung for now.

This tool isn't about ranking people or withdrawing love, it's about releasing unspoken expectations, creating emotional clarity, prioritizing where you put your energy, and making space for friendships to evolve. By regularly and consciously adjusting the ladder of intimacy expectations instead of letting resentment or confusion fester, you can honor what the relationship has been *and* what it needs to be now.

How to Have an Honest Conversation About Changing Friendships

Instead of withdrawing or making passive-aggressive comments, lead with honesty.

Try saying:

"I love our friendship, and I know life has been changing for both of us. I just want to check in. How do we want to stay connected moving forward?"

Or:

"I know we don't talk as much, but you still mean a lot to me. I want to make sure we both feel good about where we are."

Honest conversations do two things:
1. They prevent unnecessary distance.
2. They give both people a chance to create new, clear expectations.

Because friendships aren't all or nothing. They're flexible, evolving, and meant to grow with us, not hold us back.

When Hurt Happens: Navigating Conflict and Betrayal

Sometimes friendships don't just fade, they rupture. Maybe a friend crossed a boundary, betrayed a confidence, or hurt you in a way that's hard to ignore. In these moments, authenticity asks us to bring compassion *and* courage to the table.

You might say:

"When this happened, I felt hurt. Can we talk about it?"

Or:

"I care about our friendship, and I'd like to clear the air."

If you're the one who caused harm, lead with ownership: *"I realize I may have let you down. I'm open to hearing how you felt."*

These conversations can feel scary, but they often restore understanding, even if the friendship ultimately changes form.

Knowing When to Let Go

Not every friendship lasts forever, and that's okay.

If a friendship no longer aligns—whether because of toxicity, lack of mutual investment, or fundamental value shifts—letting go can be the healthiest choice.

Signs a friendship may be at its end:

- You feel drained instead of energized after talking to them.
- The relationship is one-sided, with little effort on their part.
- They don't respect your boundaries or personal growth.

Letting go can bring grief, especially if the friendship was long-term or deeply rooted. Give yourself space to mourn. Write a letter you don't send. Light a candle. Reflect on what the friendship gave you and why it's okay to move forward.

Closure Rituals and Releasing with Love

Letting go doesn't always require a dramatic ending. Sometimes, it's about quiet closure.

You might:

- Write a letter (sent or unsent).
- Have one final honest conversation.
- Create a personal release ritual to honor the friendship and say goodbye.

Friendship Through the Lens of Authenticity

Authenticity in friendships means recognizing and acknowledging when change is occurring rather than ignoring it. It involves clearly communicating expectations instead of assuming the other person understands implicitly.

By honoring the friendship while allowing it the flexibility to evolve naturally, we create space for deeper connections. When we show up honestly in our relationships, we give them the best opportunity to flourish in their new forms—avoiding unnecessary distance caused by silence and misunderstanding.

Ultimately, the strongest friendships aren't defined by constant closeness but by mutual respect, open communication, and the willingness to grow together.

Reflection: Navigating Friendship with Heart

If you're processing a shift or loss of friendship, take time to reflect on:

➢ What friendship am I holding onto out of habit or guilt?

➢ What truth do I need to express to a friend, even if it's uncomfortable?

➢ What does a healthy, aligned friendship look and feel like to me now?

Through every season of friendship, whether staying close or growing apart, trust that the love shared leaves an imprint, and that new, aligned connections will continue to find you as you walk your authentic path.

True friendship isn't just about staying connected. It's about daring to be deeply known. Let's dive into how vulnerability becomes the bridge to real intimacy.

CHAPTER 47

INTIMACY & VULNERABILITY

More than just closeness, intimacy means deeply knowing oneself and others and being fully seen and accepted without masks or pretense. It requires vulnerability, trust, and courage, yet many of us hold back out of fear of rejection, abandonment, or not being "enough." True intimacy starts within. It begins with how deeply we know, accept, and nurture ourselves before extending that same depth of connection to others. When we embrace intimacy from the inside out, we create relationships rooted in truth, resilience, and genuine connection.

Intimacy with Ourselves

At its core, intimacy is about being deeply known, not just by others, but by ourselves first. It's about having the courage to explore the depths of our own being, including our hopes, fears, desires, wounds, and dreams so that we can nurture and heal ourselves in a way that allows us to rise to our fullest potential.

As explained earlier, we are all multi-faceted diamonds. Some aspects of ourselves shine brightly in the sun, while others remain hidden in the shadows. True intimacy requires us to embrace all parts, even the ones we've suppressed, avoided, or judged. The more we integrate these hidden facets, the stronger and more whole we become.

But this kind of self-intimacy isn't always comfortable. It requires courage to look inward and witness the ways we hold ourselves back.

The Role of Self-Talk

One way to strengthen intimacy with ourselves is to pay attention to our inner dialogue. The voice in our head is our closest life partner. It's with us every moment of every day.

Ask yourself:

> ➤ How positive is the way I talk to myself?
>
> ➤ If this voice were a person, would I want to be their best friend?
>
> ➤ Would I trust them to have my best interests in mind?

If the answer isn't a confident yes, then it's time to rewrite the script.

Sometimes, the fear of change keeps us stuck in familiar patterns, even if those patterns no longer serve us. If your inner voice resists growth, thank it for trying to keep you safe and reassure it you are ready.

Ask yourself:

> ➤ What is the cost of staying the same?
>
> ➤ If I don't make changes, what does my life look like in 1, 3, 5, or 10 years?
>
> ➤ Am I willing to pay that price?

Growth requires us to confront these fears, get real with ourselves, and move forward even when it feels uncomfortable.

Intimacy with Others:

We all crave deep connection. To be seen, heard, and understood in our relationships is one of our most fundamental human needs. But we must allow others to see us to be truly known.

Vulnerability is the bridge that leads to intimacy, and for many of us, that bridge feels dangerous to cross.

Breaking the Avoidance Cycle

I had a breakthrough when I realized I take flight in romantic conflicts. If an argument arises, my instinct is to stonewall, shut down, and disengage rather than lean into the conversation with vulnerability.

I asked myself, *"Why do I do this?"* I knew that shutting down prevented the very closeness I was seeking, and it actually pulled me further from my partner rather than fostering connection.

Through deep self-reflection, I traced this pattern back to childhood. Growing up, it felt safer to stay quiet, put my needs aside, and go along with what my parent wanted. When I tried to stand up for myself, I felt diminished, like their voice would always be stronger than mine. Eventually, I learned it was easier to withdraw than to fight for what I wanted.

That pattern followed me into adulthood. In relationships, I found myself physically and emotionally closing off—crossing my arms, stiffening my face, feeling the urge to walk away—anytime tension arose.

But here's the thing: avoidance doesn't protect intimacy, it erodes it.

By shutting down, I wasn't preventing conflict. I was deepening the disconnection. The very thing I was afraid of, losing closeness, was happening because of my actions.

This realization was a turning point. Instead of shutting down, I started leaning in. Instead of avoiding, I started sharing. Each time I resisted the urge to withdraw, I built a new foundation of trust and connection.

This is what intimacy requires: the courage to stay open, even when it feels vulnerable.

Using The Intimacy Ladder to Navigate Relationships

Not all relationships require the same level of vulnerability. That's where the Intimacy Ladder comes in. This tool helps us evaluate where people belong in our lives and how much access they should have to our hearts.

- **The Top Rungs:** Reserved for the people who have earned our trust, such as those with whom we can share our most authentic selves.

- **The Middle Rungs:** Friends, colleagues, or acquaintances we connect with but may not fully confide in.

- **The Bottom Rungs:** People we interact with but keep at a distance.

This ladder isn't fixed. Relationships evolve. Some people move up; others move down. And that's okay.

What's important is that we align our expectations with reality. Many relationship conflicts arise not because of what's said, but because of unspoken expectations. When we get clear on what level of intimacy we're comfortable with, we can communicate boundaries with honesty and respect.

➢ Does this person make me feel safe to be my full self?

➢ Am I showing up in this relationship authentically, or am I playing a role?

➢ Do they respect my boundaries, or do they push them?

The people who truly belong in your life will celebrate the real you, and not try to mold you into what makes them comfortable.

The Vulnerability Leap: How to Let Yourself Be Seen

If vulnerability builds intimacy, then allowing yourself to be seen unlocks deeper connection. This doesn't mean oversharing or forcing closeness, it means taking small, courageous steps toward openness.

Ways to Practice Vulnerability:

- Express your needs out loud rather than assuming others will know them.
- Share a fear or insecurity with someone you trust.
- Be honest about your emotions rather than brushing them aside.
- Stay present in difficult conversations instead of shutting down.

Vulnerability isn't about weakness, it's about authenticity. And authenticity is magnetic. When you show up fully, you inspire others to do the same.

The Freedom of Being Fully Known

Intimacy, whether with oneself or others, centers on the desire to be fully seen and accepted. No one can truly see you if you don't allow yourself to be seen. No one can fully know you if you're hiding parts of yourself. Stepping into deeper intimacy is about having the courage to stand in your truth. It's about recognizing your patterns, breaking free from avoidance, and allowing yourself to be loved for who you truly are. Because the greatest intimacy isn't about being perfect together— it's about being real together.

Real intimacy is born from the courage to be real. When you let your heart be known, you invite a love that sees you, holds you, and celebrates you, just as you are.

When we allow ourselves to be seen, known, and loved—both by ourselves and by others—we lay the foundation for a life rooted in truth. Now, let's rise even higher.

CHAPTER 48

LIVING YOUR TRUTH

Summary

L iving with authenticity is a transformative journey, one that begins with self-awareness and unfolds into a life aligned with who you truly are. It's about having the courage to embrace your unique qualities, express your true desires, and live in alignment with your deepest values.

Authenticity isn't just about rejecting pretense. It's about stepping into your full power. It's about letting go of the masks created for acceptance, honoring the truth of who you are, and making choices that reflect your real self (and not who the world expects you to be).

Along the way, you may realize that certain aspects of your life no longer fit, whether it's a career, a relationship, or an old role you've outgrown. Change can feel intimidating, but staying stuck in an outdated version of yourself comes at an even greater cost. The more you resist growth, the more disconnected you become from your own happiness.

The Courage to Stand in Your Truth

Living authentically requires honest self-reflection and sometimes tough conversations. As you shift and evolve, some people will celebrate your transformation, while others may resist it. This isn't a reflection of your worth, it's simply a sign that not everyone walks every part of your journey with you.

By communicating your needs openly and setting healthy boundaries, you allow others the opportunity to align with the real you. Some relationships will deepen, while others may naturally shift or fade away. But authenticity isn't about keeping everyone happy; it's about honoring yourself.

Authenticity in Action: Creating Meaningful Relationships

We explored the importance of intimacy and vulnerability, both within ourselves and in our relationships. To achieve true intimacy, we must allow others to see and know us completely, without pretense. This deepens connection and fosters real belonging.

To maintain healthy relationships, we must also recognize the power of unspoken expectations and the need to adjust relationship dynamics as life evolves. The Intimacy Ladder shows us it's acceptable for relationships to change, provided expectations are communicated honestly and respectfully.

Living Authentically is an Act of Self-Respect

Choosing authenticity is an act of self-respect and a declaration of high standards for yourself and for those you allow into your life. The more you honor your truth, the more you attract people and opportunities that resonate with who you truly are.

Authenticity is a lifelong journey, but every step you take brings you closer to genuine fulfillment. By releasing what no longer aligns, embracing vulnerability, and communicating your truth, you create space for deep, meaningful connections and a life that reflects your highest self.

Live It: The 7-Day Authenticity Challenge

You've explored what it means to live more truthfully. Now it's time to bring that truth into motion.

For the next 7 days, choose one small action each day that reflects your authentic self. These don't have to be big or dramatic. Small shifts can be just as powerful.

Try things like:

- Saying "no" when something isn't aligned
- Speaking up when your truth wants to be heard
- Wearing something that feels like *you,* even if it's not "on trend"
- Admitting a need instead of hiding it
- Setting a boundary with kindness and clarity
- Creating something from the heart with no need to impress
- Taking a break from pretending or pleasing

At the end of each day, ask yourself:

➢ What did I do today that was true to me and how did that feel?

By the end of the week, you may find that even the smallest acts of authenticity create ripple effects of freedom, connection, and clarity.

You don't have to wait to be more "ready." You just have to begin.

This is where your inner truth becomes the compass for how you show up each day. As your roots grow deeper in authenticity, your ability to rise becomes stronger and more sustainable.

The Next Step:
Creating Balance in Daily Life

Now that you've gained clarity on who you are and what it means to live authentically, the next step is creating balance in your daily life in a way that supports your Life Root System. How do you structure your days in a way that nourishes your energy, well-being, and personal growth? How do you create a sustainable rhythm that keeps you grounded while continuing to rise?

In the next section, we'll explore how to bring harmony to your daily routines, ensuring that your time, energy, and priorities are aligned with the authentic life you are building. Let's move forward and create balance that serves your body, mind, and soul.

ROOT-TO-RISE INFOGRAPHIC

PHASE THREE: RISE

RISE

HUMAN NEEDS

 Transcendence

- Moving past the self to serve others
- Connecting to higher purpose
- Contribution
- Sharing
- Service
- Providing

 Growth

- Growing
- Pulsating energy
- Progress
- Learning
- Feeling momentum
- Advancing
- Breaking free

CONNECTING TO AUTHENTICITY

- Tap into Your Heart
- Aligning Others
- Your Lens

 Intimacy

- Nurturing
- Valuing relationships
- Belonging
- Feeling passion
- Having desire
- Striving for unity
- Togetherness

WITHSTANDING THE ELEMENTS

- Winds of Change
- Storms/Upheaval
- Grief & Loss

 Self

- Self-esteem
- Self-worth
- Significance
- Importance
- Pride
- Importance
- Perfection

NAVIGATING EMOTIONS

Triad:
- Body/Mind/Spirit
- Physiology/Focus/Meaning

FOCUS MIND / **MEANING SPIRIT**

PHYSIOLOGY BODY

CLEARING OBSTACLES

- Nourishing Needy Roots
- Honoring Driving Needs
- Pain Points
- Getting Unstuck
- Fears & Limiting Beliefs
- Double Binds
- Leveraging you Tap Root

 **Variety**

- Change
- Transitions
- Storms
- Challenges
- Trauma/Crisis
- Chaos
- Variety
- New/Different
- Spice of Life
- Surprise
- Fear

RESILIENCE

LIFE ROOT SYSTEM

HEALTH/FITNESS	FAMILY	RELATIONSHIPS	CAREER	FRIENDS
• Nutrition	• Parents	• Self	• Time & Money	• Introvert v. Extrovert Needs
• Food/Beverage	• Caregivers	• Romantic Partner	• Contribution	• Who are they?
• Supplements	• Siblings	• Commitment	• Heart-based/ Passion vs Corporate	• Values alignment
• Fitness/Exercise	• Partner	• Chemistry	• Hobbies/Craft	• Reflection of you
• Massage/Body Work	• In-laws	• Compatibility	• Who you are:	• What do you offer?
• Wellness vs. Illness	• Children	• Communication	• Strengths/ Weaknesses	• What do they offer?
	• Chosen		• Leader vs. Worker	• Elevate
			• Visionary vs. Operational	• Support
			• Analytical/ Data-minded	• Experience

 Security

- Certainty
- Safety
- Rootedness
- Grounded
- Comfort
- Stability
- Predictability
- Protection
- Commitment

www.glowliving.com
#glowliving
#rootorise
#lovelife

TAP ROOT
What feeds your soul deeply?

ROOTS

 GLOWLIVING
love life

© All Rights Reserved. Glow Living/Glow Marketing LLC 2025

Part Two

BALANCE

CHAPTER 49

BALANCED ROOT SYSTEM

Cultivating Stability in a Chaotic World

I n the relentless hustle of modern life, it's easy to feel like we're constantly sprinting on a treadmill, including exerting endless energy but never quite arriving at a place of peace. Between career ambitions, personal responsibilities, relationships, and self-growth, we juggle so many roles that we risk spreading ourselves too thin. The weight of it all can leave us feeling depleted, reactive, and disconnected from what truly matters.

Yet balance is not a luxury, it's imperative. Just as a towering tree relies on strong roots to stand tall against the winds, we, too, need a solid foundation to remain steady amidst life's inevitable storms. Without a well-nourished root system, even the most ambitious goals and exciting pursuits can lead to exhaustion rather than fulfillment.

Balancing Your Root System

Imagine your life as a magnificent tree. Its branches stretching toward the sky, symbolizing your aspirations, relationships, and dreams. But beneath the surface lies the root system: the unseen yet essential structure that supports everything above. Without strong, nourished roots, even the most vibrant tree can topple.

In *Root-to-Rise*, your Life Root Areas are each supported by four foundational pillars of well-being:

- **Physical Health:** The strength, nourishment, and movement your body needs to function optimally.
- **Mental Well-Being:** The clarity, focus, and mindset that shape your perception and resilience.
- **Emotional Resilience:** Your ability to process, regulate, and express emotions in healthy ways.
- **Spiritual Connection:** A sense of purpose, presence, and alignment that fuels your inner life.

When these roots are neglected, imbalance begins to grow and show up as stress, burnout, disconnection, or a quiet sense of not being enough. When you tend to each root with care and consistency, you create the stability to rise—rooted, strong, and fully alive.

The Ripple Effect of Balance

Balance is more than just managing your time, it's about aligning your life with what truly nourishes you. It's about creating harmony between the different aspects of who you are, so that one area doesn't consume you at the expense of everything else. When you achieve this alignment, the effects ripple out into every part of your life:

You become more present. Instead of constantly feeling stretched in a million directions, you show up fully for your work, your relationships, and yourself. You're engaged rather than distracted, grounded rather than scattered.

You protect your health. Chronic stress and imbalance don't just drain your energy, they take a toll on your body, leading to exhaustion, illness, and emotional depletion. Prioritizing balance helps you maintain vitality and longevity.

Your relationships flourish. When you're not drowning in overwhelm, you have more capacity to nurture meaningful connections. Your loved ones benefit from your presence, patience, and ability to give from a full cup.

Balance doesn't mean giving equal time to everything; it means giving the right energy to what matters most.

The Dance of Priorities

Balance isn't a static state, it's a fluid, dynamic process of adjusting, recalibrating, and realigning as life shifts. It's not about perfect symmetry, it's about knowing when to lean in and when to pull back.

In the chapters ahead, we'll dive deeper into how to cultivate balance across different areas of life. We'll explore strategies for managing your time effectively, setting boundaries, preventing burnout, and aligning your daily choices with your highest values. Balance isn't about doing it all, it's about doing what matters in a way that serves your well-being.

Pause and Reflect

Before we dive into strategies for realigning your time, priorities, and energy, take a moment to check in with yourself:

- ➢ What part of my life feels most imbalanced right now?
- ➢ Which of these areas feels most neglected: Physical Health, Mental Well-Being, Emotional Resilience, or Spiritual Connection?
- ➢ What's one thing you could release this week to create space for what matters most?

You don't need to fix everything at once. Start by noticing and nourishing.

Balance begins at the roots. So, how do we actually cultivate it day to day in a life that never stops moving? In the next chapter, we'll explore how to embrace balance as an art—not a rigid formula—so you can flow with life's changing seasons.

CHAPTER 50

THE ART OF LIFE BALANCE

W e explored the deeper meaning of balance, including why it matters, how it grounds us, and how imbalance often signals that we've been neglecting what nourishes us most. Now let's bring that vision to life with practical ways to care for your inner root system and move through your days with more intention, flow, and ease.

Imagine your life as a thriving garden, with you as the dedicated gardener. Each plant represents a vital aspect of your existence: work, family, fitness, self-care, relationships, passions, and personal growth. Achieving balance is about intuitively knowing which areas need watering or additional care and recognizing which are flourishing on their own. True balance lies in cultivating a garden that thrives through every season, guided by the wisdom to nurture each aspect of your life precisely when and how it's most needed.

The Myth of Perfect Balance

One of the biggest misconceptions we need to let go of is the idea that balance means giving equal time and energy to everything. That's not just unrealistic, it's exhausting. Life is full of change, interruptions, and shifting needs. If you expect to perfectly balance it all at once, you're setting yourself up for frustration and burnout.

Here's the liberating truth: balance isn't about perfection. It's about presence and adjustment. Some weeks, work will demand more of you. Other times, your relationships, self-care, or creative passions will take center stage. Balance is a living practice, a flexible dance with your priorities that shifts as you grow.

Root-to-Rise:
A Framework for Sustainable Balance

Root-to-Rise helps you create balance in a way that prioritizes what nourishes you at the deepest level. Think of your root system as the foundation of your emotional and energetic well-being. When you neglect it, your outer life feels brittle or chaotic. But when you care for it consistently, your clarity, capacity, and fulfillment grow strong and sustainable.

In this framework, balance isn't about equal time in every category; it's about intentional, consistent care for your most essential needs. That means moving your body, tending your mindset, staying emotionally connected, and making space for purpose and presence—not all at once, but in rhythm with your life.

Putting Balance Into Practice: A Weekly Plan

To bring balance into your day-to-day life, try structuring your week around your essential needs while still handling daily responsibilities. This means ensuring your energy and attention focus on what matters most, not rigid scheduling.

Here's a sample balanced week:

Monday: Start with a morning workout, then enjoy a homemade dinner with family.

Tuesday: Attend a personal growth seminar with a friend to nourish your mind and social connection.

Wednesday: Share a lunch date with your partner—create space for emotional closeness.

Thursday: Plan a double date with friends to stay connected and recharge socially.

Friday: Unwind with a yoga or meditation class to deepen spiritual connection.

Saturday: Go hiking or do an outdoor activity that supports your physical health and social life.

Sunday: Relax with a matinee or creative hobby that feeds your soul and ends the week with joy.

Pro Tip: Combine Needs for Greater Ease

You don't need to treat every need as a separate task. Some of the most powerful balancing moments happen when you combine root areas:

- Working out with a friend supports your physical *and* emotional health.
- Cooking a nourishing meal with loved ones fuels your body and strengthens your relationships.
- Taking a mindful walk outdoors nurtures your physical, mental, and spiritual well-being all at once.

When you integrate your needs rather than compartmentalizing them, balance feels more natural and sustainable.

Case Study:
Susan & John Adjust for Balance

Susan and John attended a *Root-to-Rise* seminar and realized they'd been prioritizing their romantic relationship above all else. While this brought them closer, it led to the unintentional neglect of their friendships and individual passions.

To restore balance, they made a few intentional adjustments. They planned more double dates to nourish their social lives while still spending time together. Susan took a painting class with a friend, and John joined a weekend cycling group—honoring their individual growth and self-expression. These simple shifts allowed them to meet the needs of multiple root areas, and feel more fulfilled without sacrificing their connection as a couple.

Balance Is a Moving Target
Adjust as You Grow

Balance isn't a matter of doing everything, it's about doing the right things, at the right time, for the right reasons. When you're tuned in to your energy, needs, and values, you'll sense when it's time to shift focus or slow down.

In the chapters ahead, we'll explore how to manage your time, protect your energy, prevent burnout, and build a life rooted in what truly sustains you.

You're not meant to manage it all equally. The key is recognizing what truly deserves your time and energy, and having the wisdom to let go of what doesn't.

Perfection isn't the goal. Presence is. Flexibility. Discernment. A willingness to return to what matters most.

And when life throws curveballs (because it will), how do you stay grounded in what's essential? Let's explore how to protect your balance through life's inevitable ups and downs.

CHAPTER 51

MAINTAINING BALANCE

W e've mapped out what balance looks like and how to structure your time to honor all the areas that make up a fulfilling life. However, life rarely sticks to the script. Unexpected demands pop up. Priorities shift. Some things no longer fit the way they once did. So how do you maintain balance long-term, even when life throws curveballs?

It's about learning how to adjust in real time, protect your energy, and be brutally honest about what truly matters.

Prioritization: What Really Deserves Your Energy

My friend Cynthia once told me something that changed the way I approach balance: *"Sometimes, you have to kill your darlings."* It means making hard choices and letting go of things you once loved, things you invested time or money into, or even things you thought would be part of your future. Not because they aren't good ideas. But because you can't do it all.

I've had to make these choices myself. Over the years, I had ideas for what could have been amazing businesses:

- UntamedStyle.com for goddess wear and Zen Den home decor

- GlowNaturals.com for an organic skincare line
- TravelinSistas.com for a women's travel community

And you know what? I let them go. Not because they weren't worth doing, but because they weren't worth my time and energy right now. Balance isn't about doing everything. It's about doing the right things well.

Ask yourself:

➤ What am I actually willing to commit to and see through?

➤ What's draining my energy without a meaningful return?

➤ Am I spreading myself too thin?

If something is keeping you from your core priorities, it might be time to release it.

The Boundaries Blueprint: Protecting Your Time & Energy

If you want to maintain balance, you need boundaries that stick. This means learning to say no without guilt and understanding that you don't owe anyone an explanation for protecting your peace.

Healthy boundaries start by recognizing energy leaks, including those relationships, habits, or commitments that drain you more than they nourish you. When something consistently leaves you depleted, it's time to reassess.

Setting boundaries also requires recalibrating expectations. Friendships, business relationships, and personal commitments all evolve, and it's okay to shift those dynamics without feeling like you've abandoned anyone.

It's not selfish to protect your time and energy, it's necessary. Boundaries allow you to show up more fully and joyfully for what truly matters.

Burnout Prevention: Recognizing the Warning Signs Before You Crash

To live in balance, you must be proactive, because waiting until you're completely depleted is already too late.

Burnout often begins with subtle signals:

- Feeling resentful about things you once loved
- Exhaustion even after resting
- Over committing to obligations that no longer inspire you
- Consistently procrastinating the things that matter most

Course correction starts with micro-breaks, intentional moments of rest and reset before burnout takes hold. It also means identifying the energy drainers: What's feeling forced? What have you outgrown? Then, re-prioritize what energizes you.

If something doesn't bring joy, meaning, or forward movement, ask yourself why it's still in your life. Rest isn't laziness, it's a necessary part of long-term momentum.

The Power of Rituals: Creating Stability in a Chaotic World

One of the biggest secrets to maintaining long-term balance? Non-negotiable rituals.

These are the anchors that keep you grounded, no matter what life throws at you.

Morning Rituals: Set the tone for your day

Evening Rituals: Wind down & release stress

Daily Check-Ins: Pause & reassess…are you on track?

The key is automation. When self-care, movement, or reflection become built-in habits, they don't get pushed aside when life gets busy.

Embracing Flexibility: The Secret to Sustainable Balance

Here's a truth that frees you from perfectionism: Balance is not rigidity; it's adaptability.

Some weeks, your career needs more of you. Other weeks, your relationships do. Some days, your body needs movement. Other days, it needs rest. Trying to keep everything perfectly even at all times is a losing battle. Instead, learn to pivot.

Ask yourself:

> ➤ Where does my energy need to go this week?

Be honest about what can wait. Give yourself permission to adjust. Long-term balance isn't about keeping all the balls in the air perfectly. It's about knowing which ones can be set down for a while, and which ones truly need your attention.

Balance is a Practice, Not a Destination

There's no perfect formula. There's no end goal. Balance is a living, breathing practice, and one that evolves as you do.

Some things you'll need to let go of (even if you love them). Some commitments will need to shift. Some priorities will take center stage while others step back.

And that's okay. The goal is not perfect balance. The goal is a fulfilling, sustainable life that nourishes all of you...mind, body, and spirit.

Designing a Life Root System That Truly Works for You

Now that we've covered how to maintain balance, it's time to dive deeper into how to design a life structure that actually supports you.

Ask yourself:

> ➤ What does my daily life need to reflect my priorities?

> ➤ How do I create a system that works for me, not against me?

> ➤ What adjustments do I need to make to feel more aligned?

Sustainable balance requires more than flexibility. It's also about nurturing yourself from the inside out. In the next chapter, we'll explore holistic practices—mind, body, and spirit tools—that strengthen your foundation for lasting balance, no matter what life brings.

CHAPTER 52

HOLISTIC PRACTICES FOR LASTING BALANCE

I n the pursuit of balance, we often focus on external adjustments—scheduling, prioritizing, time-blocking—yet true balance starts from within. It's not just about managing our to-do lists; it's about cultivating an inner foundation that supports all aspects of our lives.

That foundation lives in your body, your emotions, your energy, and your spirit. Aligning these aspects allows us to move through life with greater ease, clarity, and resilience.

This chapter explores holistic practices that strengthen this foundation, including practices that nourish our physical health, mental well-being, and emotional resilience. For centuries, people have used practices like yoga and meditation to promote balance. Others—like prioritizing sleep, laughter, and emotional detoxing—are simple yet profound ways to create harmony in daily life.

If you've ever felt drained, overwhelmed, or disconnected from yourself, this is your invitation to return to center. Balance is about choosing what truly supports you, not doing more.

Yoga & Meditation: The Core of Mind-Body-Spirit Connection

If balance had a secret weapon, yoga and meditation would be it. These practices calibrate your nervous system, helping you shift from stress and reactivity to clarity and peace. When integrated consistently, they improve your physical health, mental sharpness, and emotional well-being, making them foundational tools for a balanced life.

Yoga: A Moving Meditation for Body & Mind

Yoga is far more than a fitness trend, it's a practice that aligns movement with breath, creating a deep connection between body and mind. There are many styles, depending on what your body and spirit need most:

Hatha: Gentle movements with deep breathing for relaxation

Vinyasa: A fluid, breath-linked flow to build strength and flexibility

Power: A higher-intensity practice for endurance and muscle-building

Ashtanga: A structured sequence that challenges discipline and focus

Bikram: Also known as "hot yoga," practiced in a heated room for detoxification

Iyengar: Precision-focused poses using props for alignment

No matter the style, yoga helps you become more adaptable on the mat and in daily life.

Meditation: The Art of Inner Stillness & Equanimity

People often view meditation as sitting in silence, but it's truly the practice of directing your focus inward. When you meditate, you create a mental space between thoughts and reactions, allowing you to feel centered, present, and less overwhelmed by life's uncertainties.

Scientific research shows that just eight weeks of meditation can physically alter the brain, strengthening areas responsible for memory, self-awareness, and emotional regulation.

Benefits include:

- Lowering blood pressure and reducing anxiety
- Releasing tension-related pain and inflammation
- Increasing serotonin for improved mood and energy
- Strengthening the immune system

One of the greatest gifts of meditation is *equanimity*—the ability to remain calm, centered, and non-reactive no matter what life throws your way. As you practice, you learn to observe thoughts and emotions without getting swept away by them. This creates a steady inner foundation that helps you respond with clarity instead of reacting out of fear or habit. Over time, meditation becomes not just a calming practice, but a powerful tool for navigating life with resilience and grace.

You don't need to spend hours meditating to experience these benefits. Just a few minutes a day can make a profound difference. Whether through guided meditations, breathwork, or silent reflection, meditation cultivates inner balance and equanimity.

Beyond Yoga & Meditation: Daily Practices for Balance

While yoga and meditation provide a powerful foundation, balance is also shaped by the small choices we make moment to moment. From sleep to relationships, every area of life can either nourish you—or quietly drain you. Balance is about what you remove from your life, and what you add to sustain your well-being.

Here are simple, research-backed practices to enhance your physical, emotional, and social balance:

- **Prioritize Sleep: Your Foundation for Well-Being:** Lack of sleep disrupts everything, including your mood, metabolism, and cognitive function. In our go-go-go culture, people often sacrifice rest, but in reality, sleep is your ultimate reset button. Aim for 6-8 hours of quality sleep and create an evening ritual that promotes relaxation. Turn off screens, dim the lights, and wind down with meditation or journaling.

- **Move Your Body Daily (It Doesn't Have to Be Intense!):** Not every workout has to be an intense gym session. Movement is medicine, and consistency matters more than perfection. Whether it's yoga, hiking, dancing, swimming, or stretching, find an activity you enjoy and commit to it daily—not because you "should," but because it makes you feel alive.

- **Eat in a Way That Honors Your Body:** What you eat directly affects your energy, mood, and resilience. There's no one-size-fits-all diet, but a simple rule to follow is: eat whole, vibrant foods that make you feel nourished. Listen to your body and notice which foods give you energy versus which leave you sluggish. Hydration is equally vital. Drink water like your health depends on it, because it does.

- **Release Emotional Toxins:** Holding onto resentment, stress, or emotional pain creates imbalance in both mind and body. Ask yourself: *"What am I holding onto that no longer serves me?"* Whether through therapy, journaling, breathwork, or deep conversations, emotional detoxing clears the way for peace and clarity.

- **Strengthen Your Relationships:** Balance isn't just internal, it's relational. Strong, loving connections are linked to longer lifespans, better health, and greater happiness. Prioritize those who uplift you.

- **Laugh More:** Laughter is healing, not frivolous. It lowers stress hormones, boosts immunity, and releases tension. Make space for silliness, comedy, and joy.

And while the physical and emotional tools help you feel grounded, there's one more layer that brings it all together—your spiritual center.

The Spiritual Dimension of Balance

While physical and emotional practices are vital, spirituality is the soul's nourishment. It doesn't have to be elaborate or dogmatic, it just needs to connect you to something deeper. For some, this means prayer, chanting, or reading sacred texts. For others, it's gardening mindfully, watching a sunrise, or sitting quietly in nature.

Spirituality becomes especially powerful when it's personal, a practice that brings you peace, reflection, and renewal. These rituals act like tuning forks, helping you come back into harmony with your truth.

When incorporated into daily life, spiritual practices:

- Build emotional resilience
- Reduce anxiety
- Create a sense of intentional living

The beauty of spiritual balance is that it meets you exactly where you are…no altar or ashram required.

I once coached a busy father of three who always put himself last. Burned out and disconnected, he started a simple 5-minute breath prayer before the kids woke up. He described it as *"plugging back into life."* That brief morning ritual gave him patience, clarity, and a sense of groundedness that transformed his days. Spiritual connection became his fuel, not another task on his to-do list.

When we root our lives in this kind of purpose, the benefits ripple far beyond a single moment. Transcendence doesn't just feel good, it reshapes how we relate to ourselves, others, and the world.

Putting It Into Practice:
What's One Step You Can Take Today?

➢ Which practice resonates most with me right now?

➢ What's one small shift I can make today to feel more balanced?

Start simple:

- Commit to 10 minutes of meditation a few days per week
- Sign up for a weekly yoga class
- Get an extra hour of sleep tonight

Whatever you choose, the key is to start, and build from there.

Balance is a Practice, Not a Destination

Balance is a dynamic process that requires constant tuning and adjustments. Some days, work will demand more of you. Other times, family or self-care will come first. The goal is not to get everything perfect, but to stay mindful of what you need in each season of life.

By embracing yoga, meditation, and other intentional practices, you cultivate a foundation that supports your well-being from the inside out. Balance isn't about doing more. It's about being more present, more aligned, and more at peace with yourself.

When your roots are nourished, your rise becomes effortless. Rooting into balance isn't a luxury, it's your launchpad. Because once you feel balanced and grounded, something beautiful happens, you're ready for more. Ready to stretch, to dream bigger, to live with greater purpose.

As you strengthen your inner foundation with nourishing practices, you'll naturally adapt to life's changes with greater ease. Now, it's time to turn your intentions into tangible action by designing a daily schedule that feeds your roots and honors your highest priorities.

CHAPTER 53

INTENTION TO ACTION

Scheduling a Life That Feeds Your Roots

B alance isn't something that just happens. It's something you create by being intentional about how you spend your time and energy. If you want to thrive, your daily life must reflect your deepest priorities.

So let's get real. Are you actively prioritizing the things that make your life feel like an 8, 9, or 10? Or are you just hoping they'll "fit in" when you find the time? If it's not scheduled, it's not real.

It's time to stop waiting for the right moment and start structuring your life in a way that actually meets your needs.

Step 1: What Fulfills You in Each Root Area

First, take a personal inventory of what would make you feel fully nourished and fulfilled in each of these areas:

- **Physical Health:** What does your body need to feel like an 8, 9, or 10? Strength training? Yoga? More movement? Better sleep? More nutritious meals?

- **Mental Well-being:** What helps your mind feel sharp, inspired, and engaged? Reading? Learning? Time for creativity?

- **Emotional Fulfillment:** What connections or experiences make you feel deeply fulfilled? More time with loved ones? Therapy? Setting better boundaries?

- **Spiritual Connection:** What grounds you and gives you a sense of meaning? Meditation? Prayer? Nature? A personal practice?
- **Personal Growth & Passion:** What excites and expands you? A new hobby? A creative project? A course?

Ask yourself:

➢ For each root area, list two to three activities or habits that would make you feel truly fulfilled.

➢ What would make this area feel like a 9 or 10?

Step 2: Schedule Your Priorities into Your Calendar

Now, take those high-value activities and actually block time for them in your schedule.

Here's where most people go wrong:

- They intend to work out but never schedule it.
- They want to meet someone new but never make plans to go out.
- They need more self-care but only do it "if there's time."

If you want it to happen, plan for it.

- **Are you single & want to meet someone?** Schedule outings or social events each week to create more opportunities.
- **Want to build muscle?** Create a specific workout routine, scheduling different body parts for different days.
- **Need to nourish your mental health?** Plan for time to read (and finish this book!), meditate, or engage in personal development.
- **Struggling to maintain friendships?** Put friend dates, phone calls, or check-ins on the calendar.

Example: A Balanced Week That Reflects Priorities

Monday: Strength training + Meal prep for the week

Tuesday: Networking event for career growth + Reading before bed

Wednesday: Therapy session + Meditation

Thursday: Date night or social outing (emotional fulfillment)

Friday: Yoga or recovery workout + Creative hobby time

Saturday: Outdoor adventure (physical & spiritual balance)

Sunday: Deep rest + Planning next week's priorities

Step 3: Align Your Time With Your Values

Now that your priorities are in your schedule, take a step back and check for alignment.

> ➢ Does your schedule reflect what you say is most important?

> ➢ Are you giving enough energy to each root area?

> ➢ Do you feel a sense of balance and fulfillment looking at your week?

If something feels off, adjust. This is your life and you get to design it.

Step 4: Make a Commitment to Follow Through

Balance isn't about perfection. It's about consistently prioritizing what truly matters.

Tip: Keep an Accountability Check-In at the end of each week. Ask yourself:

> ➢ What went well?

> ➢ What felt unbalanced?

> ➢ What needs to shift for next week?

By intentionally crafting your schedule around what nourishes your mind, body, and spirit, you take control of your life instead of letting life control you. Balance doesn't happen by accident. It happens by design.

Protecting Your Priorities with Boundaries

Now that you've intentionally structured your life around what nourishes you, the next step is protecting that balance with strong boundaries. Without them, it's easy to let obligations, guilt, or the expectations of others pull you off course.

Your time and energy are finite resources. If you don't protect them, life will fill your schedule with things that don't serve you.

Boundaries aren't about shutting people out; they're about making sure that what's most important to you gets the space and attention it deserves.

This means:

- Saying no to things that drain your energy
- Setting clear limits on your time
- Giving yourself permission to prioritize your own needs without guilt

If you've ever felt resentment, overwhelm, or frustration in your relationships, chances are, you needed a boundary. Learning to communicate these limits with kindness and confidence will allow you to protect your peace while still maintaining meaningful connections.

Most importantly, remember that every time you say yes to something, you are saying no to something else. If you're not careful, the things that matter most—your health, your dreams, your deepest connections—can get pushed to the sidelines. Protect your sacred yes. Commit to making space for what truly nourishes your root system.

Once you've structured your days around what truly nourishes you, it's time to look at the bigger picture: how to keep thriving through all of life's seasons. Let's bring it all together and explore what it means to live in flow—balanced, grounded, and free.

CHAPTER 54

THRIVING IN LIFE'S FLOW

Summary

B alance isn't about doing it all at once or perfectly distributing your time across every responsibility. It's about intentionally prioritizing what truly matters in each season of your life, while ensuring that your root system stays strong so you can rise.

In this section, we've redefined what balance truly means, challenged the myth of perfection, and explored practical strategies for creating a life that feels grounded, fulfilling, and adaptable.

Key Takeaways:
What We've Learned About Balance

- **Balance is Not a Static State:** It's a dynamic dance that requires constant recalibration. Some days, one aspect of your life will need more attention than others, and that's okay.

- **Your Root System is Everything:** When you prioritize physical health, mental well-being, emotional resilience, and spiritual connection, you create a stable foundation that allows you to thrive in all areas of life.

- **Prioritize What Matters Most:** Instead of spreading yourself thin, identify what an 8, 9, or 10 in each root area looks like and calendar it in—because if it's not scheduled, it's not real.

- **Kill Your Darlings:** Let go of projects, commitments, or ideas that don't serve your highest priorities. Sometimes, success isn't about doing more, it's about letting go.

- **Boundaries Protect Your Energy:** Saying no isn't selfish; it's necessary. Balance requires being intentional with where you invest your time and energy.

- **Balance Looks Different in Every Life Season:** The way you prioritize will shift based on your stage in life (parenting, career shifts, caregiving, etc.). Give yourself permission to adjust.

- **Sustainable Balance is a Long-Term Strategy:** Instead of constantly fixing burnout, design a life that doesn't require constant rebalancing by aligning your commitments with your values.

- **Yoga, Meditation, and Movement are Essential Anchors:** These practices ground your energy, reduce stress, and provide an internal reset so you can stay balanced no matter what life throws your way.

- **The Power of Laughter, Love, and Community:** Balance is about joy, not just about productivity. Prioritize relationships, fun, and activities that lighten your spirit.

Balance Across Life Seasons

Balance isn't one-size-fits-all. It looks different at every stage of life.

- For a new parent, balance might mean prioritizing sleep and letting go of perfection in other areas.

- For an entrepreneur, balance might mean time-blocking personal space and setting boundaries around work.

- For someone caring for aging parents, balance might mean seeking community support and carving out moments of self-care even in a demanding season.

- For a single person looking for love, balance might mean intentionally making space to meet new people instead of just hoping it happens.

The key is to be honest about where you are, what your current priorities are, and how you can best support yourself in this season—knowing that it will evolve over time. Balance is never about doing everything. It's about doing what matters most right now. With everything you've learned in this section, it's time to put balance into action. Balance isn't the goal, it's the path to everything you desire. And now, you have the tools to walk it with confidence.

As you move forward, remember that sustainable balance is nourished not just by managing your time, but by nurturing your whole self. The practices we explored—like yoga, meditation, sleep, emotional detoxing, and joyful movement—aren't extras; they're the anchors that keep you grounded through life's demands. Building in daily rituals, protecting your energy with clear boundaries, and making space for both ambition and rest will allow you to thrive without losing yourself along the way.

Balance is created moment-by-moment, choice-by-choice. Let your roots be nourished daily, and you will rise with strength and grace.

Your A-Ha Moments & Commitments

Before we move forward, take a moment to pause and reflect on what resonated most with you in this section.

➢ What were my biggest a-ha moments about balance?

➢ What is the one commitment I am making to myself right now to create more balance in your life?

➢ What is one thing you need to release in order to make space for what truly matters?

Write your answers. Acknowledging them now will help anchor your growth as you move forward. Balance is a journey, and not just something you achieve. And every journey begins with a single, intentional step. What's yours?

You've cultivated your roots. You've strengthened your foundation. Now, it's time to stretch, expand, dream bigger, and live in full alignment with your purpose.

Welcome to your rise.

ROOT-TO-RISE INFOGRAPHIC

PHASE THREE: RISE

RISE

HUMAN NEEDS

Transcendence

- Moving past the self to serve others
- Connecting to higher purpose
- Contribution
- Sharing
- Service
- Providing

BALANCING LIFE
- Yoga & Meditation
- Gratitude
- Self-care
- Prioritizing Roots

Growth

- Growing
- Pulsating energy
- Progress
- Learning
- Feeling momentum
- Advancing
- Breaking free

CONNECTING TO AUTHENTICITY
- Tap into Your Heart
- Aligning Others
- Your Lens

Intimacy

- Nurturing
- Valuing relationships
- Belonging
- Feeling passion
- Having desire
- Striving for unity
- Togetherness

WITHSTANDING THE ELEMENTS
- Winds of Change
- Storms/Upheaval
- Grief & Loss

NAVIGATING EMOTIONS
- **Triad:**
- Body/Mind/Spirit
- Physiology/Focus/Meaning

FOCUS MIND   MEANING SPIRIT

PHYSIOLOGY BODY

Self

- Self-esteem
- Self-worth
- Significance
- Importance
- Pride
- Importance
- Perfection

CLEARING OBSTACLES
- Nourishing Needy Roots
- Honoring Driving Needs
- Pain Points
- Getting Unstuck
- Fears & Limiting Beliefs
- Double Binds
- Leveraging you Tap Root

RESILIENCE

Variety

- Change
- Transitions
- Storms
- Challenges
- Trauma/Crisis
- Chaos
- Variety
- New/Different
- Spice of Life
- Surprise
- Fear

LIFE ROOT SYSTEM

HEALTH/FITNESS	FAMILY	RELATIONSHIPS	CAREER	FRIENDS
• Nutrition	• Parents	• Self	• Time & Money	• Introvert v. Extrovert Needs
• Food/Beverage	• Caregivers	• Romantic Partner	• Contribution	• Who are they?
• Supplements	• Siblings	• Commitment	• Heart-based/ Passion vs	• Values alignment
• Fitness/Exercise	• Partner	• Chemistry	Corporate	• Reflection of you
• Massage/Body Work	• In-laws	• Compatibility	• Hobbies/Craft	• What do you offer?
• Wellness vs. Illness	• Children	• Communication	• Who you are:	• What do they offer?
	• Chosen		• Strengths/ Weaknesses	• Elevate
			• Leader vs. Worker	• Support
			• Visionary vs. Operational	• Experience
			• Analytical/ Data-minded	

Security

- Certainty
- Safety
- Rootedness
- Grounded
- Comfort
- Stability
- Predictability
- Protection
- Commitment

www.glowliving.com
#glowliving
#roottorise
#lovelife

TAP ROOT
What feeds your soul deeply?

GLOWLIVING
love life

ROOTS

© All Rights Reserved. Glow Living/Glow Marketing LLC 2025

Part Three

YOUR RISE

CHAPTER 55

YOUR RISE

Stepping Into Your Highest Potential

I n the journey from root to rise, we've built a sound foundation, cultivated balance, and learned how to withstand life's storms. Now, we turn our attention to what comes next: your rise.

This is where you step into your highest potential, craft a meaningful life, and create a legacy that extends beyond you. Rising isn't just about achieving goals or reaching milestones. It's about becoming the person you were always meant to be. It's about taking everything you've learned—about yourself, your needs, and your strengths—and using it to live with intention, joy, and impact.

Ultimately, rising is about transcending your own needs. Once your roots are strong and your inner ecosystem is thriving, you begin to bear fruit—gifts, wisdom, and contributions that nourish others. Just like the tree on the cover of this book, your life becomes generous, outward-facing, and full of meaning. Your rise is not just for you...it's for the world you touch.

Rising is a choice. Not everyone makes it.

Some people remain stuck in survival mode, caught in cycles of self-doubt, fear, or external expectations. Others wait for permission to go after what they truly want. This chapter is your invitation to stop waiting. To rise now. To embrace the urgency of life, knowing that tomorrow isn't guaranteed. To live fully, love openly, and pursue the dreams that set your soul on fire...not someday, but today.

The Rise Equation: The Formula for a Life Well-Lived

Rising doesn't happen by accident. It's a combination of deliberate choices, meaningful goals, and a connection to something bigger than yourself. In this book, we've explored many facets of growth. For truly rising, it all comes down to this:

Rising Up = Strong Foundation + Personal Goals + Higher Purpose + Meaning + Joy

Let's break it down:

- **Strong Foundation:** You've already done the work of creating a stable root system. You know who you are, what you need, and how to stay grounded through life's ups and downs. This is what allows you to rise without losing yourself.

- **Personal Goals:** Rising is about momentum and includes setting goals that excite and challenge you, whether in your career, relationships, health, creativity, or personal growth. These aren't just arbitrary checkboxes; they are the stepping stones to a fulfilling life.

- **Higher Purpose:** Beyond personal success, true fulfillment comes from connecting to a greater purpose. This isn't something you need to "find" out in the world, it's something you create and decide. Your purpose is the unique way you contribute to the world and the impact you leave behind.

- **Meaning:** Life's experiences, good and bad, carry lessons. Rising means seeing every chapter of your life as part of a larger story, recognizing the wisdom gained from even the hardest moments.

- **Joy:** Joy isn't a reward you earn at the finish line. It's something you cultivate along the way. True rising happens when you live in a way that lights you up now, not just in some distant future.

Your North Star Questions:
A Guiding Light for the Rise Ahead

As you begin the Rise portion of this journey, it's time to shift your gaze upward to the future you're building and the life you're being called to create.

But rising doesn't mean rushing. It means moving forward with clarity, courage, and deep alignment.

To help you stay grounded in your truth, I invite you to return to what I call Life's Key Questions. These are three powerful prompts that act as a guiding light, illuminating your path when decisions feel hard, energy feels low, or direction feels unclear:

➢ What do you want?

➢ Why do you want it?

➢ What are you willing to do about it?

These questions are simple but they are not always easy. They require honesty. They ask you to take full ownership of your desires, your motivation, and your willingness to rise.

Throughout the Rise section, you'll return to these questions again and again to refine your vision, reconnect to your purpose, and make bold, values-driven decisions. Think of them as stars in a constellation, always shining above, ready to realign you with what matters most.

The *Root-to-Rise* Map:
Your Personal Blueprint

Your rise is uniquely yours. There is no one-size-fits-all approach to fulfillment, which is why the *Root-to-Rise* Map is such an essential tool.

It helps you chart your own path, making sure that every step you take aligns with your values, priorities, and highest aspirations.

In the next chapter, we'll walk through how to fill out your personal map, giving you a clear vision of what rising looks like for you.

But before we begin, take a moment to reflect:

- ➤ What does rising mean to you?
- ➤ If I knew I had only a few years left to live, how would I prioritize my time differently?
- ➤ What dreams, goals, or desires have I put on hold?
- ➤ What legacy do I want to leave behind?

This is the beginning of the most exciting chapter yet.

Let's create your personal *Root-to-Rise* Map, and rise into the life that's been waiting for you.

CHAPTER 56

MAPPING YOUR RISE

Designing a Life Aligned With Your Truth

R ising isn't just about dreaming, it's about designing a life that reflects your truth, your goals, and your purpose. The *Root-to-Rise* Map is your personal blueprint to make that vision real. You've done the inner work. Now it's time to make a declaration:

"I will not settle. I will rise with intention, meaning, and joy."

Think of this map as your trail guide. You don't need every step planned. However, you do need to know and decide on your destination and what fuels you along the way.

The *Root-to-Rise* Map: A Step-by-Step Guide

You'll find the *Root-to-Rise* Map image along with my completed example on page 326 and 327. As you move through each section here, take your time answering the questions and then transfer the abbreviated version to your Map. Take your time. Reflect deeply. This is your life's design so make it count.

If you completed any of it earlier in the book, return to it now. If not, take a moment to craft a clear, meaningful statement.

You will fill in your Map from the ground up.

1.Taproot: What Grounds You

Your Taproot is your foundation and the deepest part of your authenticity. It keeps you steady when life feels uncertain and guides you when decisions get hard.

Without a strong Taproot, even your most exciting goals can feel shaky. But when you're rooted in your truth—like love, creativity, or service—you draw strength from within, not from external validation.

What value, belief, or purpose keeps me grounded and guides my path? My Taproot Is: _____

2. Answer Your North Star Questions

For each of the Five Roots of Life—Health, Family, Relationships (Self or Romantic Partner), Career, and Friends—answer these three questions and add it to your Map under Top Goals/Visions:

> ➤ **What do I want?** (Be specific. This is your truth.)

> ➤ **Why do I want it?** (Understand your motivation—this is your fuel.)

> ➤ **What am I willing to do about it?** (Intentions only become real with action.)

These three questions are your North Star and your anchor for clarity and alignment. You can return to them anytime you feel overwhelmed, unclear, or stuck. Let them be your guiding light through this next season of growth.

Don't rush this part. Give each root the attention it deserves. The more honest and specific you are here, the more powerful your rise will become.

3. Identify Your Top Driving Need

Every decision you make is influenced by six human needs: Security, Variety, Self, Intimacy, Growth, and Transcendence. Ask yourself:

➢ Which one do I want to cultivate now? If you're not sure, take the free Hidden Forces Quiz on glowliving.com.

4. Choose Your Favorite Mantra

Words carry power. A mantra is a short phrase that grounds you, motivates you, or reminds you of your truth.

➢ What phrase or quote resonates with me so deeply that I want to live by it?

5. Identify Your Top Supporters

No one rises alone. Your support system is essential for both encouragement and accountability.

➢ Who uplifts, challenges, and believes in me?

If you feel your support system is lacking, address how you can cultivate stronger connections.

6. Define Your Authentic Self Descriptors

Rising means living fully as yourself. But to do that, you need to clearly define who you are at your core.

➢ What three to five words describe your truest self? (Not the version of you shaped by external expectations.)

7. Define Your Life's Key Question

Everyone has a subconscious question that drives their actions and decisions. The quality of this question shapes the quality of your life.

Some examples:

Will it be fun? → Leads to variety and adventure

Will it make me safe? → Prioritizes security and stability

Will it make me successful? → Drives ambition but may sacrifice balance

Will it make my life meaningful? → Centers purpose and deep fulfillment

➤ What question has been guiding my life, consciously or not?

➤ What question do I want to replace it with for an empowered future? Add it to your Map.

8. Acknowledge Your Major Milestones

Before focusing forward, honor how far you've already come.

➤ What are the key moments of growth in my life so far?

These are proof of your strength and resilience. They are the foundation upon which your rise is built.

9. Define Your Goals & Aspirations

Your goals give your rise direction and momentum. They don't have to be rigid, but they should excite and challenge you.

➤ What do I deeply desire to accomplish in the next year?

If you want to create a longer-range vision, ask:

➤ What about in the next five years?

➤ How do these goals connect to your higher purpose?

10. Top Bucket List Items

Don't wait for "someday." Live your bucket list now. Your bucket list is not merely a compilation of dreams; it's a declaration of your commitment to experiencing the fullness of life. It's a reminder to cherish the moments and prioritize the things that truly resonate with your heart and soul.

➤ What experiences, adventures, or challenges do I want to embrace?

This isn't just about extravagant adventures, it's about fully living while you can.

11. Recognize Your Most Important Life Lessons

Growth comes from lessons, both painful and beautiful. Acknowledging and embracing the significant life lessons you've gleaned from your experiences is a crucial aspect of your Rise plan. These lessons are like stepping stones, guiding your way toward a future enriched with wisdom and authenticity.

> ➢ What are the most profound truths I've learned?

12. What Are You Grateful For?

Gratitude grounds you in abundance.

> ➢ List the key people, experiences, or lessons I'm most thankful for.

When life feels uncertain, come back to this list. It will remind you of all that is good.

13. Define Your Higher Purpose

Now the time has come to illuminate a concept that often shrouds itself in mystery, yet possesses profound influence over the course of our lives: The Higher Purpose.

The quest for a higher purpose can feel both simple and profound. Some discover it early as a guiding North Star; for others, it unfolds gradually through life experience. The truth that you must internalize is that there is no one-size-fits-all formula or universal truth when it comes to higher purpose. It's a deeply personal voyage, a deliberate choice that you consciously embrace, driven by your unique life experiences, values, and aspirations.

But before we embark on the path of uncovering your higher purpose, it's imperative to recognize that within the tapestry of our lives, we all play multiple roles and serve various purposes. These roles can be as multifarious as those of a loving parent, a high-achieving professional, a creative visionary, or a compassionate helper. The revelation of your higher purpose doesn't erase these other roles.

Instead, it imbues them with a deeper sense of significance and a clearer sense of direction.

One effective approach to starting the journey of uncovering your higher purpose is to begin with what you are innately skilled at and passionate about. Often, our talents and passions hold valuable clues that point the way to our unique contributions to the world. Contemplate what activities or skills ignite a fire within you, what you excel at almost effortlessly, and what offers profound pleasure and satisfaction.

One of my friends once challenged me to describe the higher purpose of *Glow Living* in five words or less, a surprisingly difficult task.

Because it can be really hard to love life sometimes, I made it my mission to figure out how to do it for myself, and then help others do the same. In the end, I still can't think of anything more important than that.

My higher purpose is simple and profound: **to help people love life**.

Your higher purpose is not an endpoint, but a guiding star that illuminates your journey. It's a commitment to living a life aligned with your deepest values and aspirations, a life that contributes positively to the world.

So, as you set foot on this transformative expedition, always remember that your higher purpose isn't something external to be sought. Instead, it's an intrinsic aspect of your being, awaiting discovery within the profound depths of your authentic self. Embrace the process, and let your passions and talents serve as your guiding lights as you craft a path toward a life brimming with meaning, joy, and purpose.

Time to develop your higher purpose…*in five words or less*.

> ➢ If I had to sum up my higher purpose in five words or less, what would it be?

Your higher purpose is the light that guides your rise and helps you create a legacy.

Making It Real

Now that you've mapped out your rise, take a moment to step back and absorb what you've created. This is your blueprint for a life fully lived.

➢ What stands out to me?

➢ What commitments am I making to myself?

➢ What's one step I can take this week to bring this vision to life?

This is it. This is your rise. And you are here for it...one step at a time.

ROOT-TO-RISE MAP

HIGHER PURPOSE

RISE

LIFE'S KEY QUESTION

TOP MILESTONES

AUTHENTIC SELF DESCRIPTORS

GOALS & ASPIRATIONS

TOP SUPPORTERS

TOP BUCKET LIST

FAVORITE MANTRA

TOP LIFE LESSONS

TOP DRIVING NEED

GRATEFUL FOR

RESILIENCE

TOP GOALS/VISIONS

HEALTH	FAMILY	RELATIONSHIPS	CAREER	FRIENDS
What I want:				
Why I want				
What I will do for it:				

ROOTS

TAP ROOT

glowliving.com
#glowliving
#roottorise
#lovelife

© All Rights Reserved. Glow Living/Glow Marketing LLC/Root-to-Rise 2025

GLOWLIVING

love life

ROOT-TO-RISE MAP

HIGHER PURPOSE
I help people love life.

RISE

RESILIENCE

LIFE'S KEY QUESTION
Will this make me feel happy and fulfilled?

AUTHENTIC SELF DESCRIPTORS
Loving
Giving
Joyful

TOP SUPPORTERS
Cleo
Tiana
See: Acknowledgements

FAVORITE MANTRA
I'm enough.

TOP DRIVING NEED
Connection/Love

TOP MILESTONES
Raised a son
Created RTR
World Travel

GOALS & ASPIRATIONS
Peak Health
Financial Freedom
Help 1M people

TOP BUCKET LIST
Travel extensively
Invest in a minority biz

TOP LIFE LESSONS
Don't boil the ocean.
No storm lasts forever.

GRATEFUL FOR
Myself and the loves in my life.
Nature.

TOP GOALS/VISIONS

	HEALTH	FAMILY	RELATIONSHIPS	CAREER	FRIENDS
What I want:	Clean bill of health. Athletic body fat %	To heal past hurts with my parents and feel connected	A committed partnership built on love, trust and shared vision.	Successfully self-employed. Time for creative projects.	Tight friend group for consistent connection & fun
Why I want it:	To prevent illness. To look fit. To be able to adventure.	I want to be clean of the past and in good place when they pass	To share my love, experience connection, and have support.	Prospect for clients. Deliver high results. Learn new skills.	To have more fun, adventure, joy and support
What I will do for it:	Exercise 4x+/week Eat whole foods Monitor weight and fat %	Go to therapy to heal myself first. Open up to them.	Discuss my needs Co-create a relationship vision.	Message 2x+ prospects per week. Learn new tech solutions.	Invite friends for activities 2x+/week. Plan trips together. Tell them they are special to me often.

ROOTS

TAP ROOT
The love of my son and helping him love life.

glowliving.com
#glowliving
#roottorise
#lovelife

GLOWLIVING
love life.

© All Rights Reserved. Glow Living/Glow Marketing LLC/Root-to-Rise 2025

CHAPTER 57

YOUR RISE IN ACTION

From Vision to Embodiment

N ow that you've mapped your rise—clarified your vision, purpose, and what you're willing to do to live it—it's time to root that vision in something even deeper. This next chapter is about integration. Because your rise isn't just a dream on paper. It's a way of living, loving, and leading every day.

To embody your rise means showing up in alignment with your North Star, even when life gets messy. It means anchoring into something greater, letting your values guide your actions, and remembering that the way you live today is the legacy you leave behind.

Spiritual Anchoring: Rising with Something Greater

"We are not human beings having a spiritual experience; we are spiritual beings having a human experience."
—Pierre Teilhard de Chardin

In every journey of growth, there comes a point when self-effort alone no longer feels like enough. You crave connection, not just to others, but to something greater. That something could be Spirit, Source,

God/Goddess, the Universe, the Earth, or simply Love. It's not about religion—it's about reverence.

At the heart of the Rise journey is the sixth human need: Transcendence—the desire to live for more than just survival or success. It's the part of us that seeks purpose, contribution, and connection to the divine or infinite.

When we nurture our spiritual life, something profound shifts. We no longer feel like we're carrying everything alone. Instead, we see ourselves as part of a larger whole, woven into the very fabric of life itself. We trust in timing and intuition, even when logic falls short. Suffering doesn't disappear, it takes on new meaning. Compassion deepens. And even when we don't have all the answers, we feel guided. Held. Supported by something both ancient and alive.

Spirituality helps us rise by reminding us: **you're not rising alone.**

A View From Above

I've always wanted to believe there was something greater than us, something beyond the surface of daily life that held deeper meaning. I remember one moment vividly: I was flying home, looking down on San Francisco from above. From that height, the cars looked like tiny specks, and I couldn't make out individual people. It struck me just how small we really are, despite living from the perspective that the world revolves around us.

That view from above shifted something in me. It gave me a felt sense of scale including how vast life is, and how humbling and beautiful it is to be a part of something so much bigger.

Later, I started co-hosting sister circles with Kristen Dessange, carving out sacred time to connect with each other and the spiritual wisdom of the natural world. We explored the wheel of the year and nature-based rituals, practices that were accessible to everyone, regardless of religion or background. These gatherings became a kind of spiritual home for me—a place to pause, listen inwardly, and remember that life is cyclical, interconnected, and always offering guidance if we're willing to tune in.

Practices That Anchor the Spirit

You don't need to live in a monastery or adopt a fixed belief system to experience spiritual fulfillment. Small, intentional practices can create a bridge to the sacred in everyday life:

- **Meditation or Breathwork**: Quiet the noise and reconnect to your inner being.
- **Yoga or Sound Healing:** sound baths, personal yoga practice, yoga in spiritual places
- **Body and Energy Work:** massage, reiki and bathing rituals
- **Prayer or Gratitude Rituals**: Speak to something beyond yourself with reverence
- **Nature Immersion**: Walk among trees, sit near water, watch the sky—let the earth realign your soul
- **Creative Expression**: Art, dance, and music can all be spiritual channels
- **Sacred Reading**: Books, poetry, or wisdom texts that stir your heart
- **Silence and Stillness**: Space for intuition and inner knowing to emerge
- **Rituals and Ceremony**: Lighting candles, journaling by moonlight, circles, or celebrating transitions
- **Spiritual Community**: Surround yourself with others on the journey of awakening

As you deepen your spiritual connection, you may become more attuned to the subtle energy you bring into the world. Your spiritual practice isn't just for your inner peace; it shapes the emotional signals, or energy arrows, you emit. When you feel spiritually grounded, your energy tends to reflect compassion, patience, and presence. In this way, your spiritual connection becomes a quiet act of service, uplifting others through how you *are*, not just what you do.

Sacred Reflection:

➤ What helps me feel spiritually connected?

➤ How do I want to invite more sacredness or spiritual grounding into my life?

➤ What have I ever experienced that I couldn't explain, but knew was meaningful?

Living Your Legacy Today

"How we spend our days is, of course, how we spend our lives."
—Annie Dillard

Imagine fast-forwarding to the end of your life. You're looking back at the choices you made, the risks you took, the love you gave—or withheld. What will you see? Will you feel fulfilled, knowing you lived fully and fearlessly? Or will you wish you had said the thing, made the move, or followed your calling? This chapter is about not waiting.

The Urgency of Life: Why We Can't Wait

The greatest lie we tell ourselves is that we have more time.

"I'll start that project when things calm down."
"I'll write the book when I have more space."
"I'll travel when the kids are grown."
"I'll say how I really feel when the moment is right."

But the truth? Life doesn't wait.

Time is the one thing we can never get back, and yet we often live as if it's unlimited. The urgency of life is about awareness and recognizing that every moment is an opportunity to create, love, experience, and contribute.

Ask yourself:

> ➤ If I knew I only had one year left to live, what would I prioritize?

Would you waste time on petty conflicts or scroll mindlessly on your phone? Or would you...

Speak your truth more freely? Make time for your creative fire? Pour love into the people and projects that matter most?

The urgency of life isn't about panicking; it's about living with clarity and courage. It's about making choices today that your future self will thank you for. The way you spend your time is your legacy.

Defining Your Legacy

Legacy is about alignment, not just achievement. It's the story people tell about how you lived, how you loved, and how you made them feel.

Take a moment to reflect:

> ➤ How do I want to be remembered?

> ➤ What values do I want to embody?

> ➤ What impact do I want to have in the world?

Legacy in Action

- Clarify your core values. Try this: "When I'm living fully, I'm embodying _____, _____, and _____."
- Choose one cause, one person, or one small act of service this week.
- Mentor someone. Share your story. Donate your time or wisdom. It counts.
- Start a legacy project: a book, a tradition, a letter, a foundation or grant, or a piece of art.

Challenge: Write Your Own Eulogy

Imagine you've lived the most courageous, creative, love-filled life.

> ➤ What would people say about me?
>
> ➤ What moments would define my story?
>
> ➤ What qualities would they remember?

Let this vision guide how you show up now.

Mini-Challenge

Pick one value to live by, one story to share, and one act of service to offer this week. Write them down—and do them.

Your Journey Has Begun

You've traveled deep into your roots, weathered emotional storms, and mapped a life aligned with your truth. You've faced your patterns, named your needs, and stepped into a version of yourself that is more whole, present, and empowered.

- You are rooted in who you are.
- You are equipped to create balance, even in chaos.
- You can weather life's seasons and rise stronger each time.
- You are no longer waiting. You are *becoming*.

Let your *Root-to-Rise* Map continue to guide you. Put it in a safe place or hang it on your wall. It's a huge achievement! Revisit it in moments of uncertainty or expansion. Let your roots keep you grounded and your vision call you forward.

You are here to create. To love. To live fully.

Rise, always.

ROOT-TO-RISE INFOGRAPHIC

RISE

HIGHER PURPOSE
What do you want to be known for?

RISING UP

- Life's Key Question
- Bucket List
- Goals & Aspirations
- Accomplishments
- Connections/Relationships
- Milestone Events

BALANCING LIFE

- Yoga & Meditation
- Gratitude
- Self-care
- Prioritizing Roots

CONNECTING TO AUTHENTICITY

- Tap into Your Heart
- Aligning Others
- Your Lens

WITHSTANDING THE ELEMENTS

- Winds of Change
- Storms/Upheaval
- Grief & Loss

NAVIGATING EMOTIONS

Triad:
- Body/Mind/Spirit
- Physiology/Focus/Meaning

CLEARING OBSTACLES

- Nourishing Needy Roots
- Honoring Driving Needs
- Pain Points
- Getting Unstuck
- Fears & Limiting Beliefs
- Double Binds
- Leveraging you Tap Root

LIFE ROOT SYSTEM

HEALTH/FITNESS

- Nutrition
- Food/Beverage
- Supplements
- Fitness/Exercise
- Massage/Body Work
- Wellness vs. Illness

FAMILY

- Parents
- Caregivers
- Siblings
- Partner
- In-laws
- Children
- Chosen

RELATIONSHIPS

- Self
- Romantic Partner
- Commitment
- Chemistry
- Compatibility
- Communication

CAREER

- Time & Money
- Contribution
- Heart-based/ Passion vs Corporate
- Hobbies/Craft
- Who you are:
  - Strengths/ Weaknesses
  - Leader vs. Worker
  - Visionary vs. Operational
  - Analytical/ Data-minded

FRIENDS

- Introvert v. Extrovert Needs
- Who are they?
- Reflection of you
- What do you offer?
- What do they offer?
- Elevate
- Support
- Experience

FOCUS MIND — **MEANING SPIRIT**

PHYSIOLOGY BODY

RESILIENCE

HUMAN NEEDS

Transcendence

- Moving past the self to serve others
- Connecting to higher purpose
- Contribution
- Sharing
- Service
- Providing

 **Growth**

- Growing
- Pulsating energy
- Progress
- Learning
- Feeling momentum
- Advancing
- Breaking free

 **Intimacy**

- Nurturing
- Valuing relationships
- Belonging
- Feeling passion
- Having desire
- Striving for unity
- Togetherness

 Self

- Self-esteem
- Self-worth
- Significance
- Importance
- Pride
- Importance
- Perfection

 **Variety**

- Change
- Transitions
- Storms
- Challenges
- Trauma/Crisis
- Chaos
- Variety
- New/Different
- Spice of Life
- Surprise
- Fear

 **Security**

- Certainty
- Safety
- Rootedness
- Grounded
- Comfort
- Stability
- Predictability
- Protection
- Commitment

www.glowliving.com
#glowliving
#roottorise
#lovelife

TAP ROOT
What feeds your soul deeply?

ROOTS

GLOWLIVING
Love Life

© All Rights Reserved. Glow Living/Glow Marketing LLC 2025

I root in truth and rise in alignment.

CHAPTER 58

CONCLUSION & CONGRATS

Congratulations on completing your transformative journey through *Root-to-Rise!* I am deeply grateful that you allowed me to walk beside you on this quest for growth, healing, and a more meaningful life. Your courage to look within, to nurture your roots, and to rise higher is a rare and beautiful thing.

As you reflect on your journey, I hope you recognize the incredible strength you've cultivated. You've explored your inner landscape with honesty, nurtured your relationships with intention, and faced life's storms with grace. You've dared to dream, to heal, and to grow. And that is no small thing.

Remember, this isn't the end, it's just the beginning. The self-awareness you've gained is now your compass. The tools you carry are seeds that will continue to grow. And your *Root-to-Rise* Map is your living blueprint, a reminder that you are never truly lost as long as you stay connected to your truth.

Now is the time to live your legacy, not someday when conditions are perfect, but today, exactly as you are. If you dream of leaving an impact, begin now. Mentor someone, share your story, offer your gifts. If love and connection call to you, answer them, make the call, have the conversation, and show up with an open heart. If adventure stirs in your soul, follow it, say yes, take the leap, and trust the unknown.

The world isn't waiting for the perfect version of you. It simply needs the real, fully alive version of you. You've built a strong foundation, envisioned your ideal life, and now possess everything necessary to rise.

You are ready. You are rooted. You are rising.

As you move forward, remember: growth isn't always smooth, but it's always worth it. Keep evaluating your needs and revisiting your Map. Consider adding your *Root-to-Rise Companion Workbook* to your self-help toolkit and continue showing up for yourself and your dreams. Embrace each moment as an opportunity to learn, love, and live more authentically.

You hold the power to create a life rich with joy, depth, and purpose. So keep your roots strong—and rise, rooted and free.

Love Life,

Chandra Lynn
Founder of Glow Living
Creator & Author of *Root-to-Rise*™

CHAPTER 59

LET'S STAY CONNECTED

T hank you for taking this journey through *Root-to-Rise: How to Love Life*. I'm honored to have shared this path of growth, healing, and rising with you.

If this book made an impact on you, would you consider leaving a review where *Root-to-Rise* is sold such as Amazon? Your words help others discover it and remind them they're not alone in wanting more from life. Even a few heartfelt sentences can make a difference.

To continue with me and other growth-oriented readers, join our Glow Living community to receive exclusive access to:

- Free updates and new editions of the *Root-to-Rise* eBook
- Bonus gifts like journal pages, checklists, meditations, and mini-trainings
- Early invitations to live workshops, online courses, and coaching programs
- Fresh blog articles on topics that complement your *Root-to-Rise* journey
- Behind-the-scenes updates from author and creator Chandra Lynn

Visit GlowLiving.com

Spread the Love

If this book helped you, share it with others to strengthen the roots of your community.

- Share it on social media using #RootToRiseBook and tag @GlowLiving and @GlowChandra
- Gift a copy to a friend or loved one
- Start a book circle or club, and use the *Root-to-Rise Companion Workbook* to dive deeper together

Work with Chandra

Bring the *Root-to-Rise* message to your event, company, or community, or explore private coaching. Reach out through GlowLiving.com and chandralynn.com to book Chandra as a speaker, trainer, or coach.

Sponsor *Root-to-Rise: How to Love Life* as a meaningful gift for your clients, employees, or community. Each copy aligns your brand with wellness, balance, and purpose while helping others strengthen their roots to live more fulfilling lives and careers. Custom branding and bulk orders are available.

Let's rise together and help the world love life...one root at a time.

ACKNOWLEDGEMENTS

To everyone listed here: you are a treasured part of my root system. Your belief in me has nourished my growth in ways words can barely capture. I rise because of you. With all my heart, thank you. Alphabetical by last name:

Kriz and Xoxa Bell, Claudia Blondin, Marcel Bordeaux, Lauren Bromstad, Michael David Brown, Benjamin Lee Brown & Family, Judi Brown, Susie Brownridge & Family, Patrick Boyer, Beth Cragun, Kristen Dessange, Julie Abono Ebding, Kai Michael Echeverria, Gabriel Echeverria, Jessica Fajfar, Laura Green, Suzette Hibble, Tom Hunting, Alia Jewel, Erik Allan Kincaid, Mary J. Lore, Erik Frodo Lashbrook, Michelle Lee, Cynthia Smith, Lisa McPherson-Keane, Disa Petrola, Erica Pacheco, Michelle Pedrotti, Maria Powers-Poole, Heather Rafter, Deirdre Rosso, Carol Rosalind, Michael Salort, Kiki Stack, Evie Sullivan, Colette Wallace, Robbins Madanes Training (RMT), Sacred Life Circle Sisters, and all who have supported Glow Marketing LLC, Glow Living and *Root-to-Rise*.

In Loving Memory of Edith & Phillip Brown, Barbara Johnston-Brown, Jeanette Lee Culp, Christopher Bock, Brenda Donato, and Faye Phillips. I carry your love forward.

COMPANION WORKBOOK

Take Your Journey Even Deeper

If *Root-to-Rise* spoke to your soul and sparked new insights, the ***Root-to-Rise Companion Workbook*** is your next step. It's designed to help you apply the framework to your everyday life…one reflection, journaling prompt, and action step at a time. With guided exercises, needs assessments, and space to map out your own rise, the workbook is your personal space to anchor what you've learned and create meaningful transformation. Visit **GlowLiving.com/RTRbooks** to get your copy and keep rising.

ABOUT THE AUTHOR

 **Chandra Lynn, M.B.A.** is a certified transformation coach, author, and speaker with a mission to empower people to love life. As the founder of Glow Living, she blends emotional resilience, spiritual growth, and actionable life strategies to help others reconnect with their authentic selves and rise into purpose.

Chandra brings a unique blend of professional excellence and soulful depth. With over two decades of experience as a marketing executive and the founder of Glow Marketing LLC, she's helped global brands connect with artists and audiences.

Her signature Root-to-Rise™ method draws from her certification in Tony Robbins' Robbins-Madanes Training program as well as yoga philosophy, nature-based wisdom, and years of coaching and teaching. Chandra has led personal growth workshops and private coaching for people seeking transformation and emotional mastery.

Beyond her career, Chandra is a proud mother, traveler, nature lover, and lifelong learner. Her journey has included motherhood, navigating personal healing and midlife transitions, and learning to thrive through life's messiness. Through it all, she's become a trusted guide for others, offering healing wisdom that's as grounded as it is inspiring.

To explore more of Chandra's work or connect for coaching, speaking, or upcoming events, visit chandralynn.com.

Every storm I survive strengthens my rise.

www.ingramcontent.com/pod-product-compliance
Lightning Source LLC
Chambersburg PA
CBHW060408130626
46555CB00005B/2001